Praise for the first edition of TRUE MAGICK:

True Magick gives the reader a no-nonsense list of all there is to know about doing magick and spells. No metaphysical double-talk here: the author minces no words and gets right down to the practical approach.

—*Dr. Hans Holzer, author of* The New Pagans

Whether you are just starting your investigation of magic or have been on the path for many years, *True Magick* is a valuable resource. Its pages are filled with information, advice, and direction, making magic an accessible tool for anyone seeking personal transformation. A wonderful blend of metaphysical and practical knowledge, this book can lead the true seeker to a better understanding of the art of magic.

—*Jade, executive coordinator,* Of A Like Mind;
co-founder of The Re-Formed Congregation of the Goddess

Bide the Wiccan Law ye must,

In perfect love, in perfect trust.

Eight words the Wiccan Rede fulfill:

An ye harm none, do as ye will.

What ye send forth comes back to thee,

So ever mind the Rule of Three.

Follow this with mind and heart,

And merry ye meet, and merry ye part.

About the Author

Amber K was born in Bronxville, New York, on July 9, 1947. She was not trained in the Craft at her grandmother's knee and does not come from a long line of hereditary Witches.

In 1978, she joined the Temple of the Pagan Way in Chicago. She has worked with Circle, New Earth Circle, and the Pool of Bast, and she helped found the Coven of Our Lady of the Woods (OLW) and the Ladywood Tradition of Wicca. She has served as Publications Officer and National First Officer of the Covenant of the Goddess, and taught in the Cella (priestess) training program of RCG, a national Dianic network.

Amber is the author of *Coven Craft: Witchcraft for Three or More* and *Pagan Kids' Activity Book*. With Azrael Arynn K, she has written *RitualCraft: Creating Rites for Transformation and Celebration; Candlemas: Feast of Flames;* and *Heart of Tarot*. She is also the Executive Director of Ardantane and serves on its faculty as the acting Dean of the School of Pagan Leadership.

She is handfasted to Azrael Arynn K and has a son, Starfire. Amber's interests include mountains and forests, dolphins, travel, science fiction, collecting large antique keys, art, reading, and all things magickal. Her role models include Doreen Valiente, Lao Tse, Xena the Warrior Princess, and Snoopy.

REVISED & EXPANDED

True Magick

A Beginner's Guide

AMBER K

Llewellyn Publications
Woodbury, Minnesota

SECOND EDITION
Fourth Printing, 2010

The first edition was published in 1990 and reprinted 14 times.

Cover design by Kevin R. Brown

Cover foliage images © PhotoDisc and Brand X Pictures

Editing and book design by Rebecca Zins

Illustrations by the Llewellyn Art Department

Tarot cards from *The Robin Wood Tarot* © Robin Wood

Llewellyn is a registered trademark of Llewellyn Worldwide Ltd.

LIBRARY OF CONGRESS CATALOGING-IN-PUBLICATION DATA
    K, Amber, 1947-
    True magick: a beginner's guide / by Amber K.—2nd ed.
        p.   cm.
    Includes bibliographical references (p.   ) and index.
    ISBN: 978-0-7387-0823-2
    1. Magic. 2. Witchcraft. I. Title.

    BF1611.K22 2006
    133.4'3—dc22

                                                                2005050440

Llewellyn Worldwide does not participate in, endorse, or have any authority or responsibility concerning private business transactions between our authors and the public.
    All mail addressed to the author is forwarded but the publisher cannot, unless specifically instructed by the author, give out an address or phone number.
    Any Internet references contained in this work are current at publication time, but the publisher cannot guarantee that a specific location will continue to be maintained. Please refer to the publisher's website for links to authors' websites and other sources.

Llewellyn Publications
A Division of Llewellyn Worldwide Ltd.
2143 Wooddale Drive
Woodbury, MN 55125-2989
www.llewellyn.com

Printed in the United States of America

Contents

Preface

Have you ever wondered about magick?

Not stage magic; not clever illusions with doves and rabbits and colored scarves; not lissome blondes in sequins disappearing from locked cabinets, but *magick*, the ancient skills and powers of the adepts who sought to transform themselves and their world. Magick chanted under the full moon by circling Witches, or performed by solemn robed wizards in candlelit ceremonies, or conjured by a skinclad shaman deep in a virgin rain forest. . . .

For magick, true magick, can change your life. With magick's aid, you can have vibrant health, prosperity, a new career. You can enhance your relationships and bring new ones into your life. With magick, you can reach deep inside yourself to find what you despaired of ever having—confidence, courage, tranquillity, faith, compassion, understanding, humor. It's not a miracle, and it's not easy, but magick works. And it can work for you.

If you're curious, you will find answers in this book. I am a high priestess of the Wiccan religion and an experienced practitioner of magick, and in this book I explain not only the history and lore of magick, but also its major varieties in the world today—from the Brujos of Mexico and the United States, to the temples of the Order of the Golden Dawn, to the sacred groves of Wiccan covens.

And if you want to practice magick to grow, to change, to heal with tools of the mind and heart and spirit—then this book will start you on the path. I will explain how to prepare yourself, how to find or create your ritual tools, how to establish a temple in your home, how to plan a ritual and cast a spell—and how to do it ethically and safely. No demons, no black masses, no hexes. Simply divine power flowing through you, intelligently applied for beneficial purposes.

Whether you are just curious, or whether you are already an aspiring magick worker—read on.

A Note about Terminology

First, I have capitalized "Pagan," "Witch," and "Wicca." Proper nouns relating to other religions are capitalized, and Paganism deserves the same respect as any other religion.

Second, throughout this book I have used "God/dess," "Goddess," or "God" to refer to the Ultimate Divine Source, and "god/dess," "goddess," or "god" to refer to certain facets or aspects of the Divine, such as Athena, Odin, or Cerridwen.

And third, I do not believe in the "generic masculine" (the sexist notion that "he" refers to people of both sexes) and have tried to avoid it. Unfortunately, it is awkward to include both genders in every sentence, such as "He or she is fortunate if he or she can design an excellent ritual for every magickal purpose." Instead, I have often used "they" and "their" to indicate the indeterminate singular as well as the plural. For example, "If a magician wants to learn magick, they had better be prepared to practice often and be willing to take risks, sometimes be disappointed, take responsibility for their mistakes, and then learn from those mistakes." I know perfectly well that this is ungrammatical by conservative standards, but it is becoming increasingly common in actual usage—and it's not sexist.

Acknowledgments

I wish to thank all those who made this book possible. They include:

My mother and father, Maxine and Bill, who believed in my writing abilities and in every person's right to choose their own spiritual path;

Ginny and Dave, high priestess and high priest of the Temple of the Pagan Way, who first taught me magick. The memory of their generosity, care, and humor still warms my heart;

Catelaine, who encouraged me during the writing of the original core of this book, then published as *Beginning True Magick*;

My coven sisters and brothers of Our Lady of the Woods, who help keep me growing;

And all the priestesses and priests of the Craft who used *Beginning True Magick* in their teaching and took the time to tell me how valuable it was.

Appreciation is due to Starhawk, because material in the back of her book *The Spiral Dance* contributed greatly to appendix II; and to Daniel Cohen, for information from his book *Magicians, Wizards and Sorcerers* that is incorporated into appendix VII.

In this new 15th anniversary edition, I add my thanks to all who have used *True Magick: A Beginner's Guide* in the past years, said fine things about it, and offered their reviews, ideas, and suggestions for improving it.

My regards to the ducks who watched me as I worked and gently encouraged me to stay on track. Even mild anatidaephobia[1] has its uses.

---

1   Anatidaephobia: the fear that somewhere, somehow, a duck is watching you (coined by Gary Larson, *The Far Side*).

Special gratitude to my beloved partner, Azrael Arynn K, who has, as always, offered her warm support and invaluable assistance organizing, editing, and critiquing this new edition.

And I thank Goddess for life and love.

Introduction to the
15th Anniversary Edition

Magick has been with us through our whole evolution-
ary journey, in every era for which we have records, and all over the world.
And even today, when the "magick" of science and technology looms so
large and transforms our cultures, the Arts Magickal are still practiced in
every nation, in many different forms.

Certainly many people believe that magick is all superstition and wishful
thinking, that our species has outgrown it, and that it is time to focus on
the solid, measurable results of modern engineering and technology. That
is understandable. The benefits of technology are immediate and tangible:
computers, a thousand portable electronic devices, cars that talk to us. Such
things have powerful appeal in a society based on accumulation, possession,
and instant gratification.

Magick, by contrast, often deals with matters of the heart and spirit. The
workings are somewhat mysterious, and the results can be gradual, organic,
and difficult to predict with precision. It takes a special kind of person to
enter this world—thoughtful, patient, disciplined, and willing to look deeply
into the nature of nonlinear, invisible, and subjective reality.

But is magick based on ignorance and superstition? Yes, frequently. A great
deal of folk magick is based on "recipes" handed down from traditional folklore and performed without understanding or self-preparation. It is an attempt
to engineer miracles "on the cheap." And it gives the illusion of more personal
power and control than that offered by simple prayer. It is similar to the fantasy
magic of movies and novels, where a twitching nose or ancient incantation
changes reality in the blink of an eye. And it works only as a placebo.

But is *all* magick based on ignorance and superstition? I wondered that once, long ago. Are we as a species so desperately self-delusional that we would cling to a practice so universally, in every civilization throughout history, if there was really nothing to it? But ancient peoples who practiced magick were not stupid just because they had not invented air conditioning; they produced brilliant thinkers and ageless art, among other things. And primitive societies existing today are often wiser spiritually, socially, and politically than our much-vaunted Western civilization. All the creations of these cultures—including magick—deserve more thoughtful, open-minded examination and reflection than most of us have been willing to give them.

Here in the West, many thousands of people practice magick. They are not hopeless losers grasping at straws to achieve success and happiness without talent or practical skills. They include medical professionals, technical staff for scientific projects, astronomers, physicists, computer technicians, educators, and business owners. They practice magick because they were open-minded enough to try it and because they discovered that it works.

To bring it to a personal level, I have been working magick for about twenty-seven years now, and I like to believe that I am not so silly as to hang on to something that long if it was nonsense. (I have had jobs, cars, and relationships that didn't work, and I was able to let them all go.) But time after time, I have seen people healed, lives changed, and even weather transformed through magick. The results never seemed supernatural; that is, they did not flout gravity or produce something from nothing. Often they seemed synchronistic, almost coincidental; but the excuse of coincidence only stretches so far. In any case, whether I am practicing magick or "causing coincidence," I am content as long as it works.

Occasionally the results of magick are dramatic—even spectacular. Such experiences tend to sweep away any lingering doubts about the reality of magick.

So it works, and like any tool it can be used for good or ill. As with any tool, some people have a natural affinity for it and develop their skills quickly; others have to work harder for results. As with any field of human learning, it contains its share of mistaken notions and charlatans. But there is a core of truth to magick that has kept it alive for millennia, and I hope you will find some of that truth in this book.

When I began my training as a Wiccan priestess in the late 1970s, I was frustrated by the lack of straightforward books about magick. It seemed to me that most of the available books either repeated superstitions from folklore or taught complex systems buried in layers of magickal symbolism specific to particular traditions. So I wrote a booklet, *Beginning True Magick*, that was designed to be simple, clear, and concise. A lot of people liked it, and Llewellyn asked me to expand it into a book. When *True Magick: A Beginner's Guide* first came out in 1990, I did not realize that it would sell more than 200,000 copies and become a standard textbook in Wiccan covens all over the United States.

Now, of course, there are many new books about magick—and some are excellent. But "the little green book," *True Magick*, seems to have found a special place in the hearts of many, and I was glad to have the chance to revisit and polish it.

Most of the book has stood the test of time, and it needed little change. But today's readers are a more sophisticated lot, with more training and resources readily available to them, so it seemed appropriate to expand the boundaries of the book into somewhat more advanced magick. Therefore I have added the sections on intrinsic and inner magick—and, by the way, coined these terms to stand for forms of the Art that every adept knows, and practices, and calls by different names. There is also more information on natural magick and new chapters on nature magick and everyday magick.

I have also added exercises and learning activities—lots of them—because magick is learned by doing, not just reading about it. Here for the first time I have published an exercise called the Elemental Star, which students over many years have assured me is an extremely useful tool for analyzing and tracking balanced personal growth. I have also listed many good books on various aspects of magick that have appeared over the past fifteen years, so that readers may pursue their special interests in depth.

And I have introduced material on quantum physics, because scientists are beginning to find evidence that the universe is even more mysterious and amazing than anyone had guessed—anyone but magicians, that is. It is wonderful to see the revelations of the laboratory converging with the intuitive knowledge that has been the province of magick for so long. It confirms what we have known for ages: that magick is not supernatural or miraculous, is much less devilish, and is simply a reality beyond the frontiers of known science.

My aim has been to preserve what was valuable from the first edition of *True Magick* and to add a great deal of additional material that would give it more breadth and depth, as well as the exercises to improve it as a practical learning tool. I do appreciate all the encouraging comments that readers have made over the years, and I have done my best to include the constructive suggestions you have shared.

There are different ways to read this book, depending on your temperament and need. You can:

+ breeze through the whole thing without stopping, then go back and begin doing the exercises;

+ read one chapter each week, doing the exercises at the end as you come to them;

+ read the whole book and then come back to explore the parts that really intrigue you in more detail;

+ read a chapter and then discuss it with your teachers, if you are part of a group or class, comparing the concepts here with what you have been taught; or

+ form a study group and use the book as the outline for your program, doing the exercises together or in parallel.

Hopefully I will have discovered much more to share with you by the time the 25th anniversary edition of *True Magick* appears. I am not concerned that we will ever run out of new material, for the wonders of magick are as infinite as space.

Please enjoy this book, and write to me about it if you wish. I cannot answer every letter, but I do read every single one that I receive.

In your practice of the Arts Magickal, may you be blessed by the Lady of the Moon and the Hornéd One of the Wilds, and by the Guardians of the Watchtowers, and by all spirit beings attracted to your rites.

Blesséd be,

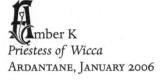

mber K
Priestess of Wicca
ARDANTANE, JANUARY 2006

With harm toward none

and for the greatest good of all

so mote it be!

About Magick—and You

Why do you want to do magick?

This book is for you—if you want to:

+ know in what direction your life is headed, so that you may consciously guide your own destiny;

+ make wise decisions and solve difficult problems;

+ cleanse yourself of ignorance, fear, and hatred;

+ heal yourself mentally, emotionally, and physically;

+ find new strength, happiness, and skill within;

+ have all the necessities of life;

+ protect yourself from harm;

+ help others when they request it;

+ help create a more loving world;

. . . and, ultimately, if you want to find spiritual fulfillment and joy in sharing the essence of divinity.

If you want magickal skill in order to harm another, or to control or manipulate anyone, then this book is not for you. Put it down or give it away before you endanger yourself.

If you seek the ancient skills of the adepts for only ethical, beneficial purposes, and primarily for your own growth, then read on.

What Magick Is Not

Magick is not an array of tricks or stage illusions. The "k" at the end of the word serves to distinguish it from the "magic" of nightclub acts. Magick is not for show.

Magick is not supernatural. As Janet and Stewart Farrar, prominent Irish witches and Craft teachers, point out, "Magic(k) does not break the laws of Nature; when it appears to do so, that is because it is obeying laws that the observer has not yet understood."[1]

Magick is not the medieval art of summoning demons to do one's will, at least not to intelligent and ethical magicians. Though it is possible to establish communication with beings on other planes of reality, trying to coerce them into service is both immoral and dangerous.

Magick is not based on a pact with "the Devil." Most magicians, including Wiccan priests and priestesses, do not believe in Satan and would certainly have no dealings with such an entity if he did exist.

Magick is not a good way to get revenge on enemies or force a former lover to return to you. Indeed, there is no "good" way to accomplish such nasty and immature things; but the penalties for misusing magick can be far greater than the consequences of these actions on the material plane.

Magick is not available only to a few talented individuals born with special gifts. It can be learned and mastered to a great degree by anyone with self-discipline and persistence.

Magick does not reside in ritual tools, amulets, magickal swords, etc., unless and until they are charged by a magician. The skill and power lie always in the magician, not in the tool.

Magick does not generally result in spectacular "special effects" on the material plane: strange entities materializing, showers of gold falling from the sky, locked doors bursting asunder, and so forth. Dramatic physical effects are possible and occasionally occur, but most magick aims at internal growth, where results are harder to see. Even magick for material-plane purposes tends to manifest in more or less quiet, gradual, natural ways.

---

1   Janet and Stewart Farrar, *The Witches' Way* (London: Robert Hale, 1984), 110.

And magick is not easy to learn or to practice. It is not an instant fix for life's problems, nor is it a shortcut to fame and wealth. It is a set of specialized tools, uniquely well-designed for inner growth and spiritual development. It can be used for more ordinary purposes, but sometimes that is like trying to pound nails with a screwdriver. Magick can be used to bring you safety, wealth, or loving relationships, but it is not a substitute for wearing a seat belt, getting a job, or being sensitive to your lover's needs. And no matter what it is used for, magick requires hard work and discipline.

What Magick Is

A definition of magick is in order. We have already rejected that of *Webster's* dictionary: magick as "the use of means (as charms, spells) believed to have supernatural power over natural forces." Here are some other definitions by magicians:

"Magic is the science of the control of the secret forces of nature."
—S. L. MacGregor Mathers

"Magic is a comprehensive knowledge of all nature."
—Francis Barrett

"Magick is the art and science of causing changes to occur in conformity with will."—Aleister Crowley

"Magic is the art of effecting changes in consciousness at will."
—William Butler

"The work of magic involves transformation, and the first transformation is the shift of perception."—Marion Weinstein

"The movement of natural energies . . . to create needed change. Energy exists within all things—ourselves, plants, stones, colors, sounds, movements. Magic is the process of rousing or building up this energy, giving it purpose, and releasing it. Magic is a natural, not supernatural, practice, though it is little understood."
—Scott Cunningham

So we can see that magick involves using natural forces to effect willed change, often changes in our own perceptions or consciousness. But what is the goal?

What Magick Is For

Stewart Farrar puts it this way: "The stage-by-stage development of the entire human being is the whole aim of magic."

According to Marion Weinstein, magick can help "get your entire life in harmony mentally, emotionally, physically, spiritually and psychically . . . And what is the ultimate purpose of the work? To fulfill the self on an even higher level. To transform, uplift, and so fully develop the self that the whole Universe may benefit thereby."[2]

William G. Gray, another well-known occultist, says: "Magic is for growing up as Children of Light. Sane, sound, healthy, and happy souls, living naturally and normally on levels of inner Life where we can be REAL people as contrasted with the poor shadow-selves we project at one another on Earth."[3]

Thus magick exists to expedite, guide, and enhance change. Wiccans might say it is the work of the goddess within: "Everything she touches, changes . . ."

It seems a peculiarly human process, as far as we know. Other creatures can change their environments, but only sentient, self-aware beings can change themselves. Perhaps the cetaceans attempt this too—one day we may explore the spiritual paths and magickal traditions of the dolphins and whales.

Change ourselves? But to what? To a fuller range of possibilities, a broader spectrum of spirit. Not change to something else, but to something *more*. First learn to know ourselves, and then we expand, stretch our hearts and minds and souls, and explore and develop new territories within ourselves.

We are part of All That Is. With magick, we can experience existence from the perspective of other parts and know that we are One. We can experience at-one-ment with the immanent Source.

Perhaps this is the goal of all spiritual paths: to reconnect with the Source, to bridge the chasm of illusion that makes us feel separate and alone, to come Home.

---

2 Marion Weinstein, *Positive Magic* (Custer, WA: Phoenix, 1991), 3.
3 William G. Gray, *Inner Traditions of Magic* (New York: Samuel Weiser, 1970), x.

But the quest requires us to change, and magick is an effective tool for this. The scary part is this: we can't know who we are changing into until we actually experience the change. By then it's too late for second thoughts. We cannot change back; we can only keep changing, or wither.

Because we give up our old selves, any change is a "little death" that is the necessary first step to rebirth. To choose this, to will it, and to seek it out is an act of incredible courage. Magick requires daring. Not to change is to stagnate and die; but to willingly offer up the life we know is to find a greater life.

In "The Charge of the Goddess," she says, "Nor do I demand aught of sacrifice, for behold, I am the mother of all things and my love is poured out upon the earth." On one level this is true: killing a lamb on an altar stone does not lead to inner growth.

Yet on another level, sacrifice is required: self-sacrifice, the surrender of your old self. This is the meaning of the Hanged Man of tarot's major arcana (below) and of Odin's act in Norse mythology: "Nine days and nights I hung on the Tree, myself sacrificed to Myself . . ."

To the conscious mind unaware of the immortal Spirit within, this kind of sacrifice, the loss of the isolated little persona-self, seems terrifying indeed. Yet through it one regains the lost wholeness of the Greater Self, which is all of us, which is God/dess.

The Robin Wood Tarot

Thus far our focus has been on that branch of magick called theurgy; or as Isaac Bonewits defines it, "The use of magic for religious and/or psycho-therapeutic purposes, in order to attain 'salvation' or 'personal evolution.'" Though this is generally the best and highest use of magick, we will not ignore thaumaturgy, again defined by Bonewits: "The use of magic for non-religious purposes; the art and science of 'wonder working'; using magic to actually change things on the Earth Plane."[4]

Thaumaturgy might include magick to heal physically; to travel safely; to obtain satisfying employment or a new home; to purify and bless a house or one's tools; to draw an adequate income; and so on. If such matters are accomplished without harm to others (as in seeking *a* job rather than *Sam's* job), and the magick is performed to supplement material-plane efforts rather than replace them, then there's nothing at all wrong with the practice of thaumaturgy.

Acting in Accord

Understand this: magick is not miracle-working. After you do a spell or ritual to achieve your purpose, you must still take practical steps to allow the magick to manifest. This is called "acting in accord" with the magick. You can do healing magick to get over an illness, but you must still rest and drink liquids. You can do a spell to get a better job, but you still must ask friends if they know of openings, and then apply for them. If you fail to do the logical follow-up steps, you will be like the legendary blonde who prayed night after night to win the million-dollar lottery, until after some weeks a great and weary voice thundered from the heavens: "O my daughter, I will consider your request; but you could help by buying a lottery ticket."

Magick and practical action reinforce each other; but you must do both to make the magick work.

Blesséd be.

---

4   Isaac Bonewits, *Real Magic* (Berkeley, CA: Creative Arts Book Co., 1971), 268.

A Brief History of Magick

Through most of the human history that we know, human cultures included a mix of magick, religion, science, philosophy, and trickery or illusion. Magick was often performed in the name of, or through the power of, a deity: the pharaoh blessed the crops as Amon-Ra incarnate; Moses parted the Red Sea in Jehovah's name; the Delphi oracle delivered the wisdom of Gaia and, later, Apollo. All gods and goddesses performed miraculous feats, but certain deities are especially patrons of magick: Isis, Hecate, and Inanna were among the first.

Often enough, the practice of magick was confined to a priestly class. They alone could enter the inner sanctum of the temple, read the omens in the stars, and receive the commands of the gods. Occasionally they impressed their congregations with "secret" skills that were actually rudimentary science, as in predicting eclipses. Sometimes they used blatant trickery to make idols "speak" or great temple doors swing open at a word from the king. And sometimes they performed magick that was true, real, and effective.

But all was intertwined as part of the human quest for understanding the world and our place in it. It was not until very recently that a historian could say, "Along with magic and science, religion makes up the third point of an eternal triangle of ideological warfare."[1]

---

1   Anthony Aveni, *Behind the Crystal Ball: Magic, Science and the Occult from Antiquity Through the New Age* (New York: Times Books, 1996), xi.

Magick Everywhere

However blended with other endeavors, humans have done magick in all cultures throughout history; each culture has created its own special techniques and understandings. In many African villages, according to Malidoma Patrice Somé, all positive magick and ritual were community endeavors; the solitary magician was suspect, and probably working to harm the village. Among the Norse, the written letter was a thing of mystery and awe, and the magick of runes and bindrunes became a high art. Hindu magicians developed the tattvas, those combinations of elemental symbols and colors that could become gateways to other realms of energy and consciousness. The *strega* of Italy saw magick as a way to fight oppression by the wealthy and powerful, and developed it as a weapon.

Always there have been commonalities, because all magicians are human and share the same structure of mind and emotion at the deepest levels of being. Magicians everywhere know that invisible forces can be concentrated and channeled to change the world, whether they do it with dance, song, pranayama breathing, or words of power. They know that other worlds exist close to ours, accessible through the mind: the underworld of the shaman and the astral planes of the ceremonial magician. They know that higher powers can be invited to inhabit our bodies and speak through our lips; hence the oracles of Gaia and Apollo at Delphi, who counseled the kings of Greece; the Asatru priestess speaking for the Norse gods in *seidhe*; the Vodoun *mambo* being "ridden" by the love goddess Erzulie; and the modern Wiccan priest aspecting the hornéd god, or the priestess Drawing Down the Moon.

Let us look at a few of the highlights of magick in various times and cultures, and let us begin as close to our beginning as possible.

Magick at the Dawn of Humankind

Most of the story of our species occurred before written history. Humans and our hominid ancestors go back two million years and more: eighty thousand generations at least. Writing has only been in common use, in some cultures, for one-fifth of one percent of those long eons. We will never know most of the struggles, experiments, discoveries, and traditions that comprised the magick, science, or religion of our ancient forebears.

We have found a tiny fraction of the artifacts from our Paleolithic ancestors, though doubtless there are thousands more remarkable objects buried beneath windswept desert dunes, hidden deep in unknown caves, or sunk in the sediments of lakes and coastlines. What can we learn from the cave paintings, carvings, artifacts, and graves?

We see paintings in deep caves where no reasoning being would live that depict animals, hunters, and people dancing in masks and the skins of animals. We find sculpted and carved images of women, either pregnant or fat, with large breasts, hips, and bellies. We find bones incised with records of the changing phases of the moon, or with plants and animals (in one remarkable blade, seeds and a bull bison on one side, and flowering plants and a cow bison on the other). We find small bone and ivory carvings, usually of animals, that are perforated as though to hang on a leather thong. We find ancient flutes, again of bone, and images of bows that may have been made for music rather than hunting. We find the skulls and bones of cave bears carefully collected and arranged. And we find skeletons sprinkled with red ochre and buried in a fetal position with grave goods close by.

If these long-ago people thought like us, then their magick may have been to honor the spirits of their prey, gain success in hunting, revere a mother goddess and a hornéd god of animals, seek the strengths and protection of animal spirit allies, and prepare the dead to be born again into a new life. But all we really have are a few silent, enigmatic clues, and a great deal of imagination and speculation.

Magick in the Fertile Crescent

The ancient civilizations of Sumer, Babylonia, and Assyria were places of learning, science, and magick. The science of Mesopotamia included astronomy, writing, arithmetic, irrigation, and architecture. The magick of Mesopotamia included the power of the spoken word. A thousand years before the Common Era, Babylonian exorcists could invoke the powers of benevolent gods, banish demons of illness, and heal with words and hands.

Their astrologers could interpret the signs of the night sky; their wise men or *baru* were among the first to divine the future by reading the entrails or livers of animals. Many magicians specialized in the creation of amulets, charms, and talismans for protection.

Life, Death, and Magick in Khemi

Egypt was known as Khemi or "the Black Land" in the days of the pharoahs. Their magickal arsenal may have been vast and elaborate, but what has survived are occasional documents such as the Book of the Dead, artifacts such as their mummies, inscriptions on papyrus documents and temple walls, and thousands of amulets or talismans.

Their magick was intimately tied to the cycles of nature. They knew that the human spirit followed a similar cycle of life, death, and rebirth, and their magick was designed to aid the process. Magick was used to protect the body, which continued to be home to part of the soul after death; it could provide resources for the spirit to survive the journey to the underworld and ensure prosperity in the next life. Magickal amulets could protect body parts, stand in for the mummy if it was damaged or destroyed, and help procure a positive judgment at the Weighing of the Soul. The most popular forms were the *udjat* or Eye of Horus, the scarab beetle, the *djed* or Pillar of Osiris, and the ankh, symbol of life.

The *shabti* were another form of magick: these were tiny servitors made of clay who would grow and harvest the crops in the next life, and serve the deceased as commanded. This reflected the Egyptians' belief in the magick of replication and substitution: a clay figure, painted eye, or false door was as effective as the real thing, since all matter was living, organic, and spirit-filled.

Redundancy was built into Egyptian magick: if one amulet was good, two or twenty were better. Creation myths were not replaced, but new ones were added. A spell or incantation might be used, and then another performed for the same purpose, just to be safe. Deities multiplied and overlapped. The Egyptians welcomed new magick but discarded nothing.[2]

The Magick of Old Europe

In central, western, and northern Europe, all too little was recorded. We have the stone circles and other megalithic monuments of the pre-Celtic peoples; we have some folklore recorded by early Christian monks in the Celtic enclaves of Wales, Ireland, and Scotland; and we have the Eddas and runic inscriptions of the Norse. Later, fragments of Druidic lore were recorded by the Romans, their bitter enemies.

We can guess at many things. That they worked a magick of animal totems seems clear, because many clan and family surnames are those of animals, and they danced with horned masks. Old herbal compendiums suggest that plants were used for magick as well as healing, and certainly the Druids believed that each species of tree contained its own symbolism and powers. Folklore tells us that amulets and talismans were popular, from hag (or holey) stones to rowan twigs or iron nails. The use of "witches' bottles," "witches' ladders," and "witch balls," lingering into historical times, tells us that unseen energies were trapped, directed, or diverted.

Protective magick was extremely important, for the world was filled with uncanny spirits and creatures: boggarts and brownies; the Fair Folk, *seelie wicht* or Gentry; *pookas* and goblins; spectral black dogs and great *orms*; giants and trolls; and the shades of the dead. So people memorized spoken charms and carried amulets, and later hung magickal brass ornaments on their horses and nailed horseshoes or Brigit's crosses over their barn doors.

Here, as elsewhere, religion and magick went hand in hand. During autumn thunderstorms, Odin or Herne led the Wild Hunt through the dark sky, and goddesses lived in every spring and holy well. Much magick was used to placate, propitiate, and protect.

---

2   Dan Burton and David Grandy, *Magic, Mystery, and Science: The Occult in Western Civilization* (Bloomington, IN: Indiana University Press, 2004), 9–34.

Science and Magick in Greece and Rome

Some say that science really began with the Greeks. They gave us the study of logic, geometry, the concept of the atom, the formation of cells and planets, and the whole view of the cosmos as an orderly machine operating by fixed laws.

And yet Plato, Aristotle, and most of the great philosophers of that era also firmly believed in magick. They spoke of divination, the elements, astrological horoscopes, the evil eye, and the correspondences of bodily organs with celestial objects. All around them were practitioners of thaumaturgy or "low magick for a price," magickal healers, and quacks, as well as theurges who taught of the spirit. Greeks invented or rediscovered the magick wand, spoke to the dead through necromancy, and sometimes pushed nails into clay images in a Vodoun-like curse.

The culture of Rome continued the Greek mix of science and folk magick, much of it concerned with healing. The naturalist Pliny and others list a thousand remedies that involve rubbing strange substances on the body at the correct phase of the moon. Some worked because the healer and patient expected them to, and some were actively harmful. Today we would view such remedies as a mixture of practical herbalism, psychology, magick, and rank superstition. Throughout the Roman Empire, magick and religion were still intertwined: often a legionnaire would wear an amulet sacred to Mars to help him in battle, or one sacred to the Celtic horse-goddess Epona if he were a cavalryman.

When Christianity appeared on the scene, one of its early branches was Gnosticism, whose believers knew the search for knowledge was the best path to God and that all faiths had wisdom to offer. With sufficient esoteric knowledge, humanity could fight past demons and evil forces and come to a direct experience of divinity. Magick had an important place in Gnosticism, but there wasn't much need for the authorities and dogmas that existed elsewhere in the emerging Roman Church.

Magick Versus the Church

New forces were afoot that would strike a heavy blow against all forms of magick. Emperor Constantine of Rome converted to Christianity and declared magick illegal throughout the Empire. He was followed by a long string of Christian monarchs who reviled magick. Perhaps they saw magick as deceit and trickery, the game of charlatans who preyed upon the gullible; some so-called "magick" certainly was. Possibly they wished to reserve magick for the church: the transformation of the wine to the blood of Christ is certainly a magickal act. Perhaps they feared that magick came a little too close to the miracles of Jesus, such as healing, walking on the Sea of Galilee, or changing the water to wine at Cana. Certainly Constantine was serious: "There shall be no more divination, no curious inquiry, forevermore."[3]

Early Christianity was only one of many, many religious sects, and it soon set aside the passivity of the early martyrs to attack its competitors. As the new faith spread through Europe, zealous churchmen and rulers lashed out against any who did not accept the authority of the church.

The Crusades against the "infidels" who held the Holy Land were followed by the Inquisition that aimed to destroy heresy within Europe. Gnostics and Pagans, Jews and Muslims, Cathars, Albigensians, Waldenses, the Knights Templar, homosexuals, and Witches all became targets over the following centuries. Some were attacked for their "heretical" beliefs, some because they practiced magick (and non-Christian magick must have come from the Devil), and some because they held land, wealth, or power. Folk magick was still practiced in the rural corners of Europe, and wise women and cunning men continued their healing in the villages; alchemists and a few magicians with wealthy patrons quietly sought the Mysteries. However, for all practical purposes, spiritual and temporal control was in the hands of the Church of Rome.

But by the sixteenth century, the church had other rivals for the minds of humanity. Experimentation and measurement led to the advance of science, and the Reformation in Christianity took Western society away from the

---

3   K. Seligman, *The History of Magick and the Occult* (New York: Harmony, 1948), 73–74.

more magickal, Pagan-based practices of the Roman Catholic Church to a more abstract religion based on faith and dogma—which still, like the Roman Church, forbade the practice of magick.

Between the hammering of the Roman Church, the impressive advances of science and engineering, and the austere beliefs of the Protestant churches, the study of magick seemed doomed. But across the sea from Europe lived a different world.

Magick Comes to the New World

In North America, Native American cultures were no strangers to magick. For most tribes, it was closely bound up with their spiritual practices, except for the renegades who used magick to harm the community: the malevolent sorcerers who could change their skins and move like animals, who knew the secrets of poison and curse.

When other peoples arrived in the New World, they brought their beliefs and their magick with them. The German immigrants, called "Pennsylvania Dutch," had their hex signs for protection and good fortune; the settlers of the Ozarks and the Appalachian Mountains practiced the "pow wow" folk magick of their ancestors. Black slaves brought the religions of Africa and blended them with Catholic beliefs to create new Afro-Caribbean magick and spirituality: Vodoun, Santeria, Candomblé, and more. Jewish immigrants brought knowledge of the Qabala, and others came who held the lore of their Witch or Norse ancestors.

Despite the headlong rush of technology in the nineteenth century—the railroads and telegraph and factory—a curious thing happened: the Spiritualist movement appeared. The gaze of the American public went from science to séances, table-rapping, communication with the dead, ectoplasmic apparitions, levitation, and other mystical phenomena.

The Western Tradition Rises

Back in Europe, the Enlightenment was eclipsed by the Romantic Movement. As though in reaction to the Industrial Age, many people began looking to a (largely mythical) past and matters of the spirit for their inspiration. Suddenly medieval romances, including the legends of King Arthur, were popular again. New orders of Druids arose and gathered at Stonehenge (not originally a Druid temple) in white robes. Folklorists began gathering the old legends and customs of the countryside, and Egyptology bloomed to the point that mummies were shipped to England and viewed at "unwrapping parties." The Society for Psychical Research was founded in London in 1882.

Divination became quite stylish, and dream interpretation, palmistry, physiognomy, phrenology, tarot cards, and Gypsy fortunetelling became all the rage.

In the meantime, magickal orders thrived. The Masons and Rosicrucians, who had been around for a long time, reappeared; and the Hermetic Order of the Golden Dawn was created to teach the Western Tradition of ceremonial magick to initiates. That the "Western" tradition was based on a Jewish mystical system (the Qabala) and on the mythology of Egypt, mixed in with esoteric Christianity, struck no one as odd. It was "dedicated to the ideal that a select brotherhood of adepts would reform the entire world by perfecting both self and nature as illuminated through secret doctrines passed down through the ages."[4]

The Golden Dawn grew and splintered under the impact of several strong and willful leaders, and was succeeded by a string of other temples, lodges, and orders more or less in its image. A few still exist today, while others lasted only as long as their charismatic founders.

Wicca and Paganism: "We're Back"

Back in America, the Spiritualist movement had faded and people were distracted by a World War, the Great Depression, and another World War in rapid succession. But the 1950s and '60s brought a youth culture that turned on with rock-and-roll, sexual freedom, the hippie lifestyle, marijuana, and so-

---

4   Aveni, 208.

called New Age practices—a motley collection of channeling, crystal healing, organic gardening, tarot reading, meditation, and spirit guides.

About the same time, a retired British civil servant named Gerald Gardner
was reinventing Witchcraft as the religion of Wicca, a form of nature-oriented spirituality that included the practice of magick. Through the efforts
of Ray Buckland and others, Wicca spread to the United States, and soon
cropped up in Canada and Australia as well. Other varieties of Neopaganism appeared concurrently, such as Asatru (the Norse religion of the Vanir
and Aesir gods), new Druid organizations, feminist Goddess spirituality, and
other magico-spiritual groups based on the practices of ancient Egyptians,
Hebrews, Sumerians, Celts, Picts, and so on.

Though the New Agers, Neopagan groups, and occasional family-tradi-
tion Witches were far from identical, they did and do have overlapping atti-
tudes and beliefs, in particular an openness to magick and a self-empowered
spirituality quite unlike the churches on Main Street.

The Triumph of Science and Religion

For all the interest within the youth counterculture and in rare pockets of
mature freethinkers, it seemed as though Western society in the late twentieth century was firmly non-magickal. The power centers belonged to science
and technology, which had brought us the Good Life of fast cars, television,
and scented toilet paper; to the merchant class, whose spirituality focused
on profit and market share; to the mainstream churches, whose doctrines
had become traditional and comfortable; and to the conservative Christians,
suspicious of science and intolerant of the occult.

It was into this mixture that the New Agers, the Pagan priestesses and
priests, and the new magicians came. Some exist in the economic mainstream as nurses and computer technicians and real estate agents; others live
on the fringes, making arts and crafts in out-of-the-way nooks. Those who
practice magick (and let it be known) are sometimes dismissed as kooks by
the excessively left-brained, or are feared by conservative religionists. But
bold and imaginative thinkers, whether shamans or scientists, have always
been on the fringe of society. The value of magick is proven by its effect on

the individuals who practice it and its capacity to improve society, whether or not it is understood or given credit by the majority of people.

Magick lives. It lives in the hearts of those who preserve or revive their traditional cultures, and it lives in the minds of those who are curious and open-minded enough to explore its possibilities.

Science Discovers Magick

But wait. Who are those others who march this way, conjuring with invisible forces and reciting arcane incantations? They are the quantum mechanic mages, the prestidigitory physicists, the—scientists?

As we discuss in chapter 4, the more we explore the foundations of matter and energy, the farther we reach into the vast reaches of space, the more wonders we encounter: things that are neither particle nor wave, reality transformed by the eye of the beholder, instantaneous communication that cannot be measured or traced, neutrinos, gluons, photinos, selectrons, charm, strings, branes, muons, and quarks, oh my!

It seems that the old Arts, once scorned and nearly exhausted, may yet receive validation and renewal by scientists who dare to look deeply at the fabric of reality—and see magick there.

Exercises Toward Mastery

1: Artifact Meditation

Find a book or online article that shows interesting artifacts of stone, bone, ivory, or wood from before recorded history. Pick one and meditate on it; ask yourself how it might have been used in magick, and give your imagination free rein.

2: Research the Magick of an Ancient Culture

Pick one culture—Greek, Chinese, Sumerian, Norse, African, Polynesian, whatever interests you—and do some research, online or in the library, until you feel you have a beginning understanding of how magick fit into their lives. If you feel motivated, write an essay on it and submit it to a Pagan or magickal journal or 'zine.

3: Read About Famous Magicians

Appendix VII, "Magicians Through the Ages," briefly introduces some real and legendary people who are remembered as great practitioners of the Art. Read about them and see if there is one who especially intrigues you. Then find a biography (or autobiography) for that person. Think about their experience with magick and whether you might have made any different choices than they did.

Blesséd be.

To follow this path further, read:

Behind the Crystal Ball: Magic, Science and the Occult from Antiquity Through the New Age by Anthony Aveni (Times Books, 1996)

Magic, Mystery, and Science: The Occult in Western Civilization by Dan Burton and David Grandy (Indiana University Press, 2004)

The Rise of Magic in Early Medieval Europe by Valerie I. J. Flint (Princeton University Press, reprint ed. 1994)

The Secret Teaching of All Ages (An Encyclopedic Outline of Masonic, Hermetic, Qabbalistic and Rosicrucian Symbolical Philosophy, Being an Interpretation of the Secret Teachings Concealed with the Rituals, Allegories, and Mysteries of All Ages) by Manly P. Hall (Philosophical Research Society, Diamond Jubilee Edition, 1988)

The Occult: A History by Colin Wilson (Random House, 1971)

First Steps in Magick

So it begins. The steps that follow will lead you into another universe, in a gradual and logical way. Later you will encounter experiences (if you haven't already) that are anything but gradual and take you far beyond logic, but at least you can begin with a sense of order. If you are already an experienced practitioner, you should still read this chapter; it's very useful occasionally to go back to the essentials, fill in the gaps, and reinforce good habits that may have drifted into disuse.

A Time for Magick

Find a time of day, preferably every day, when you can work on your magick. If you wish, you can combine magickal training with a daily spiritual practice—prayer, meditation, chanting, or whatever your faith suggests or requires. Early birds may choose the hour of dawn, others may use the first hour after returning from work or school. Just before bedtime is possible, but you may be too tired, and the magickal exercises may leave you too excited to sleep well at first.

Make this daily work a habit; it has been said that if you do something for twenty-one days in a row, the habit is fairly well established. An hour at a time should be sufficient. Do not attempt too much on any single day; save some of the adventure for tomorrow! But if you feel tired on a given day, and are tempted to skip your practice, then promise yourself, "I'll just spend ten minutes or so, centering and re-energizing." (The "or so" may turn into an hour, once you get started and see how good it feels.)

You will also perform rituals at special times, depending on your needs and correct magickal timing (a certain day, hour, phase of the moon, or astrological conjunction often helps magick along). But on all the other days, do your practice until the pattern is established.

A Space for Magick

You need a place to do the work—your own personal temple or sanctuary. This can be a room in your home or a private space outdoors, but it should ideally be a quiet and private place dedicated solely to your magickal training and practice.

The first reaction to this idea is often "That would be great, *but* . . ." "BUT I don't have room in my apartment." "BUT I don't have a yard." "BUT I don't have any place that's really private."

It's time to move your BUT. Take all the obstacles and problems, stuff them in a sturdy cardboard box in your mind, tape it securely with heavy packing tape, and tuck it out of the way. (The next time you open it, if you ever notice it again, it will be empty.)

Now find a place. If you don't have the resources to find a few square yards of space on a planet this size, how will you do everything else required to become a competent magician? So do it.

Get creative. Is there a room in your house or apartment that really doesn't get used much? Take it. Clear out stuff, have a garage sale, donate to a charity, make room.

You may eventually want shelving, a chest, or a cupboard for supplies such as candles, oils, herbs, incenses, and ritual tools. Some magicians keep them under the altar or in it. A small table or wooden chest may serve as your altar; I used a wooden television cabinet at one time, with the appliance removed and shelves installed inside.

You may wish to decorate the room with magickal paintings, statuary, photographs, or wall hangings. These might depict your favorite deities, power animals, religious symbols, or anything that touches your heart and spirit and helps to empower you.

Some ceremonial magicians decorate their temples in a very formal and elaborate style. They may have black and white pillars flanking the altar (representing the two great principles or polarities that uphold the Qabalistic Tree of Life), great brass or silver candlesticks, complex wall hangings for each of the elements, and a personal computer for working out astrological charts. (In most magickal homes, however, the computer would be in another room; many practitioners find technology useful but prefer that their temple areas have a more archaic/romantic look. Also, magickal energies can sometimes disrupt electrical appliances, including watches and computers.)

Is there NO "extra" room? Do you have a chair? Put a room divider or folding partition around it, then sit in the chair and do magick in your head.

If you live in a nice year-round climate, you could do most of your work outdoors; some magicians work outside whenever possible, to be close to the rhythms and power of nature. Find a corner of your yard, screen it with lattices, fencing, and plants, and call it your temple. Maybe a storage shed or part of your garage could be cleared.

If you are able to set up a permanent outdoor ritual area on your own land, you can design it to be as elaborate as you wish. You can surround your circle with standing stones, or herb or flower gardens. You can outline it in rocks, or erect candle posts at the four cardinal points. You may wish to build a covered shrine to shelter a statue of your favorite goddess- or god-aspect. If you like, hang wind chimes, magickal talismans, or protective wards from nearby trees. Or you can leave the space simple and natural.

If you are uncertain how to arrange or decorate the area, use your divinatory skills (pendulum, tarot, etc.) to decide, or simply trust your instincts. It is more important that the area feel right to you than that it follow any standard layout or decor.

No space inside or out? Find a secluded spot in a nearby public park, a national forest, or other public lands, and make it yours. You already own it, so use it. Clean and bless the space, and get a small suitcase or backpack to carry books and supplies back and forth.

By the way, forget the movie stereotype of a wizard's workshop as dark, cobwebby, and cluttered with skulls and ancient manuscripts. Mess and magick don't mix. Indoors or out, keep your temple very clean and unclut-tered. It should be one place in your life where you can find solitude and simplicity.

Your Magickal Journal

You will need a written record of your rituals, results, observations, tarot readings, dreams, new knowledge and insights, and so forth. Wiccans or Witches call this a "Book of Shadows." Others may call it simply a "magick-al journal," or follow Scott Cunningham's suggestion and call it a "mirror book," because it is "a mirror of your spiritual life. As such it is quite valu-able in assessing your progress in Wicca and life itself. Thus, when reading over the book, you become your own teacher. Notice problem areas and take steps to resolve them."[1]

A stationery store can provide you with a simple, inexpensive book of blank pages; or you can visit a metaphysical shop or Internet store and find beautiful blank books with embossed leather covers. There is some advan-tage in having a book you can touch—as a tangible, solid object, it may bol-ster your subconscious faith in magick. However, it is also possible to keep a virtual journal on your computer, and some people love the idea of record-ing thoughts on astral experiences in cyberspace. Just back up your electron-ic files frequently.

A Purpose for Magick

One of the first things to record in your journal is a statement of why you wish to learn magick. (Look again at chapter 1 to see if anything there reso-nates with your heart.) If your motives are wise and good, you can re-read them from time to time and reaffirm your direction. It is also possible that you will look at this statement years later and say to yourself, "I have cer-tainly grown since then! My purposes now are deeper and more profound than anything I could have imagined then."

---

1   Scott Cunningham, *Wicca: A Guide for the Solitary Practitioner* (St. Paul, MN: Llewellyn, 1990), 79.

Your Family and Neighbors

Unless you live by yourself in the country, you may have to brief other people on your plans to study magick. If you are married, certainly your spouse needs to know and hopefully is a full partner in this project. If you have roommates, at least explain in general terms what you are doing, and perhaps offer to lend them some good books if they are interested. If your activities are likely to be noticed by neighbors (chanting, torchlight processions, etc.), and if you are on good terms with them, you might give them enough information to allay any fears or misconceptions: for example, "I'm doing a ceremony of blessing for my house tonight, in case you hear singing or whatever; I'll try not to disturb you."

If you have small children, explain what's happening in simple terms. Occasionally do simple little rituals with them, like lighting a candle to help someone get over their illness more quickly—with permission from the sick person, of course! Older children may be more intensely curious and want to be deeply involved. You can certainly teach them the basics, such as grounding and centering, without permitting anything that could possibly get too complicated for them. There are good books on Pagan parenting that discuss children and magick in more depth.

Last but not least, consider your animal friends. Some animals love magickal energies and ritual, others get nervous and uncomfortable. Talk to them about what you are doing (they may not understand all the words, but your voice is reassuring and they like the attention). Decide whether you will allow them in your circle or whether that's too distracting for now, and make sure they have a comfortable place to be elsewhere if they choose not to participate.

Choosing a Magickal Name

When you cast a circle "in a place between the worlds, in a time outside of time," you become someone different. For the duration of that experience, you set aside your everyday persona and become a magick-worker.

Some magicians choose to recognize and enhance this shift in consciousness by taking a new name, for use only during ritual or only among other
"magickal" folk. Assuming a new name is a message to your Deep Mind that
you have embraced a new facet of yourself. Being called by this name is a
signal that you are to shift into that persona and make the inner preparations
necessary to work magick.

This is not a universal practice among magicians. The high priest who
initiated me used the name "Dave" in the circle and out of it. Many magicians prefer not to have a clear-cut distinction between their magickal and
mundane personas, on the theory that it is harder to incorporate magick
into their daily lives if they emphasize the difference by adding a new name.

You must decide for yourself whether a new, additional name will help or
hinder your magickal growth. If you are uncertain, then experiment with it.

Usually I recommend that you choose a name representing qualities you
would like to grow into. If you are a very "earthy" person, but lack energy,
passion, and enthusiasm, then you might choose one associated with the element of Fire that corresponds to those qualities. A man might choose a Fire
god name like Agni (Hindu), Hephaestus (Greek), or Sol (Roman). A woman
might choose Vesta (Roman), Brigid (Celtic), or Bast (Egyptian).

Alternatives include fiery herb names such as Cinnamon, Cayenne, or
Ginger. More direct still are Flame, Flambeau, Ember, or Niedfýr. Related
animal names would include Salamander, Dragontongue, and Red Mare.
Such a fiery name can help you discover and express the Fire energy that is
hidden within you.

Many people need to meditate and read a lot before the perfect name
comes to light. I must have considered hundreds of possibilities before I
chose "Amber," because it looks like sunlight and seems a combination of
Earth (the life-blood of a tree) and Fire (the sunlight which gave the tree
energy to live). This happened before "Amber" became a popular name; and
a few months after I chose it I was shocked to learn that there was another
Witch named Amber who lived nearby. So I chose "K" as a surname, because
I liked that letter and wanted my name to be unique. Later it occurred to me

that my "K" was the K in magick . . . and the difference between *magic* and *magick* is the difference between illusion and transformation.[2]

Your new name can come from a book of ancient mythology; from another language important to you; your power animal; a sound you have heard in nature; a list of herbs, flowers, or gemstones; a fantasy novel; an acronym (first letters of the words in a phrase); a star chart; the name of a person you admire; or anyplace else. The crucial thing is not the source, but how you feel about it.

Choose a name filled with power and magick. If it wears well, then carry it proudly. If it does not, then change it. Tell your friends and family when you would and would not like them to use it, and patiently remind them until they remember. Be sensitive to the changes you feel within when the name is used, and live in such a way that you do the name honor.

Your Magickal Apparel

Because ritual is a special and often sacred activity, most magicians feel it is appropriate to dress in a distinctive way when they are about to work an important magickal operation. That something "distinctive" might be your naked self, it might be a special robe, or an elaborate costume with headgear, jewelry, a staff, etc. As you dress (or undress), the deeper levels of your mind realize that something special is about to happen, and prepare psychologically and emotionally.

Let's begin with the "skyclad" option, which is a Pagan term meaning "clothed by the sky"—that is, nude. Some Wiccan traditions prefer working skyclad, for several reasons. First, they feel that psychic energy flows more freely if it is not impeded by clothing. Second, it expresses the belief that the human body is natural and good, that it is the temple of the Spirit and not to be hidden in shame. Third, differences in income and social status are minimized when all in the circle are skyclad, as no one is wearing either expensive or cheap clothing.

---

2 Many true magicians use the *magick* spelling to distinguish theurgy and thaumaturgy from stage illusions. However, it should be noted that many practitioners do not follow this usage, and retain the spelling *magic* when they write of the art.

Skyclad Wiccans still wear their "Witch jewels," traditionally a silver brace-let and either a necklace (for women) or a torque (for men). High priestesses may also wear a crescent crown and garter, and high priests a hornéd mask or headgear.

Special jewelry is often worn by those who work magick. You should not wear the Witch jewels mentioned earlier unless you are an initiated priest/ess of Wicca and thus entitled to them. However, you may still want to wear jewelry that reflects your religious path (such as a pentagram, crescent moon, Star of David, cross, or whatever). You may also find or design jew-elry of particular metals, with certain gemstones set in it, to enhance your growth with their special energies. Lists of colors and gemstones, together with some of their traditional correspondences or associations, can be found in the appendices of this book. All jewelry worn during ritual should have magickal significance—and no watches, please.

Probably more magicians work robed than skyclad, either to stay warm or because the robe has symbolic meaning. The most common style is an am-ply cut robe with long sleeves and a hood. The robe should be loose enough so that one can dance and move freely, and sit down cross-legged. Avoid very long, flowing sleeves, since they tend to drag in the wine chalice or catch fire on the candles. You can use the hood to block your outer vision when you meditate and thus avoid distractions.

Robe designs can be found in pattern books at your local fabric store. They will not be called "ritual robes," of course. Look in the leisurewear sec-tion for caftans, or in the costume section, or try to find a pattern for a choir robe. If you want something very simple, make a "T pattern," as shown in the illustration on the right.

Natural materials such as cotton, rayon, or wool are generally recom-mended because they allow your skin to breathe. However, if your rituals don't run too long and the room's ventilation is good, you can use anything that looks attractive and can be cared for fairly easily.

If you work with a coven or magickal lodge, it may have a tradition that certain clothing is worn in ritual. For example, the color of your robe may reflect your degree of attainment within the group. In my home temple,

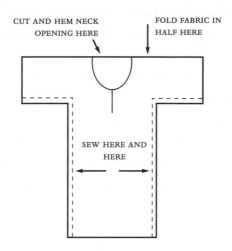

Earth-degree initiates wore Earth colors; Water-degree initiates had robes of watery green; Fire-degree wore red; and so on. But the Ladywood Tradition of Wicca asks all its students to obtain green robes, long-sleeved and hooded, but of any shade of green, to reflect the range of greens in a natural forest. Ask your teacher what is customary in your group.

If you are working as a solitary or with a partner, you can choose or design whatever you wish. If you don't plan to work skyclad, you may make or buy any color robe that feels healing, balancing, or empowering. One favored combination, as shown in the Magician card of the Rider-Waite-Smith or Morgan-Greer tarot decks, is an inner white shift or robe, and an outer robe or cloak of bright red. The white stands for purity of heart and spirit; the red symbolizes will and courage.

Still not sure? Then a simple white cotton robe is quite suitable to get started.

Most magicians wear a cord, also called a girdle or cingulum. In many covens and lodges this is awarded at initiation, and the color may represent the degree of initiation attained. If you are working alone, a simple white cord may be the best choice. You can sometimes find appropriate satin cord at a fabric store, or you can weave your own from several lengths of thinner cord. Make it at least as long as you are tall; a nine-foot cord is traditional in many groups.

It is important to keep your robe (as well as your body) clean and neat for every ritual. This shows respect for the powers you will be invoking and for yourself. When a robe becomes stained or worn out past repair, burn it or bury it with respect.

We have not mentioned footwear, for the simple reason that most people do not wear any during ritual. Having your bare feet on the earth or floor helps to keep you grounded. If you must wear footwear, you may choose anything you like, but sandals or comfortable shoes are preferred. Sore feet can be an unnecessary distraction.

Though clothes do not make the magician, dramatic and attractive apparel (or jewelry if you work skyclad) can enhance your confidence and subtly improve the power and quality of your work.

Dedication Ritual

You may wish to perform a short ritual to formally mark the beginning of your magickal studies. Many covens and magickal lodges require such a ritual because it impresses upon the student that this is an important step in life, and it spells out their responsibilities to themselves, the group, and the Art. Students are then formally known as dedicants, candidates (for initiation), seekers, neophytes, or some other term special to the group.

You can do a dedication ritual even if you are a solitary student. You may keep it simple, on the theory that the gods are impressed by sincerity and simplicity, or you may play it up with fancy robes and decorations, for the benefit of your Younger Self/Inner Child (more on this in chapter 5). Do what feels right to you. Here is a suggested outline:

1. Find a private place outdoors, or in your temple, sanctuary, or "magick room."

2. On your altar—or any small table or clear surface—place an image or symbol of your deity. On either side of it place candleholders,

one with a red candle for courage, and one with a white candle for purity. In front, place a small dish of salt, a little bowl of water, and a goblet or chalice with a little wine (or more water) in it.

3. You can dress in a simple robe or be skyclad, or dress in any clothing that is special to you.

4. Sit before the altar, and think about magick and why you want to learn it.

5. Stand, mix a little salt in the water bowl, and sprinkle some over yourself. Say, "I cleanse myself of all that is negative that I may walk this path with pure heart, mind, and spirit."

6. Say, "Powers of Air, Fire, Water, and Earth, be present and help me in my journey."

7. Invite God, Goddess, and deities by name to witness your dedication. If you don't have a relationship with a named deity, you can invite "the Creator" or "the Source of All Things."

8. Perform the self-blessing spell (rite) described in chapter 16.

9. Raise your arms up and out to the sides, and speak in a firm, strong voice: "Here in the presence of (deity) and the elemental powers, I dedicate myself to the study of the Arts Magickal. May I learn well, proceed from love, act with wisdom, and use my powers only for good. With harm toward none and for the greatest good of all, so mote it be!"[3]

10. Thank the elements and deity or deities. Sit quietly for a while, noticing anything about yourself or your surroundings that seems different.

Note that this ceremony does not bind you to the study of magick for any particular length of time. Should you ever decide not to pursue these studies, you can do a short ritual to release yourself from this path.

---

3   "So mote it be": traditional words of power meaning "It must be as I have said."

Music

Often you will make your own music in ritual, using a rattle, drum, or other instrument. At other times, recorded music is very helpful as a background to meditation, preparing the altar, or anything that does not require silence. If you wish, collect some inspiring, beautiful music and a simple sound system. You might consider music by Kitaro, Constance Demby, Patrick O'Hearn, Ken Davis, or Patrick Ball. Do not use popular music or anything that is sad, discordant, or angry in tone. At first, instrumental music alone is fine; later you might add *a cappella* choirs and music from various cultures and eras. Find your favorites and play them often during your practice.

Books

Do not buy a mass of books all at once, which you may not get around to reading for years. (There are enough of us already doing that.) First finish this book, and do all the exercises. Then pick one other book—perhaps from the recommended reading list in the appendices—and read that carefully. Perhaps you can get a copy through interlibrary loan or borrow it from a teacher, rather than buying it. If it's wonderful and you know you will refer back to it, you can always buy your own copy. If it's not so good, or too advanced, or just doesn't interest you, then you have saved some money.

Read critically, asking yourself lots of questions about the material in the book. Don't just swallow everything the writer says, even a well-known author, even this one. Compare, challenge, think it out for yourself. Everyone has a piece of the puzzle and their own special perspective on the universe; no one has the whole truth.

Tools

If you want to collect ritual tools, jewelry, props, and costumes, do it gradually. Make or find or buy one thing at a time, and get used to using it before you get another. Find all the meaning, energy, and uses of an object before you stuff it in a closet and reach for the next wonderful thing that you want.

Please do not approach it as we did; my partner and I like magickal stuff and collected it gleefully everywhere: some we made, some we bought from catalogs, some we discovered in metaphysical shops, some we found at yard sales or in the woods or on the Internet. A few thousand dollars later, we have enough magickal tools and supplies to equip six covens and a tower full of wizards for a hundred years. The only answer was to start a Pagan college (Ardantane) so that someone could use all this wonderful paraphernalia—we sure don't have the time to do so.

At any rate, the tools and costumes are great fun, and can be useful, and will be discussed later in this book. But they are not the heart of magick. So gather things—thoughtfully.

Supplies

The same advice applies for supplies such as herbs, candles, oils, incenses, and other consumables. Make or buy them as you need them.

The Journey Begins

Not everyone chooses to shape themselves or their world; some drift passively where the winds of fate blow them. If you choose to learn magick, it means that you have empowered yourself to take charge of your life. You haven't taken responsibility for becoming more and better than you are now, and perhaps you have chosen to make the world a better place. This takes courage and strength, and I salute you.

Exercises Toward Mastery

1: Your Temple or Sanctuary

Choose a place. Now. You can always change it later. If careful thought convinces you that there is no space in your home, then head outdoors.

2: Your Time for Practice

Choose a time when you can continue to study and practice magick. Pick a time now, and try it out for a week. You can always change it later.

3: Your Magickal Journal

Obtain a blank book. Put your name in the front (or your magickal name, once you have one), and the date of your dedication ritual. Then write your purpose in learning magick, and your initial thoughts and feelings as you begin this journey.

4: Your Magickal Name

Decide whether you will adopt a new (additional) name. If so, write down ideas. Unless you have a clear favorite, ask your deity to give you a sign as to which one you should use for now—a dream, a message from nature, or other portent.

If you choose to keep only your original name, then meditate on its meaning (or research it if you don't know), and find the magick and power that it holds.

5: Your Magickal Apparel

Decide whether you want to work skyclad or with a robe or other special garment. Make or buy something to get started. You can always change it later.

Blesséd be.

To follow this path further, read:

Wicca: A Guide for the Solitary Practitioner by Scott Cunningham (Llewellyn, 1990)

Positive Magic by Marion Weinstein (Phoenix Publishing, Inc., 1980)

Spiritual Gardening: Creating Sacred Space Outdoors by Peg Streep (Time-Life Books, 1999)

Gardening with the Goddess: Creating Gardens of Spirit and Magick by Patricia Telesco (New Page Books, 2001)

Magick and Science

Magick is based on certain premises that we might call the "Foundations of Magick." These are akin to the laws of physics, but physicists are just beginning to find scientific validation for some truths known to adepts for millennia. We can sum up these foundational ideas by saying that:

+ energy is abundant;
+ everything is connected;
+ possibilities are infinite;
+ the path lies within you;

. . . and that magicians can use their understanding of connections and available energy to turn possibility into actuality, by following that inner path. We will explore each of these points, but first a disclaimer.

The Limits

If anyone says that they understand *exactly* how magick works, they are probably an Ascended Master (and therefore not physically present) or kidding themselves.

The truth is that no human being really understands the workings of magick. To use an analogy, most people can walk and talk and drink a glass of water without having any real clue how their nerves and muscles and sinews are constructed. Likewise, almost anyone can flick a light switch and make the lights come on in the living room. But touching the light switch doesn't make you an electrician, and being an electrician doesn't mean you have a master's degree in electrical engineering, and having that degree doesn't mean that you understand how electricity works down to the sub-atomic level and beyond.

The same is true for magick. Anyone can work a simple spell, projecting energy toward a goal, and billions of people do it daily without having any training—or even calling it "magick." Doing this doesn't make one a magician: we reserve that title for people with training and intention. Being a magician doesn't make you an adept: that takes years of training and practice, and probably some natural aptitude for the Art. And even adepts don't understand everything about magick—not by a very long shot.

Now, we have models aplenty, which are working analogies. For example, kahunas (traditional Hawaiian shaman/priests) visualize psychic energy as being like water. Many Witches and others model the human Self as having three levels or personas. Using such models, we can all work magick, just as anyone can turn on the lights and pretty much anyone can learn to wire a table lamp. Some of us—quite possibly you—will become very, very competent at working magick, and transform our lives for the better. And a very few will become adepts, and change the world of humanity. And isn't that enough?

But totally mastering magick would be like completely understanding physics. You probably know in general terms how many breakthroughs have occurred in the last century or so; yet in 1890, Albert Michelson, distinguished former Head of the Physics Department at the University of Chicago, who won a jillion science awards, including the Nobel Prize in Physics (1907), and who was the first to accurately measure the diameter of a star, stated firmly that "The more important fundamental laws and facts of physical science have all been discovered and these are now so firmly established that the possibility of their ever being supplanted in consequence of new discoveries is remote."[1]

---

1   Quoted in Jargodzki, *Mad About Physics*, 133.

Today many scientists have a more realistic view of the matter. Thomas Carlyle said, "I don't pretend to understand the universe—it's a great deal bigger than I am."[2] And the famous physicist J. B. S. Haldane added, "My suspicion is that the universe is not only queerer than we suppose, but queerer than we can suppose."[3]

We will never completely understand physics or magick. Not you, not me, not the greatest adept alive. As far as we can tell, the realm of possible understanding is limitless, and there will forever be a frontier to our knowledge, beyond which lies . . . mystery.

None of this should discourage us from learning everything we can. Just don't expect simple or complete answers, like the astronomy professor who told his students, in the final exam, to "Describe the universe, and give two examples."[4]

Having said that, we can explore some working principles and models that will help you become a magician. Just remember, what follows is not "The Truth"—it just contains enough truth or resemblance to reality to work. And remember, too, that other models for magick also work perfectly well, we just can't fit them all in one book.

The Nature of Reality

On one level, believing in magick at all seems a little crazy; it's right on the library shelves between Bigfoot and fairies on one side, and unicorns and vampires on the other. Solid, respectable, commonsensible people don't believe in such things—do they? They're not real—are they?

To decide what might be real, we have to take a look at "reality." Can you answer these questions?

> **TRUE or FALSE:** There is real stuff out there that exists even if we don't see it (like Paris, or air).

> **TRUE or FALSE:** If we observe carefully and do lots of experiments, we can predict what will happen next (this particle is here, moving in that direction, so it will soon be there).

2   Quoted in Jargodzki, 39.

3   Ibid., 22.

4   Jargodzki, 145.

TRUE or FALSE: Nothing can travel faster than the speed of light (Einstein, right?).

TRUE or FALSE: There are certain laws of physics we know that govern matter in all times and places (laws like gravity and entropy).[5]

Did you answer "true" to all of these? Sorry; according to a lot of respected physicists, the answer is "maybe, maybe not" for every one.

We all would like the universe to behave in "normal," predictable, commonsense ways, but at the deepest levels we can see, it doesn't. Frank Herbert said it well: "Deep in the human unconscious is a pervasive need for a logical universe that makes sense. But the real universe is always one step beyond logic."[6]

So here are some best guesses about the nature of reality.

The "Laws" of Nature Are Not Universal

The world we know seems to operate by certain natural laws that we think of as universal and unchanging. Life is based on carbon atoms rather than silicon, for example. Water runs downhill. We can't see in the dark . . . and so on. But many of the "laws" we count on are based on random accidents that occurred when the universe started to expand, or when Earth was formed. In another universe, or galaxy, or even on another planet, the rules may be different. "A law of geology, biology, or human psychology may stem from one or more amplified quantum events, each of which could have turned out differently."[7]

There Are an Infinite Number of Kinds of Particles (Most of Which We'll Never See)

How many different building blocks of the universe can you name? Well, there are protons, neutrons, electrons, and a few weird ones like quarks and muons. So, maybe ten or twelve? According to Superstring theory, there are not only a lot of different kinds of particles, there may be an infinite number.

---

5   True/False questions are from Gribbin, *In Search of Schrödinger's Cat*, 222–223.

6   Quoted in Jargodzki, 71.

7   Gell-Mann, *Quark and the Jaguar*, 134.

We just don't know anything about most of them, because most have such high masses that we'll never get them into a laboratory to look at.[8]

There Is No Difference Between Matter and Energy

At the smallest level we can measure, "things" sometimes act like waves of energy and sometimes act like particles of matter. Mostly they behave like whichever one you expect them to . . . which is very courteous and cooperative of them, but just a tad frustrating if you want your universe to be simple. Simple or not, this works just fine for magicians. We *know* we can manipulate energy, and we do it all the time in rituals. And if even solid things are really (or sometimes) energy waves, then they are not as rigid and static as they seem, but susceptible to change by the power of imagination, will, and directed energy.

Mostly, Everything Is Empty Space—Which Is Very Full

How much did you pay for this book? Did you know that it's composed mostly of empty space—like 99.99999 percent of it? If you think that's bad, so is your car's engine block. Every "solid," material object is built of particles (or waves) that are more space than stuff. But that doesn't mean nothing is happening in that empty space, or that it looks like Sunday night at Starbucks. Scientist John Gribbin tells us that actually "it is seething with activity, a maelstrom of virtual particles . . ."[9]

The World Is Only Real Because We Are Watching It

Remember the "big bang"? Well, you're probably too young, but you know that's when everything started, right? Not exactly. Quantum theory says that it wasn't *really* real until someone observed it—or at least observed the leftover radiation from the event. In other words, the universe existed only in potential, even after it was created, for billions of years, until we evolved to the point that we noticed. At that moment everything became real, back to

8   Gell-Mann, 129.
9   Gribbin, 260.

the beginning. In a sense, we created all that exists by seeing it.[10] Remember that mean fourth-grade teacher you had who kept saying, "Pay attention— look at me!"? Poor thing, she just wanted to be real.

As Gribbin puts it, "the whole universe may only owe its 'real' existence to the fact that it is observed by intelligent beings . . . the fundamental axiom of quantum theory [is] that no elementary phenomenon is a phenomenon until it is a recorded phenomenon."[11]

There's Not One Universe; There Are Infinite Universes

If you read science fiction, you must have encountered the idea that there are "parallel universes" that are mostly like ours, but different in some key aspect. For example, our hero Captain Kirk of the Enterprise is an evil person in the universe next door; there, he actually walks around rumpled and unshaven and even sneers. Only there are more "universes next door" than we can imagine: one where Kirk is only captain of a beach volleyball team, one where he's a druggist in Iowa, etc. Physicist Bryce DeWitt suggests that "every quantum transition taking place on every star, in every galaxy, in every remote corner of the universe is splitting our local world on earth into myriads of copies of itself."[12]

Time Isn't Real

Explain this to your boss the next time you're late for work. Albert Einstein himself said that "the distinction between past, present, and future is only a stubbornly persistent illusion." It seems that everything is happening at once—but our brains aren't configured to process all the input simultaneously, so we build clocks, pretend time is linear, and handle one crisis at a time. It makes life much simpler, really. Of course, now and then the illusion breaks down and we can be heard muttering, "WHY does everything have to happen at once?"

---

10 Ibid., 212.
11 Ibid., 209–210.
12 Bryce DeWitt, article in *Physics Today*, 1970, quoted in Gribbin, 244.

The Universe Is Not Predictable

If you knew everything about the state of the universe at its beginning and understood all the laws of physics, you could pretty well predict everything as it unfolds, right? Wrong. The best you could do is to calculate "probabilities for various alternative histories of the universe . . . Information about which of those sequences of events is actually occurring can be gathered only from observation."[13] In other words, there is randomness and chaos in the universe, and no matter how much you know about your cat, you cannot know which way it will jump—until you see it happen.

The Speed of Light Is No Limit (Think Instantaneous)

Did you ever see the bumper sticker that says, "186,000 Miles Per Second—It's Not Just a Good Idea, It's the Law"? For a long time, everyone thought that nothing could travel faster than the speed of light, and that was kind of comforting, especially if you had teenagers with driving permits. Just another self-delusion, it seems. Quantum mechanics tells us that everything throughout time and space is linked by "a web of electromagnetic radiation that 'sees' everything at once."[14]

Does all this seem a little disturbing, or downright paradoxical? The great scientist Richard Feynman said that "the 'paradox' is only a conflict between reality and your feeling of what reality 'ought to be.'"[15] Well, what *do* we know—or seem to know—that allows for the existence of magick?

Energy Is Abundant

From a certain perspective, everything can be said to consist of energy vibrating in various wavelengths. Thus energy manifests as solid matter, liquids, gases, plasma, and still more subtle energy fields. Because we are energy forms existing in an ocean of energy, we are generally unaware of the intensity and variety of the energy about us—we can't "see the forest for the

---

13 Gell-Mann, 131–132.
14 Gribbin, 191.
15 Richard Feynman, *Lectures*, quoted in Gribbin, 231.

trees." But energy is abundantly present, at least on the planet we are most familiar with.

We might recognize this more clearly if we could experience the environment of Earth from the perspective of, say, a hypothetical lichen-like creature from Pluto's moon, Charon (hardly likely, but play along with the notion). Let's name our pretend creature *"wh,"* which is a nice low-energy name. Now *wh* is used to three things: darkness, stillness, and extreme cold. One night (it's always night there), *wh* wins a fabulous all-expense-paid vacation to Earth in the Charonian National Sweepstakes. It embarks on a Plutonian passenger spaceliner, which looks something like a wrinkled gray cantaloupe. Sunward to Earth, for a carefree rest among the primitives!

Some four hundred years later, right on schedule, the ship arrives and *wh* crawls out onto planet Earth—and into a nightmare! Burning solar radiation pours down in torrents; turgid gases howl and tear at *wh*, thunderous noises batter his tender earholes, and corrosive liquids and stinging silicate particles lash his body. This is not at all what *wh* expected! He immediately retreats into the ship and begins composing a strong letter to his attorneys. Back on the beach, human bathers enjoy the sunny skies and mild sea breezes of a perfect summer's day.

Now that's just one spot on one little planet. Imagine how much energy is being poured out by the sun right now; multiply that times billions of galaxies with trillions of stars.

What about all that cold, dark space between the stars? No energy there, right? Wrong. Scientist John Gribbin points out that "the energy density of the vacuum is infinite."[16] So there is a huge supply of energy waiting to be used, if we can only harness it.

But does a magician need to wield great forces in order to work magick? Well, no. It's all around us, but we don't really need very much. You may have heard the idea that a butterfly flapping its wings in China could trigger a hurricane two weeks or two months later in the United States. Thanks to Chaos theory, that's not really far-fetched. Murray Gell-Mann explains that "chaos . . . introduces, in certain situations, *indefinitely large sensitivities of*

---

16 Ibid., 260.

outcome to input [emphasis added]."[17] In other words, a little nudge at exactly the right time and place can have an enormous impact later.

So yes, magick requires energy, and there is a very great deal of energy out there; but the best magicians don't even think in terms of hurling thunder and lightning. They use finesse—a little nudge.

Everything Is Connected

You are connected with events everywhere. Comedian Steven Wright gives an amusing example: "In my house there's this light switch that doesn't do anything. Every so often I would flick it on and off just to check. Yesterday, I got a call from a woman in Germany. She said, 'Cut it out.'"[18]

Everything is connected. A lovely metaphor for this model of reality is Indra's Web. Imagine for a moment that you are drifting in the velvet blackness of deep space. Stretching out before you and receding behind you into infinite distance are myriad parallel silver threads. Crossing them right and left are endless banks and layers of more silver threads, touching each other as they cross. Reaching up and down as far as you can see, also criss-crossing, are countless more curtains of threads, so that the entire universe is filled with a silver fabric or webbing in multiple dimensions.

At each of the infinite number of points where the threads touch, a little clear crystal sphere is attached. The spheres are glowing, and their combined light illuminates the cosmos. Further, the polished surface of each sphere reflects every other sphere within it; in fact, it reflects the entire pattern of the web. Each reflects all that is reflected from every sphere; reflections reflected in reflections, images of images of images, all linked and sharing their light in limitless brilliance.

The poet Francis Thompson expressed the concept beautifully:

All things by immortal power,

Near or far,

Hiddenly

---

17 Gell-Mann, 131–132.
18 Jargodzki, 77.

To each other linked are,

That thou canst not stir a flower

Without troubling a star.[19]

When you know what this means—when you feel it, on a level deeper than the conscious mind can go—then you have one of the keys to magick.

It has been so since the beginning of time. The particles that make up the universe have existed from the big bang at the beginning. John Gribbin explains:

> The atoms in my body are made of particles that once jostled in close proximity in the cosmic fireball with particles that are now part of a distant star, and particles that form the body of some living creature on some distant, undiscovered planet. Indeed, the particles that make up my body once jostled in close proximity and interacted with the particles that now make up your body. We are . . . parts of a single system . . . If everything that ever interacted in the Big Bang maintains its connection with everything it interacted with, then every particle in every star and galaxy that we can see "knows" about the existence of every other particle.[20]

A variant of this insight about connections is expressed in the phrase, "As above, so below." Microcosm reflects macrocosm. Whatever exists on a greater scale of magnitude, or as a thoughtform on subtler planes of being, has its counterpart or equivalent on the human scale and in the material plane.

The *separateness* of things that seems so obvious to us is, frankly, not real. But we believe it and act on that belief in ways that may destroy us. Listen to Fritzjof Capra:

> The natural environment is treated as though it consisted of separate parts to be exploited by different interest groups. The fragmented view is further extended to society, which is split into different nations, races, religious and political groups. [This] belief . . . can be seen as the essential reason for the present series of social, ecological, and cultural crises. It has alienated us from nature and from our fellow human beings. It has brought a grossly unjust distribution of natural resources, creating economic and political disorder; an ever-rising wave of violence, both spontaneous and institutionalized, and an ugly, polluted environment in which life has often become physically and mentally unhealthy.[21]

---

19 Francis Thompson, quoted in Jargodzki, 50.
20 Gribbin, 231.
21 Capra, *Tao of Physics*, 9.

We talk about the "other sex," or those "other people" in "other places." When we learn that the "other" is not other, that it's us, that we are all intimately connected, *then* we can do magick. Better yet, we can survive as a species.

Possibilities Are Infinite

Yes, infinite. Looking at this statement from a cosmic perspective, we can see that in an infinite universe, everything we can dream of will manifest somewhere, sometime. "All possible things do happen, in some branch of reality."[22]

Is the universe infinite? Astronomers say that our galaxy alone has about one hundred billion stars in it, with an uncounted number of planets circling them. What's more, they can see, so far, at least one hundred billion galaxies, each with about that many stars. This means that the part visible to us includes more than 10,000,000,000,000,000,000,000 stars . . . and we can see no end to them.

Time is also a factor, of course. Given more time, more things become possible. Our galaxy seems to have been around for roughly seventeen billion (17,000,000,000) years, and for all we know this could simply be the latest in an infinite number of recyclings.

Yet the scope of the universe may be far vaster than even this information implies. What if whole galaxies exist on a microscopic scale in each grain of sand, each drop of water? What if all the galaxies we can see with our greatest telescopes are drifting in a mote of dust on some much larger world? What if there are whole worlds in the subtler planes—"the astral," "the Realms of the Mighty Ones"—or in other dimensions of reality?

Somewhere, as you read these words, centaurs dance by moonlight, and torchlight glints from a golden hoard where dragons lie dreaming in their caverns.

---

22 Gribbin, 250.

You may be tempted to reply, "Maybe so, but I'm interested in the possibilities for my life here and now, not in whatever may be happening on distant planets or other planes."

But the possibilities are here, too. Modern science has educated us to some of our potential; but you don't need a doctorate in physics to work wonders. The world is full of people who have transformed their lives and found courage, love, and beauty where before there was despair and pain. Others engage in showier wonders such as psychic healing, fire walking, or bending spoons by mind power. Most of these people are not consciously practicing magick. How much more they could do if they had the understanding and disciplined skills of an adept!

What are the possibilities for your life? Do you need relationships that are loving, creative, and stable? Do you want a career that is more challenging and financially rewarding? Is there an old injury, physical or emotional, that you are ready to heal? Do you have fears or thought patterns that make you unhappy and block your best efforts? Is there an addiction you would like to release—to junk food, cigarettes, alcohol, drugs, overwork, or television? Is there an art or skill you've always wanted to learn, but did not because you feared you didn't have the talent?

Magick can help you with any or all of these efforts. Imagine life as it could be for you. Imagine with your Younger Mind, for which colors are brighter, sounds more clear, tastes more vivid, and anything seems possible. It is possible. All your dreams are possible. You have chosen certain paths, but other paths still lie open to you, and magick is the door.

It will not be easy. You are learning that magick is not miraculous or supernatural. A few mumbled incantations or gestures with a wand will not get you where you want to go. To become a magician requires study and hard work, both in the astral realms and here in the material world. It also requires faith and imagination. But if you can believe, and dream, and work, then your possibilities are infinite.

Scientists as Magicians

Did you know that Isaac Newton, who "discovered" gravity, considered himself to be a magician? And not just an ordinary magician, but "part of the *aurea catena*, the 'golden chain' of magi, or unique figures designated by God in each age to receive the ancient Hermetic wisdom."[23] He actually wrote far more about alchemy than about physics. Morris Berman tells us that "the centerpiece of the Newtonian system, gravitational attraction, was in fact the Hermetic principle of sympathetic forces . . . his unpublished writings reveal his commitment to the cornerstone of all occult systems: the notion that mind exists in matter and can control it."[24]

In a much more recent era, Albert Einstein believed that "astrology is a science in itself and contains an illuminating body of knowledge." He went on to say, "It taught me many things, and I am greatly indebted to it . . . astrology is like a life-giving elixir for mankind."[25]

What about the most modern of present-day scientists? John David Ebert explains:

> Ideas like the Gaia hypothesis, Chaos theory, Ilya Prigogine's self-organizing struc-
> tures, or David Bohm's holographic cosmos all exhibit the presence of images from
> earlier, more mythic cosmologies . . . [Scientists at Princeton have] meticulously
> documented the reality of such paranormal phenomena as telepathy, psychokinesis
> and remote viewing. Rupert Sheldrake's morphogenic fields are a kind of scientific
> transformation of the ancient *anima mundi*, the soul of the world which . . . infused
> the minutest particle with teeming, sentient consciousness. Medical doctors such
> as Richard Gerber, Larry Dossey or Deepak Chopra . . . [see] in thought systems
> like Kundalini yoga or acupuncture the rudiments for a whole new science of vibra-
> tional medicine, in which the pranic channels and pathways of the subtle body can
> become superconductors for states of consciousness leading to higher health.[26]

It seems we are coming full circle: the ancient magicks have emerged again as the cutting-edge theories of modern science.

---

23 Jargodzki, 31.

24 Morris Berman, in Jargodzki, 92.

25 Quoted in Jargodzki, 125.

26 Ebert, *Twilight of the Clockwork God: Conversations on Science and Spirituality at the End of an Age* (Council Oak Books: Tulsa, OK, 1999), 4–5.

But Does It Really Work?

Does magick always work? Yes, but not always with the result that you intended. That is, a spell or ritual will always have an effect, but flaws in the design or performance, or interference, can cause a different effect than you had hoped for.

For example, suppose you do magick to win the lottery, and then, very properly, you act in accord with your magick by buying a ticket. Granted, the odds of winning might be 1 in 50,000,000. However, you did magick! Yet you don't win. Why?

Perhaps magick improved the odds in your favor, say to 1 in 1,000,000. You improved your chances of winning by a factor of fifty, and that's impressive. The magick worked, to a degree. But it's not enough—the odds are still heavily against you, and it's not surprising that someone else wins the jackpot. After all, several million other people were wishing very hard that they would win, which by itself is a sort of diffuse, unconscious magick, and at least a few hundred were actually doing focused, intentional magick. Your spell is a drop in the bucket, and chances are it will not overcome all that desire and intent. Luck exists, too.

Usually when you perform magick, you don't have hordes of people actively working against you. Usually, a well-crafted spell or ritual is quite successful. However, you should also know that magick rarely manifests with dramatic special effects. True magick doesn't look like Hollywood magic. Your result will often be subtle and quiet, and it may seem more like a coincidence than a miracle.

Yet that's not always true. I have been part of a working that involved two rings of nine magicians each, great incantations (partially in Latin), a crystal-tipped magickal staff, and a dragon's egg, where lightning, thunder, and rainbows embellished the rite at all the appropriate moments. That's very satisfying, but it's the exception rather than the rule.

Do you wonder, "Why isn't everyone out there practicing magick?" As Chuang Tzu said (of the Tao), "If it could be talked about, everybody would have told their brother."[27] Magick is not well understood. What little we know is not easy to explain, much less to master. Besides, we live in a culture that long ago decided to follow science and religion, but not to explore the Arts of magick (with the exception of a few of us). When you mention magick to your friends, they may think you mean card tricks or making pigeons appear out of a scarf. If you explain further, they may look at you blankly. If you start to draw parallels between thaumaturgy and quantum mechanics, they may get very confused and turn on the television to escape.

And that's okay; magick is not an adventure that everyone wants to experience. Magick is mostly *terra incognita*, the Unknown Land, even to the tiny handful of adepts among us. But if you have courage, you can explore that land and just maybe fill in a blank space on its vast map.

Exercises Toward Mastery

1: Abundant Energy

Do some research in a library or on the Internet: try to find out how much energy our sun produces in one minute. See if you can convert that into some measure that makes sense to you, like horsepower or light bulbs. Now multiply that times the number of stars in our galaxy. That gives you the radiation from the stars of one galaxy in one minute. Think about it.

2: Minimal Energy

Consider how much energy it takes to change a human life; for example:

+ Saying "I love you"
+ Signing a contract to buy a home
+ Cutting a cancerous tumor from a human organ
+ Reaching out to shake hands with a former enemy

Now, how much energy does magick require?

3: Connections

It has been said that there are no more than six degrees of separation between any two people on Earth. For example, you probably are not personally acquainted with the Premier of the People's Republic of China. But you

---

27 Capra, 17.

might know, for example, your cousin Marty, who knows a car mechanic named Fred, who knows the governor's chauffer, who knows a senator, who knows the Chinese ambassador, who knows the Premier. Six steps get you to the Premier's office in Beijing. It's a theory that might or might not be true, on average. But just for fun, explore it. Ask your friends who they know who knows someone famous.

4: Infinite Possibilities

Meditate on the following question until you can answer it: What would you attempt if you knew that you could not fail? Now think of three reasons why it might be possible.

Blesséd be.

To follow this path further, read:

Stalking the Wild Pendulum: On the Mechanics of Consciousness by Itzhak Bentov (Destiny Books, 1977)

The Tao of Physics by Fritzjof Capra (Bantam Books, revised edition, 1984)

Natural Magic: The Magical State of Being by David Carroll and Barry Saxe (Arbor House, 1977)

Twilight of the Clockwork God: Conversations on Science and Spirituality at the End of an Age by John David Ebert (Council Oak Books, 1999)

The Quark and the Jaguar: Adventures in the Simple and the Complex by Murray Gell-Mann (W. H. Freeman and Co., 1994)

In Search of Schroedinger's Cat: Quantum Physics and Reality by John Gribbin (Bantam Books, 1984)

Mad About Physics: Braintwisters, Paradoxes, and Curiosities by Christopher P. Jargodzki and Franklin Potter (John Wiley and Sons, 2001)

How to Meditate: A Guide to Self-Discovery by Lawrence Leshan (Little, Brown & Co., 1974)

Everyday Miracles: The Inner Art of Manifestation by David Spangler (Bantam Books, 1996)

The Magician's Companion: A Practical & Encyclopedic Guide to Magical & Religious Symbolism by Bill Whitcomb (Llewellyn, 1993; see especially "What Is Magic?" on pp. 1–17)

Mind into Matter: A New Alchemy of Science and Spirit by Fred Alan Wolf (Moment Point Press, 2001)

The Path Lies Within You

Now we come to a key concept, which adepts understand and most others do not. It is summed up in the Lovers card of the major arcana in a traditional tarot deck, like the Rider-Waite-Smith deck. In this card, an angel hovers above a couple while the man looks at the woman and the woman looks up at the angel.

In *Tarot Revealed*, Eden Gray says of this card that the self-conscious intellect represented by the man does not establish direct contact with superconsciousness (the angel) except through Eve (the subconscious).[1] All three figures in the card represent different aspects of one person, and all three must connect, communicate, and cooperate to make magick happen.

As the Farrars point out in relation to this passage,[2] it is the secret of Wicca. Quite obviously it is an open secret at this stage, since the same insight (in different terminology) has been published more than once. But reading it is one thing, while understanding and using it are something else.

We begin by exploring this three-part model of the Self. It is not the only model of the way we humans are organized, but it is one that has been used effectively within the Huna religion of Hawaii, the Faery Tradition of Wicca, and by giants in the field of psychology, notably Sigmund Freud and C. G. Jung. Although these three components of Self have different names in different schools of thought, we shall call them Middle Self, Younger Self, and Higher Self.

---

1   Eden Gray, *Tarot Revealed* (New York: Signet, 1988), 162.
2   Janet and Stewart Farrar, *The Witches' Way*, 169.

The Middle Self

The self-conscious intellect is that part of our Self where rational thought and much of the personality reside. It can be referred to as normal waking consciousness, the Middle Self, the very descriptive talking-head self, or just Talking Self. It is the part of you that is reading these words right now, and its power is an important part of what makes us human. It is the man in the Lovers card of the tarot.

Middle Self thinks, decides, and judges. It is strong in the elements of Air and Fire, Mind and Will. It controls conscious movement, but has little to do with the moment-by-moment operation of the physical body: breathing, circulation, the nervous system, the endocrine system, etc. It recognizes emotions sometimes, but it is not the source of our deepest feelings.

Unfortunately, most people act as though the Middle Self is all we are, and that is far from the truth.

In *The Tao of Physics*, Fritzjof Capra discusses how a seventeenth-century scientist, Rene Descartes, managed to warp our perceptions of who we are:

> Descartes' famous sentence *Cogito ergo sum*—I think, therefore I exist—has led Westerners to equate their identity with their mind, instead of with their whole organism. As a consequence of the Cartesian division, most individuals are aware of themselves as isolated egos existing "inside" their bodies. The mind has been separated from the body and given the futile task of controlling it, thus causing an apparent conflict between the conscious will and the involuntary instincts.[3]

Imagine the captain of an ocean liner who believes that the ship and everything in it is subject to his control alone. He forgets all the crew working below decks—maintaining the engines, preparing food in the galley, doing myriad activities that actually keep the ship functioning (Younger Self). Further, he forgets that the schedule, destination, and ultimate fate of his vessel depend on the decisions of the owners of the shipping line (Higher Self) and ocean currents, storms, etc. (laws of nature).

This captain may sail in blissful ignorance for a long time, until the engines break down, the crew mutinies, the owners fire him, or an exhausted radar operator misses the iceberg that wanders into the ship's path. Then suddenly the

---

3   Fritzjof Capra, *The Tao of Physics*, 9.

illusion of control is shattered, and our captain realizes how very dependent he is on the good will, cooperation, and efficiency of others.

The Younger Self

Let's look at the part below decks that our captain neglected. It is variously called the subconscious, the Lower Self, or the Younger Self. Since Freud began discussing this level as the id, it has received a rather bad reputation as a sort of psychological slime pit of odd sexual fantasies and savage impulses, which is quite distorted and unfair. But this level is generally ignored by the conscious level, Middle Self.

The id image is not only undeserved, it is also a major obstacle to the successful practice of magick. In point of fact, the Younger Self is a valuable ally to the conscious mind. It is in charge of the physical body, emotion, memory, and sensation. All that you feel, remember, or experience in your body comes from this deeper part of you; and if you think that's not power, just recollect the last time you were in love or sexually aroused, and just how little your brain was involved at that moment.

Younger Self is a powerful generator and channel of psychic energy, but it often requires the guidance of the conscious self in order to use this energy constructively. It is the bridge between Middle Self and Higher Self; it is the woman on the Lovers card.

In many respects it is childlike, though in the Hawaiian Huna tradition it is represented as an animal spirit, with a mammal's deep instincts, intuition, and immediate awareness of the sensate world. In this model, the animal soul has evolved to the point where it is ready to become part of the Self of a sentient creature—you—but it could not function in a complex human society without Middle Self's thinking ability.

The Higher Self

There is yet a third aspect to the Self, which Starhawk in *The Spiral Dance* characterizes as the Higher Self or God Self, which does not easily correspond to any psychological concept. The Higher Self is the Divine within, the ultimate and original essence, the spirit that exists beyond time, space, and matter. It is our deepest level of wisdom and compassion and is conceived of as both male and female, two motes of consciousness united as one.[4]

"Two motes" because in Faery Wicca and Hawaiian Huna, the Higher Self is thought of as a pair of spirits who guide and protect us, as well as taking raw magickal energy and shaping it into manifested results. They speak to us through the still, small voice within, our intuition and sense of right and wrong.

This is the part that many religions represent as an angel or deity "out there," rather than within-and-without. They might also depict it as the soul, which is understood to be immortal but essentially passive. In our model, however, it is the part of Self that is our connection to divinity, and that can channel immense power into creation and transformation when approached correctly.

The Magickal Team Within You

Now the important part is this: all three aspects of the Self must work as a team in order for magick—that is, guided transformation—to occur.

Often, would-be magicians fail because they address the Higher Self directly, without going through Eve or the Younger Self. This is, of course, why most prayer is ineffective (except as a means of mild catharsis or self-comfort): there is no direct channel of any consequence from the Middle Self to the Higher Self or God/dess within.

Some aspiring magicians, still more limited in their understanding, even leave out the Higher Self, believing that they can do magick through the unaided power of the intellect. But this is simply ego talking to itself, which accomplishes nothing.

Effective magick works like this: the Middle Self chooses a purpose in harmony with its True Will; it communicates this purpose to the Younger Self, triggering emotion and physical activity to raise power; the Younger Self

---

4   Starhawk, *The Spiral Dance* (HarperSanFrancisco, 1989), 35.

boosts the power and channels it to the Higher Self, along with a clear image of the goal; and the Higher Self uses the power to manifest the desired result. Middle Self experiences the result, and the circle is complete.

For all this to work, a free flow of communication, trust, love, and energy among the three levels of Self must be created.

Creating a loving and aware relationship among these three is not a task quickly done. It is the work of a lifetime or many lifetimes. Yet, you can make great strides in just a few weeks or months if you work at it persistently.

Clearing the Path: Phase One

Begin with the relationship between Middle Self and Younger Self. If you are like many Westerners, you (or more precisely your conscious intellect) have pretty well ignored your Younger Self. You might be uncomfortable with your sensual nature and afraid of whatever needs and impulses are hidden deep inside you. Or you might label Younger-Self aspects as childish and convince yourself that mature adults do not indulge in play or dress up for rituals. If this describes you, then you are well on your way to fossilization.

Set aside such nonsense and begin to make friends with Younger Self. Talk to it not because the words will impress it, but because the images and feelings accompanying your words, and your tone of voice, and the mere fact that you are paying attention, will make a difference. Listen to it, whether you are doing meditation and trancework, dreaming, working with the pendulum, or using the tarot. Be still, be open, pay attention.

Court the Younger Self as you would seek to win the trust of a small child or an animal: patiently, lovingly, gently. Ask its name; when sufficient trust has been established, it will come to you. If you wish to adopt a Huna technique, ask it to show you its animal form during meditation, trance, or dreamwork. You will see a mammal, and not necessarily your favorite species, your totem, or your power animal. Look it in the eyes and ask if this is a true representation of Younger Self. If it cannot meet your gaze, or disappears or runs away, then Younger Self is being shy or mischievous and misleading you. In time you will find the correct animal, and by understanding the characteristics of that species you can gain valuable insights into the character and personality of your Younger Self.

Though not childlike in every respect, Younger Self enjoys the same things children do: bright colors, music, toys, treats, games, cuddling, pretty clothes, nice smells, and so on. When you indulge your sensual, playful, and childlike needs, you are pleasing Younger Self and improving the inner relationship so necessary to your growth and happiness. Of course, fulfilling every desire of Younger Self would not be appropriate and could be harmful. You must decide as a team or partnership what is best, using your Talking-Self maturity, intelligence, and foresight to balance the spontaneity and direct the energy of Younger Self. Eventually you will add the wisdom, love, and power of the Higher Self to this working partnership.

Let's go back to Younger Self for the moment. Soon your efforts at building communication and trust will begin to clear the path of obstacles such as misunderstanding, indifference, or suspicion. Through ritual and other means you will learn to communicate more clearly and vividly with Younger Self, and to listen more carefully. You will have discovered a new friend in yourself.

Clearing the Path: Phase Two

That is one step. However, the path between Younger Self and the Higher Self must still be cleared. Younger Self, as the guardian of memory and the wellspring of feeling, has stored many negative emotions that are all obstacles to communication with the Higher Self. If a small child breaks a dish, then out of shame it will hide from its parents. Your Younger Self remembers every dish you ever broke, and every transgression, and all the feelings of shame, guilt, fear, or self-contempt that resulted from this lifetime and former ones. All these block the path to the Higher Self—NOT because Younger Self is too sinful or impure for the Higher Self, but because it feels bad and therefore does not reach out to the Higher Self.

How do you remove such feelings? This can be difficult. First you must be in touch with them, identify them, know their shape and color and intensity.

You can learn much through trancework and divination, but you will probably need outside help as well: co-counseling with a friend, or therapy with a professional counselor. Hypnosis and age regression can provide much information; these are channels to the memory banks of the Younger Self. If your conscious communications with Younger Self are very clear, you may be able to simply ask in meditation, "What hurts?" A reply may come in the form of flashes of memory or vivid images, or in tastes, smells, or physical sensations that provide clues to old traumas.

Once you know what you are dealing with, then the balancing, cleansing, and healing can begin. Your old, negative emotions stem from mistakes of past lives, the errors of childhood, and from more recent acts that left you feeling guilty or embarrassed. The key is to correct what you can—to balance your karma. Where you have stolen, restore; where you have broken, mend or replace; where you have harmed, heal.

If you cannot locate the person originally involved in an incident (for example, if you stole a toy from a playmate when you were five, and now have no idea where they live), then direct your actions toward a substitute. For the toy example, you might buy a similar toy and give it to a needy child at Yule or Christmas. Before you do, hold a colorful ritual, with the toy in a prominent place on the altar, and vividly demonstrate what you plan to do, and why. When you present the toy to a child, do it in person, and if possible join in play with the gift. This sort of direct involvement has much more impact on Younger Self than if you simply mail a check to a fund for needy children. To finish this particular episode, you might contact the spirit of your original playmate—in meditation, in trance, or on the astral—explain what you have done, and ask forgiveness. I suspect that it will be granted.

Aside from balancing the scales for your own errors, it is very useful to rediscover old issues where you were the injured party, and find ways to forgive those who hurt you.

Continue clearing the path with more cleansing and purification: ritual baths, aura cleansing exercises, smudging (as done in some Native American traditions), ceremonial sweats in a lodge or sauna, and fasting, if your healer or physician concurs. Do self-forgiveness and self-blessing rites, and use positive affirmations frequently.

Gradually, over time, the old, negative feelings will dissolve and disappear, leaving the way clear for images, love, and energy to flow freely between Younger Self and Higher Self.

Clearing the Path: Phase Three

This leaves but one of the triple paths to clear: that between the Higher Self and Midlle (Talking) Self. The Higher Self will gladly shower fulfillment and blessings on you, but you must be ready to receive them. If you doubt that you deserve them, or believe them to be impossible, then you have blocked the path. You can open it by developing higher self-regard and the faith that all things are possible for you.

Beyond this, you must be able to tell when the blessings have arrived. How easy it is to become so wrapped up in life's difficulties that we are oblivious to the really wonderful things occurring around us! Know also that you may receive the essence of what you asked, but in a form you did not expect. The Higher Self is wiser than the conscious mind, and often gives us what we really need rather than what we ask for.

In your magick, seek that which is wise and appropriate, and then immediately afterward be alert and open to its manifestation. If you see clearly, you will not be disappointed. Be ready to celebrate.

Exercises Toward Mastery

1: Name Younger Self

Do you imagine your Younger Self as your childhood self or, in the Huna manner, as an animal? In either case, find a quiet time and place to meditate, visualize Younger Self, and ask his or her name. It may be a childhood nickname. Your animal self may have an animal name that you cannot pronounce, but with a little urging will choose a human-language nickname for you to use. Be patient if Younger Self is shy.

2: Play with Younger Self

Again, enter a light trance, and visualize Younger Self. Talk to it gently. Project feelings of love. In your mind, play with it however it likes, be it splashing through puddles in the rain, building with wooden blocks, or romp-and-chase games with your animal self. Begin to create trust.

3: Clear the Path to Higher Self

You may need help for this one, either with an experienced meditation guide or a therapist. Regress through time to the event where you first felt shame or guilt. Out of trance, explore the incident and determine whether you really did something wrong or were just made to feel that way. Design and perform a simple ritual to forgive yourself or others involved, and release those negative feelings. Follow up, if necessary, by balancing your karma, performing some concrete act, as discussed earlier in this chapter. Then repeat the process, several times if necessary, until you cannot find any more sources of guilt, shame, or self-hatred. *Note:* This is an ongoing process, and you do not have to put your magickal training on hold until it is finished. But the more you clear the path, the stronger your magick will become.

4: Send a Gift of Energy to Higher Self

Compared to Younger Self, the Higher Self is rather independent and certainly less needy. Nonetheless, it is good to occasionally send a gift of free energy to Higher Self, no strings attached, just as a way to show your appreciation for its love and guidance. First visualize Higher Self, perhaps as a beautiful, glowing couple, filled with unconditional love for you and very closely connected to your life. Then raise power by dancing, singing, breathing deeply, or any other way, and working with Younger Self, send it to Higher Self with feelings of gratitude, appreciation, and love. In response, you will probably feel a wave of loving, tingling energy, especially in your heart chakra.

Blesséd be.

To follow this path further, read:

Fundamentals of Hawaiian Mysticism by Charlotte Berney (Crossing Press, 2000)

Hawaiian Magic and Spirituality (2nd edition) by Scott Cunningham (Llewellyn Publications, 2002)

Huna: A Beginner's Guide by Enid Hoffman (Schiffer Publishing, 1997)

Clearing Your Lifepath and Kahuna Wisdom by Allan P. Lewis (Homana Publications, 1983)

Essential Huna: Discovering and Integrating Your Three Selves by Arlyn J. MacDonald (Infinity Publishing, 2003)

Hawaiian Wisdom by Clark Wilkerson (Clark & Dei Wilkerson, 1968; out of print)

Ethics and Hazards

If you are going to work magick, then hopefully you want to work good magick. If you have no particular morals or ethics, then you are going to get hurt because our actions always rebound on us. Presumably you also want to work safely, and there are simple precautions you can take beyond working responsibly and ethically.

Part 1: Ethical Guidelines

Begin by taking responsibility for your life and everything in it. This is part of coming into your power. You cannot be a lifelong victim, the pawn of others' schemes, and the plaything of fate, and be a magician too. Accustom yourself to the idea that nearly everything in your life—every event, relationship, thought, and material object—is there because you chose it. Rarely do we choose consciously; always, however, we choose. What we have considered to be acts done to us, or coincidences, or accidents, are often events chosen or at least accepted by us on a level below the conscious mind. The choices may be wise or foolish, but they are ours.

In *Medicine Woman*, Agnes Whistling Elk says this:

> Every act has meaning. *Accident* is a word born of confusion. It means we didn't understand ourselves enough to know why we did something. If you slip and cut your finger, there is a reason why you did it. Someone in your moon lodge wanted you to do it. If you knew how to listen to the chiefs inside your moon lodge, you would never do such a foolish thing . . . "Accident" is a way to lay down the responsibility for your action and ask another to pick it up.[1]

---

1   Lynn V. Andrews, *Medicine Woman* (HarperSanFrancisco, 1983), 132.

The Wiccan Rede

This book is about magick in general, not just Wiccan magick. However, the same principles apply to all magickal practice, and the primary guideline is most concisely summed up in the rule that guides Wiccan (and other benevolent) magicians. It is called the Wiccan Rede, and it states "An ye harm none, do as ye will." In modern language, "Follow your True Will as long as you don't hurt anyone (including yourself)."

Why? Because we are all One, connected in ways more deep and subtle than the conscious mind can know—so much so that to harm another is to harm ourselves. Harm can be physical, mental, or emotional, and can also include anything that interferes with another's free will or karma.

The Rede says "Harm none," and it means exactly that: harm no person, no animal, and no plant, unless it is to protect yourself or preserve your life. If you harm someone or something unnecessarily, there will be consequences . . . which leads us to the Law of Return.

The Law of Return

The Law of Return says, "What we send out returns to us." Send a curse, you will be cursed. Send love, you will be loved. Some call this the Threefold Law and say that what you send returns to you three times over.

Most of us can easily understand that it is wrong (and foolish) to harm an innocent person with magick, or to force a former lover to return to you if they freely chose to leave. But what about using magick to punish a wrongdoer—the thief who steals your car, or the rapist who terrorizes your neighborhood? Harming even these, out of anger or vengefulness, can do no good. Use your magick to call back your car (or a new one), or to protect yourself and your loved ones from attack. Leave judgment and retribution to a higher power.

Magick Only with Permission

Even well-intentioned magick can do damage if you intervene in someone else's life without that individual's permission. For example, your Aunt Molly becomes ill, and because you care about her you are tempted to do some healing magick without asking her, perhaps because she doesn't approve of magick.

Before you intervene, think. She has something to learn or to gain from that illness; otherwise her Younger Self and Higher Self would not have permitted it. Perhaps she needs to learn that she can trust others in the family to keep the household going when she is not active. Or that she is loved, and that people will rally around to care for her when she needs help. Or maybe that she can trust her body's strength to help her recover from even a severe illness. Maybe she simply needs extended rest, and this is the only way she can allow herself to have it. Whatever you think of the strategy (getting sick), there is a reason for it that should be respected.

As a general rule, ethical magicians will do ritual work for others only if asked and if the request seems wise and proper.

If you are uncomfortable doing any particular magick, don't do it. Listen to your intuition; it is your internal moral compass and guide. It will rarely (if ever) steer you into doing magick that will interfere with someone else's free will or cause harm to anyone.

Refusing to Charge Money

Wiccan priestesses and priests do not charge for work done in the circle, and the same rule may be recommended for any magician. (The exception might be certain forms of divination, such as water dowsing or reading the tarot, which do not usually involve the invocation of higher powers). Ritual magick-for-hire seems to have ill effects on both the magician and the quality of the magick. And how not? We have all seen the effects of commercialization on other crafts: money becomes the goal, instead of service or excellence. At any rate, consider these couplets:

> *If you would pay coin for a magick spell,*
>
> > *better to throw your purse in a well.*
>
> *If you would ask coin for a magick spell,*
>
> > *better to throw your wand in the well.*

Part 2: Hazards

Can magick be dangerous? Well, yes; but so can painting your house or driving to the supermarket. Just because magick is unusual and somewhat exotic in our culture doesn't mean it resembles fantasy novels or the special effects in movies. Do not worry about unleashing demons or transforming yourself into a toad. Be aware of realistic hazards, use common sense, work carefully, and do really major workings in a circle with other experienced magicians to help. Then proceed with courage and confidence.

Let's explore some problems potentially involved in the use, or rather misuse, of magick—so you can avoid them.

Energy Imbalance

As a magician, you channel a great deal of power through your body. If the power is drawn from your own reserves, you will be left feeling depleted and weak. No need for that! Energy is abundant all around you; draw on that and use it well, then ground the excess. If the extra energy is not sent into the earth or somewhere else, it continues to circulate in your own energy system. This can cause you to be jumpy, like drinking too much coffee, and keep you awake or give you a headache. In time the excess energy will dissipate, but it may take several hours. See chapter 8 for more about this.

Excessive Introversion

It is possible to become so involved with activity on the inner (and astral) planes that you neglect Earth-plane affairs: your job, family, meals, and so on. Healthy spirituality requires a balance between inner and outer activity, so keep in touch with the things of this world. Are you spending quality time with the people you love? Are you eating right? Is the house clean, and have you checked the oil in your car lately? You may become an Advanced High Thaumaturgical Poo-Bah of the Nineteenth Degree, but you still need to remember to buy toilet paper when you go shopping.

Temptation to Act Unethically

Along with power of any kind, magickal or mundane, comes the tempta-tion to use it in negative ways out of anger, fear, or greed. Stand by the rules of ethical practice, and when in doubt listen to your "inner bell." If you are having trouble getting clear communications from within, then go to your teachers or respected elders, and ask their counsel. Temptations will come from time to time, but your moral strength will grow each time you face a challenge successfully.

Interference from Nonmaterial Entities

The energies used in magick tend to draw the attention and presence of creatures from other planes of existence. Remember that the magickal circle exists between the worlds, overlapping both this level of reality and the astral planes. The cone of power acts as an energy beacon on these other planes, and naturally entities living there will notice and investigate. Some will be benevolent, a very few might be mischievous or even malignant, and most will simply be curious. So don't be surprised if you have visitors to the circle. But neither should you be alarmed.

There are basically three kinds of nonmaterial beings you might encoun-ter, apart from deities. These are elemental spirits, nonhuman life forms, and discarnate humans ("ghosts").

The elementals, of course, are invited. When you call "the powers of Air," then the airy spirits or sylphs will be present. The sign of the air-invoking pentagram, or rather the energy and intention associated with it, both invite and hold them just beyond the circle's boundary. You want their energies present and available, but not overwhelmingly active within the circle—you don't need sudden gusts of wind blowing out all your candles. At the same time you draw air energies to the circle from outside, you are also evoking air qualities, such as intellect and imagination, from within you.

Like the sylphs, the elemental spirits of Fire (salamanders), Water (un-dines), and Earth (gnomes) are wild and powerful in their pure state, living but not especially intelligent. Treated with respect, firmness, and care, they are allies rather than threats.

Other entities may come to your circle uninvited. These are alien beings that live in other dimensions of reality and normally have nothing to do with humanity. But some are very curious and will draw near just to see what's happening. Although they may, rarely, cause physical phenomena, such as drafts that make the candles flicker, they cannot or will not enter a properly cast circle.

These entities probably account for many of the medieval tales about conjuring up demons, which were then compelled to serve the sorcerer calling them. Possibly some of these aliens were just going along with the gag, humoring the silly human's demands in a spirit of mischievous fun.

Yet there is no doubt that the medieval magicians were afraid of these entities: they took elaborate precautions, working from within a triple circle and placing a triangle of manifestation outside to confine the entity when it appeared. If these life forms were forced to cooperate, then the sorcerers may have had good reason to be afraid: nobody, human or otherwise, likes to be coerced.

Normally such creatures are invisible in the wavelengths apparent to human eyes; indeed, they exist wholly on another vibrational level. When they manifest visually on this plane, this usually means that we can see them psychically with the third eye. Because such vision can be powerfully influenced by individual subjectivity, the creatures may appear in various forms to different observers. If you expect to see a demon with red eyes and long teeth, you probably will; if you expect an angel, you will see that instead. In either case, the life-energy of the same entity is sensed: but the way this experience is interpreted by our brains varies, according to the beliefs and emotions of the perceiver.

If you see or sense a presence watching your ritual from outside the circle, remember that it is probably curious and harmless, and will disappear once the circle is opened, if not before.

Is there any real danger from astral entities? Ordinarily not; but there could be if you:

- have a weak or damaged energy field due to substance abuse or trauma;

- are mentally confused or incapacitated by certain drugs;

- are "dis-spirited" in the shamanic sense (have vacated your body and left it open); or

- work outside the protection of a well-cast circle with some intense kinds of magick.

Then it is possible that you could be affected or even possessed by an outside entity.[2] Therefore, it is always wise to do major work within the circle; and if you are mentally, emotionally, or spiritually unwell, then concentrate on getting yourself healed first, before you attempt any unrelated magickal work. Healthy, balanced people do not have difficulties with visiting entities.

The third type of entity is a discarnate human that has not yet moved on to the afterlife. Ghosts are not uncommon in old houses, at crossroads, or near cemeteries. Often they are people who don't yet realize that they are dead and so linger, disoriented and lonely, in places that were familiar to them in life. As a rule ghosts are silent, and reveal themselves only in the subtlest ways: a half-seen glimpse of movement, a slight chill, or a sense of presence in an empty room. It is quite possible to communicate with them, or even help them along to the next world (though that is a subject for another book). The main thing to remember is that ghosts may be distracting, but they are harmless except perhaps in extraordinary circumstances.

Success in the Wrong Endeavors

If you plunge into magickal work directed toward your superficial conscious goals without serious effort in understanding your deeper karmic needs and direction, you can waste a great deal of time and energy running down false trails.

---

2   This, by the way, is very different from invoking God/dess, which is, in part, an expression of the divinity already and always within you.

"Know thyself" is good advice. Invest substantial amounts of time in self-exploration through meditation, dreamwork, past-life recall, divination, and communication with your Younger Self and Higher Self. Then you can focus your magick on goals in harmony with your True Will, rather than just the goals that seem attractive or "sensible" to your conscious mind.

Fortunately, there is a built-in safeguard against using magick toward an inappropriate goal: if the goal is wrong for you, usually Younger Self or Higher Self will sabotage your efforts and keep doing so until Middle (Talking) Self "wises up." But if Talking Self refuses to pay attention, they could let you achieve an inappropriate goal since you are too stubborn to learn except by experience. For example, you might finally achieve your conscious goal of becoming a wealthy plastics manufacturer, only to miserably realize that you might have been far happier pursuing your old fantasy of becoming a forest ranger.

Persecution

Practicing magick is definitely suspect behavior in modern Western society, and that goes double for Wiccan magick. Reactions from neighbors may run the gamut from "Isn't that—er, quaint!" to "Definitely a mental problem!" to "Devil-worshipper!" It is possible that one could lose a job, have property vandalized, or even be physically attacked for practicing magick, even in the "enlightened" Western civilizations.

Some magicians avoid this through great discretion, even secrecy. Others flourish by being extremely cheerful and open about it, usually after establishing a solid reputation as a good friend and neighbor. It is the in-between state that seems most dangerous, where people know that "something weird" is going on, but not much more. This situation allows imagination and fear to run wild, so avoid dropping veiled hints or cultivating an air of mystery.

One thing is certain: as long as you are legally an adult and no one is being harmed, you have the right to practice magick. And you always have the right to protect yourself from anyone whose ignorance and fear would lead them to hurt you. If you are attacked, perform protective magick, call on the law, and mobilize your network of friends and relations. Do all that is ethical and legal to keep yourself and your family safe.

Yes, magick has its risks, as does any challenging and worthwhile activity. To practice this ancient Art safely and successfully, however, you need simply follow commonsense guidelines: Proceed slowly and carefully. Keep your priorities and your goals clear. Stay centered, balanced, and grounded. Don't try anything but self-healing if you are ill. Work magick only for worthy goals, and never to influence another without permission. Be discreet, but not furtive or afraid.

You have chosen a way of power that few understand or would attempt. Many choose to amass money, or status in a large corporation, or political influence. While these things can be used for good purposes, we have all seen how often they become corrupted and result in great harm.

Unlike these, magick tends to be swiftly self-correcting when it is misused. If you make a mistake, you will know it sooner rather than later. And that is a blessing; you won't have to wait until the end of this life to know whether you have done well.

Exercises Toward Mastery

1: Ethical Scenarios

Discuss each of the following situations with your teacher; if you have no teacher, ask a friend whose character and judgment you respect.

a. A teenage friend says her boyfriend has lost interest in her, and would you please do a spell to rekindle his love for her. Do you agree?

b. An uncle whom you love is very ill, and you would like to do some healing magick for him. However, he is part of a religion that discourages magick, and you don't think he would give you permission to work on his behalf. Would you do some remote healing work anyway?

c. You have been having a lot of problems lately with your job, your health, and your marriage or primary relationship. A friend sends you an e-mail saying, "My group is doing magick to get your life straightened around." You did not ask for magick and don't know what she means by "straightened around." How would you reply to her?

d. Someone has been doing a lot of vandalism in your neighborhood—breaking car windows, tagging houses with spray paint, even hacking at trees with a hatchet. A member of your magickal study group suggests that you do a "karmic dumping run" to bring all of the vandal's negativity back on them right now. You don't know exactly how that would manifest in the culprit's life. Would you do this working?

e. You would like to buy a neighbor's car, but the price he is asking seems steep. A friend suggests you do a little spell just to nudge him mentally, so he is open to bringing the price down to something more reasonable. Does that seem like an acceptable use of magick?

f. You suspect that a neighbor is abusing her children, though you have no direct proof—just occasional yelling and some unexplained bruises. You read about binding spells that can stop a person from acting. Would you perform one on your neighbor?

g. Your country is at war in a foreign land, and a relative is over there in the military. His wife asks you to "do some of that magic stuff to smash the bastards" he is fighting. If you could figure out how, would you do attack magick against the enemy soldiers?

For discussion of these scenarios, see appendix VI, "Discussion of Ethical Scenarios."

2: Hazards of Magick

Next to each potential hazard, write down H if you believe you are at High Risk for that problem, L if you think the risk is low for you, and ? if you have no idea what the level of risk is. Then re-read the sections of this chapter that pertain to any High Risk or unknown factors, and discuss safeguards with your teacher, if you have one.

_____ Energy imbalance

_____ Excessive introversion

_____ Temptations to act unethically

_____ Interference from nonmaterial entities

_____ Success in the wrong endeavors

_____ Persecution

Blesséd be.

To follow this path further, read:

The New Wiccan Book of the Law by Lady Galadriel (Moonstone
Publications, 1992)

An Ye Harm None: Magical Morality and Modern Ethics by Shelley Tsivia
Rabinovitch and Meredith MacDonald (Citadel Press, 2004)

Positive Magic: Occult Self-Help by Marion Weinstein (Phoenix Publishing,
1978)

The Pyramid of Magick

Before you can begin to practice magick successfully, it is necessary to prepare yourself thoroughly—indeed, most of the work of magick is in the preparation rather than in the ritual. This is important because, after all, you are the most important element in magick. The crucial tools are your mind, will, body, and so on, not your athame and candles. Few magicians would enter the circle wearing a torn robe and carrying a dirty pentacle, yet many people perform rituals every week with muddled minds, weak wills, and unconditioned bodies. Instead, train and prepare as though you were an athlete, if you want to perform star-quality magick. You can begin with the pyramid.

According to Clifford Bias in *The Ritual Book of Magic,*

> The Magus, the Theurgist, the True Witch stand on a pyramid of power whose foundation is a profound knowledge of the occult, whose four sides are a creative imagination, a will of steel, a living faith and the ability to keep silent, and whose internal structure is love.[1]

A Profound Knowledge

Let us explore each point. Your knowledge will come from many sources, but one of the most desirable is an experienced and ethical teacher or teachers. Look for those who have used magick successfully for their own spiritual development, whose inner lights shine as beacons. An ethical teacher will never ask for money for teaching you in a coven or as an apprentice, i.e., in a

---

1 Clifford Bias, *The Ritual Book of Magic* (New York: Weiser, 1981), 1.

context of spiritual growth. However, it is usually considered acceptable to charge fees for public workshops on skills such as reading the tarot, or in an academy setting where fees cover the expenses of facilities and materials. In any case, when fees are not charged it is appropriate for the student to offer energy or skills to a teacher to "balance the scales."

An ethical teacher will never demand sexual favors or that you do anything you consider unethical in return for teaching. A good teacher will be confident without being boastful or self-centered; will be attentive to you without being dominating or invasive; and will require hard work and self-discipline, but not subservience. (These issues will be discussed in more detail in chapter 18.) Many excellent teachers may not even call themselves magicians; they may be devout individuals from many different spiritual paths, or teachers of "mundane" topics that are revealed as magickal in their hands. They may be truck drivers or waitresses or budget analysts or forest rangers.

Knowledge can come from books. Caution and discrimination are the watchwords here, since there is a great deal of misinformation published on the subject of magick. "Recipe books" of spells and incantations are of little use until you understand the way magick works and have developed basic skills such as visualization, concentration, and channeling energy; avoid completely any book that offers spells to dominate and manipulate others. For some excellent books, see the suggested reading list in appendix IV.

Knowledge comes from nature. Great wisdom and peace can be discovered in the woods or fields, or on lonely beaches. You must be open, receptive, observant, and sensitive in order to learn, since nature's secrets are not in words. The rewards are spiritual treasures beyond reckoning. As a country Witch puts it in a popular Pagan song, all the tomes in an occult bookstore "don't amount to an acre of green."

Knowledge comes from observing people who have found love, wisdom, fulfillment, and personal power. See how they live, how they respond to life. Talk to them, but pay more attention to their lives than their words. Many "magickal" people can't explain in words what has worked for them.

Knowledge can come from you. Your dreams, your visions, your intuition or "inner bell," your deep-buried wisdom garnered in past lives—all are worthy of attention. Trust yourself; not necessarily the self that is grouchy because your feet hurt or jittery from too much caffeine, but the calm, wise, loving Self deep within. You know the difference.

Knowledge comes from the experience of practicing magick a little bit at a time, starting with simple things and carefully paying attention to the results and to your feelings as you do it.

A Creative Imagination

Imagination is the first side of the pyramid. If you cannot clearly imagine the goals you intend to achieve through magick, then do not expect to achieve them. To put it another way, "If you don't know where you're going, you'll probably wind up somewhere else." You must be able to vividly experience your goal in your mind and sense the image, sound, smell, taste, and feel of it. Further, you must be able to imagine the steps that will bring you to it, both within the circle and on the mundane level.

Many exercises can help you to develop your imagination. For example, when you read a descriptive passage in a novel, don't just skim on ahead to the bedroom scene. Pause and try to create the described environment in your mind. Experience each detail the author describes, then add details of your own. Then move on to the bedroom scene, and imagine that in detail.

Or, the next time you have any particularly moving and memorable experience—a gourmet meal, a moonlight swim, cuddling a newborn—take some time immediately afterward to relive it with all the detail and intensity you can muster. Then write about it in your diary or Book of Shadows, again in great detail.

Storytelling is another way to develop your imagination. In order to vividly evoke images and experiences in others' minds, you must experience them vividly in your own mind. Try this: read a short story, fable, or parable, then go through it again, living it in your mind; then tell it to a friend; and then tell it to a group.

A Will of Steel

Will is the second side of the pyramid. First know what you really want—what you yearn for passionately, with all your heart. This is your True Will, not your whims or petty desires. Magick works best on things that really matter to you, because the intensity of your need makes them far easier to imagine and to raise power for. Many people talk about "will power" as though it is the key to all achievement, but they usually mean a sort of mental pig-headedness, which is not what will is about. True Will is about heart and passion: a sword of Fire, not a plodding bulldozer.

Start by watching your words. When you say you will do something, do it; immediately, if possible. Set a small goal and accomplish it quickly and decisively. Then congratulate yourself, and consider how it felt to do that. Set yourself another goal, a bit more challenging. Gather your energy and do it as quickly as possible. Keep stretching and challenging yourself, one task at a time, one day at a time; your will is a muscle that must be exercised repeatedly to grow strong.

And "assume the virtue if you have it not"—practice holding yourself in a self-assured manner and speaking with strength and decisiveness. Your Younger Self will watch and learn.

A worthy companion to will is focus: being able to put all your energy and attention on to one thing alone, like a laser beam. It is also called one-pointedness. It is the polar opposite of scattered and diffuse; it is Focused Will, and there is little that can withstand it.

A Living Faith

Faith is the third side of the pyramid: "A rock-firm faith in your own powers and the operability of your spell," as Paul Huson says.[2] We might say faith "in your own powers and the reality of magick." This takes time and experience to build. If you can simply maintain an open mind at the beginning, you are doing well. As you progress, applaud and record your successes, and look for the causes of failures without blaming yourself or getting discouraged.

---

2   Paul Huson, *Mastering Witchcraft* (New York: Berkeley Windhover, 1970), 26.

Often it bolsters faith to read about past and present magicians who have achieved noteworthy results. You can do the same by looking at your own successes!

As part of a program to develop faith in yourself, Huson suggests that you

> must never break your word. If you do not think that you are going to be able to fulfill a promise, do not make it, even if there is only the faintest possibility that you may not be able to come through. You are trying to cultivate a state of mind . . . whereby it is absolutely . . . in accordance with the nature of things that whatever you say is going to come true. Each and every time you break your word . . . you chip away a little . . . faith in yourself.[3]

To Keep Silent

Now we have come to the fourth side of the pyramid: the ability to keep silent. Discretion and containment are the keynotes; thoughtless babbling drains power. As Bias elegantly puts it, "The real magus has neither the compulsion to parade in full magical regalia before the uninitiated, ranting pontifically on 'Cosmic Consciousness,' nor the need to buttonhole people at parties, muttering darkly about attending a Black Mass."[4] Not that you will be attending Black Masses (hopefully), but the principle applies to positive magickal work as well. Talking about it to anyone but a co-adept simply invites disbelief, if not outright harassment.

Another level of meaning is this: a magician must be able to keep silent—become still within and without—in order to become sensitive and receptive to very subtle signals on this plane and others: currents of psychic power, shades of emotion, the presence of unseen spirits. The loud and busy personality will miss all these and blunder through rituals in ignorance of what is occurring around and within them.

As the great Hindu spiritual leader Mahatma Gandhi said, "In the attitude of silence the soul finds the path in a clearer light, and what is elusive and deceptive resolves itself into crystal clearness."

---

3   Ibid.
4   Bias, 3.

There is a third and much deeper meaning to this side of the pyramid: you must learn to "enter the silence." At the center of each of us is a place that is utterly still and profoundly deep. It is the same silence that is in the fallow and frozen soil, at midnight in the depths of winter. It is the silence in the far reaches of intergalactic space, where nothing seems to move, the straining ear hears nothing, and no star twinkles. It is the silence that existed before the Beginning, when Goddess slept dreamless, where time and space were not.

In your busy life, full of sound and sensation, you may never have touched this place. Why would anyone want to? Because it is beyond fear and distraction, pettiness, anger, and all that litters the path to the Source. Because it is the center of your power. Because here, where there is nothing, there is the *potential* for everything.

You will understand when you go there.

And Love Within

The internal structure of the pyramid is love. Magick motivated by love heals old pain, encourages growth, eases transitions, and moves mountains. Magick motivated by fear, greed, hatred, etc., can only poison or damage the magician. Remember, too, that magick depends on the connections between all things (Indra's Web—see chapter 4) for its effectiveness. Love recognizes and cherishes connections, hatred repudiates them; this is another reason why the magick of love simply works better.

In designing rituals and working magick, therefore, always seek a way to approach your goal with love. For example: suppose a stream runs past your home, and a factory upstream begins dumping pollutants into it. Perhaps your first reaction is anger at the factory managers, and you are tempted to lash out at them magickally. Don't do it! You will harm yourself without enlightening them or stopping the pollution. Instead, focus on your love for the stream, and for its once-and-future clarity and beauty. Design a mighty ritual of protection, invoking the spirit of the stream, the Guardians of the Watchtowers of the West, and all the goddesses and gods of water, within you and without. Then act in accord by speaking to the factory officials, and if necessary organizing the neighbors and drawing in the resources of environmental groups.

What should be your attitude toward the factory people? Set aside your hatred. First, because it is misdirected: if you truly hate anyone, what you really hate is their ignorance and careless greed, which are fleeting manifestations of their outer personas. You do not hate the people themselves, which is to say the shining, eternal spirits within them. If a child spills a cup of juice, you dislike the mess but still love the child.

Secondly, set aside hatred because any strong emotion strengthens your psychic ties with its object, and presumably you do not wish to set up lasting karmic bonds with the ignorance of the factory managers. Therefore, reject the pollution without hating the polluters. Say to yourself, "I now embrace a clean environment and cast out pollution from my life: as I will, so it must be." Then with great power and purpose, as the Mother Goddess/Father God firmly and lovingly correcting an errant child, do what is necessary to correct the situation "with harm toward none and for the greatest good of all."

These six qualities, then, compose the pyramid. Master the pyramid and power is yours. Use it wisely.

Exercises Toward Mastery

1: Making a Model

Did you ever build model animals or airplanes as a child? Or even do cut-and-paste projects with construction paper? If so, this could be fun. Photocopy the illustration on page 80 onto thin white or ivory card stock, available in any copy shop. Color in the elemental symbols as follows:

> Spirit (egg): Purple
>
> Earth (square): Yellow
>
> Air (circle): Light blue
>
> Fire (triangle): Red
>
> Water (crescent): Silver

Then cut out the entire shape, and score and fold along the edges of the triangles and the tabs at the bases of the triangles. Now you have a pyramid; but before you seal it, place inside some little symbol to represent "Love." It might be a pink paper heart, a heart-shaped candy, or a short poem expressing love. Now close the pyramid with glue or transparent tape.

Place it on your desk or where you will see it often.

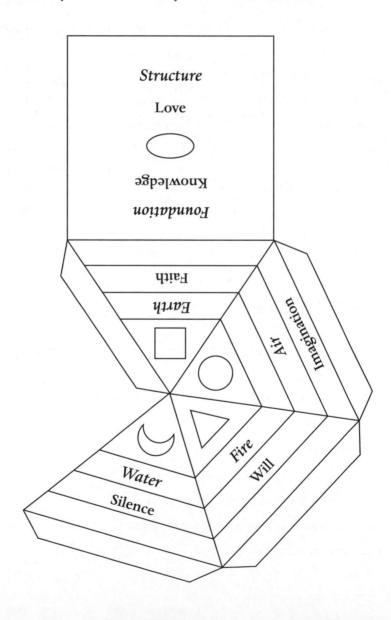

2: Exploring Ways of Knowing

Think about something you know from a source other than books and classes. Write each answer down—perhaps in your magickal journal or Book of Shadows. What have you learned from:

- nature? (a tree, a storm, a natural disaster, moss, a stone, the wind, the stars, a stream . . .)
- a relationship? (with a parent, friend, lover, leader, teacher, student, co-worker . . .)
- a life experience? (tragic, blissful, peak . . .)
- the elements? (Earth, Air, Fire, Water)
- an ancestor?
- an animal? (pet, wild, neighbor's . . .)
- a dream?
- a spirit? (a deity, an angel, a spirit guide, an animal ally, a plant deva . . .)
- a teacher or mentor who knows you well?
- a role model whom you have never met?
- a past life?
- your possessions or belongings?
- a particular kind of light? (sun-, moon-, star-, an incandescent lightbulb . . .)
- your Younger Self/inner child/inner animal spirit?
- your Higher Self?
- your anima or animus?
- a work of art? (painting, sculpture, dance, music . . .)
- a divination someone has performed for you?
- a divination you have performed for yourself?
- a personal success or triumph?

- a personal failure?

- an incident in the news?

- a sport you have participated in?

- a hobby or pastime you enjoy?

- your school experiences, apart from what was formally taught in the classrooms?

- the experience of being a child?

- the experience of being an adolescent?

- people you have known? (the best, the worst, the funniest, the oddest, the wisest . . .)

- experiences in your life? (most empowering, loneliest, funniest, most embarrassing, most uplifting, most boring . . .)

- your breath?

- your body?

- silence?

If the answer to any of these is "Nothing," then a learning experience awaits you.

3: Stretch Your Imagination

Sit in a quiet place, and imagine a vast desert landscape with a four-sided pyramid in the foreground. Now see the pyramid begin to revolve, and notice that each side is a different color; as it turns, you see them: pale blue . . . crimson red . . . sea green . . . earthy brown . . . pale blue . . . and so on. Become aware of music playing softly, but keep watching the pyramid. The music is that of distant trumpets, clear in the desert air. As you watch the rotating pyramid and listen to the trumpets, smell the scent of cinnamon; and realize too that you are growing warm. Then you may become aware of the taste of butterscotch in your mouth, contrasting oddly with the cinnamon smell, as you hear the music and watch the colors of the pyramid, and float upward until you are watching the pyramid turn directly beneath you. Try this several times, with variations, and remember to hold each sensation as you add the next.

4: Strengthen Your Will

Begin with an extremely simple action—for example, touching your nose. Say aloud: "I shall touch my nose. As I will, so mote it be!" Then do it.

Choose a slightly harder action: for example, doing three pushups. Say aloud: "I shall do three pushups. As I will, so mote it be!" Do the pushups.

Continue this, choosing slightly more difficult (and productive) actions each time. Move to tasks that take several minutes, then jobs that require an hour or two. In each case, complete the task immediately after you have spoken the words.

Each morning for several days, start with a simple action and move to more challenging tasks—but always something you can accomplish that day, even if other responsibilities intervene. Get into the habit, every day, of choosing some task that is within your power and helps you achieve your goals. Use the same words, and never ever allow anything but a dire emergency to keep you from fulfilling the task. Train your deep mind that your will is irresistible, and that your word is law.

5: Meditate on Faith

Find a stone, preferably about fist-sized; a smooth river stone works well. In a quiet place, sit holding the stone in both hands. Breathe deeply and clear your mind. Now think about someone you know whose word is always good, someone who always keeps their promises, always speaks the truth as they understand it. Then think about a time when you promised something and kept your word; and how you felt knowing that you had been true to your promise. Now think about the laws of nature that you trust, like gravity: always present, always consistent. Now take all this faith in your friend, in yourself, and in nature, and roll it into a glowing ball. Visualize yourself, perhaps in a ritual robe, standing within a magick circle at your next ritual, and place the glowing ball within the circle, so that it lights and infuses everything there—most especially you. Say aloud, "Faith in knowledge, faith in power, faith in silence, faith in love, faith in magick, faith in myself. As I have faith, so mote it be!" Place the stone where you will see it often. Hold it sometimes, and let it represent all those things you have found to be trustworthy, reliable, and true in life.

6: Practice Silence

In a quiet, darkened room, lie down, breathe slowly and steadily, and imagine moving into a tunnel that leads inward. Follow the tunnel, deeper and deeper, farther and farther from the busy, noisy upper world. Notice that all around you is quiet. Keep going in silence until you can hear your breathing and heartbeat. Imagine that you move past even those sounds until you enter a chamber of stillness. There, sit and be. When stray thoughts or images drift into your mind, gently release them and let them float away. Remain in the chamber until it is time to retrace your steps and come back to the world.

If a deep tunnel makes you nervous, you can replace it with a mountain trail that leads to a peak where there is no sound but the sighing wind, and then allow the wind to fade to stillness.

If you fall asleep, that's all right. You probably need the rest. Try the exercise again later.

7: Experience Love

Stand before your altar, or some symbol of your God/dess/Divine Spirit/Source and Creator. Say aloud, "Help me to do magick only from love. May my tools shatter and my powers desert me if I should ever enter the circle to work the Art with malice or hatred in my heart. Empower me to remember who and what I love, and raise the cone of power only for them. So mote it be!"

Now be seated and think on what and who you love. In your mind's eye, see the face of one person you love dearly, and whisper, "I love you. For you I would raise and command the powers of Earth and Air, Fire and Water. I would work magick for you." Do it again with another person, and another. Then visualize other beings or realities you love: this beautiful blue-green planet, your favorite place in the world, a beloved animal companion, a worthy cause that affects the lives of real people. For each, say the same words. After a while, stand and say to your deities, "Thus may I ever work from love, and only from love. So mote it be."

Blessèd be.

To follow this path further, read:

The Ritual Book of Magic by Clifford Bias (Weiser, 1981)

Mastering Witchcraft by Paul Huson (Berkley Windhover, 1970)

These may be out of print, but it's well worth finding old copies.

The Energies of Magick

Energy is within you and all around you, both your personal energy and the energy field that permeates the universe. We'll start on a personal level.

If you're alive, you are generating energy and using it constantly. (The energy of your soul or spirit seems to exist independently of your body, and we won't be exploring that here.) Your body's energy field should be strong, clear, and balanced for you to do the best possible magick, but it is not what powers your magick. The cone of power raised in ritual, and the power that makes even the smallest spell operate, comes from the ambient energy field.

The energy that powers your body, sometimes called chi, forms your etheric body. It permeates your whole physical body and extends out beyond your skin a little. The "glow" that radiates out even further from your body is your aura. Most people can see the aura with a little training; some see it in black-and-white and some in full color. A few people can't see it at all, but can sense it kinesthetically as a kind of change in pressure or temperature. Your aura reflects your energy level and general health.

Within your etheric body are several energy centers or nodes called chakras. There are many of these—perhaps hundreds—but most metaphysical traditions deal with five to seven major ones. The most common system includes these seven:

The seven common chakras and the energy taproot for grounding

Crown (top of the head): Spiritual connectedness

Third Eye (between the eyebrows): Psychic sensitivity

Throat (at the base of the throat): Communication

Heart (at the heart): Emotional condition

Solar Plexus (beneath the rib cage): Energy, overall vitality

Sacral (between the ovaries or above the penis): Sexual drive

Root (base of the spine): Survival; basic life functions

The chakras are points where certain kinds of energy are concentrated within your energy body. They can be visualized as spheres of light, and their color, intensity, and clarity reflect the health and functionality of different human systems, as shown in the list above. When you train yourself to sense or visualize your chakras, you might see, for example, that your solar plexus or energy chakra is small, dim, and muddy—meaning that your general energy level is very low, and you are probably feeling fatigued and lethargic. A large, bright, clear heart chakra, on the other hand, would indicate very strong, loving relationships.

Any magician—actually anyone who inhabits a human body—should monitor and maintain the health of their energy field. If your energy body is debilitated or injured, you will become physically and perhaps emotionally ill.

There are some common problems with energy fields. People who don't watch their health through good nutrition and exercise will often have an anemic, weak energy field and a small, dim aura. This leaves you vulnerable to nonphysical creatures that attach themselves to your etheric body and feed off your energy, rather like astral mosquitos. They can be easily removed, but unless your energy improves, they will return.

Illness, injury, and the use of hard drugs, including hallucinogens, can leave thin places or tears in your energy field, through which your energy leaks. As you heal or give up drug use, your energy body will repair these holes.

Then there are energy vampires. These are living people who you may know as relatives, friends, acquaintances, or irritating co-workers. They are people who have low personal energy and often damaged etheric bodies, and they habitually suck energy from others around them—including, quite possibly, you.

Please note that we are not talking about conscious malice. Most energy vampires are not remotely aware of what they are doing. It is a subconscious process, and they would be shocked to realize their effect on others. The effect is very negative, but without the high drama, visibility, or intentional evil of Count Dracula. That is almost unfortunate: in some ways, an obvious villain would be simpler to deal with than a banal, subtle, unintentional habit.

If you think about the people you know, you may recognize one or two who leave you feeling drained and depressed after every visit. Sometimes they grab on to you, leech-like, and pour their troubles into your ear. Sometimes they are morose and quiet. Because their etheric bodies are damaged, they cannot actually hold on to the energy they have taken for very long. It's exactly like pouring water into a bucket with cracks and holes in it; soon the pail is empty, and they must find more water somewhere.

Frequently such a person will have an energy connection to your etheric body, a chord or energy tube to the chakra that best defines your relationship or their need. Such chords are entirely appropriate in some relationships: your baby depends on you for survival and will be connected to your root chakra; your spouse will connect with your heart and sexual chakras. But in other cases, it's not at all appropriate. An old lover may still connect to your heart chakra and leave you unable to heal the loss of the relationship. Energy vampires often attach a chord to your energy chakra at the solar plexus.

The best strategy is to disconnect the chords—your teacher or an experienced energy healer can help with this—then strengthen and heal your energy field overall. Also, avoid the company of people who leave you feeling weak and drained.

Cleansing and Balancing Your Energy Field

Whether you are mowing the lawn or working high magick, it is good to keep your energy field clear and clean. Use the exercises at the end of the chapter and make them part of your daily magickal discipline.

Other exercises are similar, in that they usually involve visualizing each chakra and breathing energy into or through it. The way you see/imagine/visualize each energy center may be different from the experience others have. Books may suggest that each chakra should be a certain color, or be visualized as a lotus with a certain number of petals. Fine, if that works for you; but if you see them in black and white, or in colors different from those described in the books, or as animals instead of flowers, that's fine too. The main thing is to get better acquainted with your own energy field, no matter what it "looks like."

The exact form of the exercises is not as important as that you pay attention to your energy body and the chakras, and do some balancing or healing when something is not right. It's like cleaning your house: you can use a canister vacuum cleaner or an upright, or a broom and dustpan; but you can't ignore your house completely and assume it will remain clean and functional.

Centering and Connecting

If you pay attention at all to your insides, you know whether you are feeling a little off-balance, harassed, confused, uncertain, weak—or whether you are feeling strong, confident, solid, sure of yourself, grounded, tranquil, and centered. It is extremely important that you be aware of your inner state, no matter what outside distractions or duties demand your attention. If you realize that you are drifting "off center," *stop*, and take time to center and connect yourself.

Again, use the exercises at the end of the chapter, both grounding and centering, as well as *bhramari* breathing.

Remember, your connection with the great web (God/dess) is at your center, and as long as you are centered, all the power, peace, and resources of the web of life are yours.

The Power Within You

Raising power is not easy in this society. From an early age we are taught that power is "out there," not within us. One person seems like small potatoes indeed, in comparison with giant corporations, the military might of governments, the demanding tentacles of huge bureaucracies, and the self-assurance of large churches.

Yet reflect: all those great organizations were created and are run by individual people like you. People who sweat, burp, and make dumb mistakes. Folks. The only difference that is relevant here is that leaders and executives have a sense of their own personal power—and use it.

You, too, have power within you. All the strength you could ever need is there, including the strength to draw in more power from all around you. Learning that you have it, and learning to use it, is like exercising weak, flabby muscles. You begin with small challenges, practice frequently, challenge yourself more as your strength grows; one day you will achieve things that you can scarcely dream of today.

Raising power demands emotional intensity. As indicated earlier, there is energy available for goals you feel strongly about, and for needs and desires passionately felt. Lukewarm feelings will not serve. Get into the gut feelings that make you yearn, cry, shout, and tremble. It's not easy if you happen to be a middle-class, proper, civilized person who has been taught that strong emotions are messy and socially inappropriate. You must break through your conditioning, find the flame in your heart and the fire in your belly, if you are to change yourself and your world. Let yourself feel. If necessary, open the floodgates by reliving the tragedies and triumphs of your life and the events that brought you heartache or joy.

Raising Power from Without

Remembering and reliving can raise power. Raise more power by drumming, chanting, clapping, pounding, breathing, singing, dancing, or any other active method you favor. Let the feelings flow free; let the power surge through you. Visualize your goal and experience it as real and accomplished. See it, hear it, touch it, smell it, taste it. You will know when the energy peaks or gets as high as it is going to get; at that instant, release it into the reality you have created in your mind.

Throughout, remember to draw the power from Earth, the sun, the moon, or other natural sources. You must be an open channel for energy. If you are closed, then you will use only energy from your own reserves, and thus will exhaust yourself quickly.

Sending the Power

The energy can be released directly into the mind-image of your goal or into a physical object, called a witness or object link. For example, if you are doing healing work (only with the permission of the ill or injured person, of course), you might use a photograph of that individual or a lock of their hair. You visualize the person as whole and healthy, raise the power, and channel it to them through the hair or photo.

Of course you can also channel the power directly into the sick individual if they are sitting in front of you. If they are not present and you have no object link, visualize the person and use their name.

If you are working to obtain land for a home, you might again use a photo, or some earth from the site, or even a drawing or painting. If you are working for essence and don't have a particular form or object in mind, then picture yourself enjoying an activity associated with this goal—walking on the land, building a home, gardening, or whatever.

Earthing Excess Energy

After you have raised and sent the power, you will probably feel keyed up, as if you were vibrating. This happens because extra energy is still circling through your nervous system, and you have actually raised the vibrational level of your whole body.

This is fine for brief periods, but your nervous system is not used to this level of energy, and there may be adverse effects if you don't bring the level down to normal. You might feel uncomfortably tense, or get a headache, or be unable to sleep at your usual bedtime. You might be hyperactive and run around in fast-forward mode until you collapse from exhaustion. Eventually your energy will rebalance, but there is no need to suffer; you can "ground" or "earth" the extra energy almost immediately.

Sit or lie down, rest quietly, and allow the excess power to drain into the earth through your skin and especially your hands. It may help to have a big, rough rock on hand: you can hold it in your lap and channel the energy into it until you feel balanced again. Then put the rock outdoors on the ground to discharge. Another method, "sending down roots," is covered in the exercises at the end of this chapter.

In many magickal rituals, everyone is helped to ground with "cakes and wine," the ritual term for any food and beverage shared in a mindful, spiritual way. Holding a potluck feast after the ritual will accomplish the same thing. When your body has to digest solid food, it returns to its normal energy level more quickly.

Protecting Animal Companions

If you have animals sharing your home, they may have strong reactions to the unusual amounts of energy around your ritual. Depending on the nature of the energy and the animal's individual needs, they may either hide or want to snuggle close. If they hide, focus on the power you've raised and channeled to be quite sure it is positive energy. Of course, an animal might run away from even very positive energy if the energy is simply too intense for its nervous system to handle comfortably. If your animal companion is clearly upset, during your work you may have to put it in another part of the house, outdoors (if you are in), or at a friend's home.

If your animal wants to cuddle, you might have to remove it for a while. Never channel energy into an animal unless you are a very sensitive healer, since the sudden influx can upset its energy field and do more harm than help.

If you have fish, caged birds, or other trapped animals, put a large quartz crystal or a pattern of smaller ones between the circle and the creature's habitat to intercept and filter the energies.

Recharging Talismans and Wards

Occasionally you will need to charge an item so that it can radiate the energy gradually over a period of time. For example: a hag stone (a stone with a hole in it) or rowan twig worn as a protective amulet; a little bag filled with dried herbs, created as a healing talisman for yourself or someone who requested it; a piece of rose quartz or a Brigit's cross placed by your door as a ward, to protect and bless your home.

Just as you replace the batteries in your smoke alarms, you need to re-charge the energies in these magickal items from time to time. First, do a quick cleansing with salt and water or by "smudging" the object with burn-ing sage. Then raise energy by breathing, chanting, or other means. Touch or hold the item with your dominant or projective hand and pour the energy into it, visualizing or speaking the purpose of the item: "I charge you, O ward, to protect this house and all who dwell within it, to allow within all that is blessed and good, and to turn away all else from our door! So mote it be!" Then visualize sealing a "cocoon" of energy around the object to keep the energy from dissipating too quickly.

We are all filled with the energy of life and surrounded by more energy in vast quantities. Yet we have grown used to thinking of energy as something strictly outside ourselves—something generated by technology or perhaps weather, beyond our control except when we operate a machine.

As a magician, you need to consider first the energy closest to home, that which is in your body. Care for your body, pay attention to your personal energy field, and it will serve you well. Surrounding you is the ambient field, the energy of the cosmos, there for you to use. And in fact, at the deepest levels there is no real distinction between energy and matter: you are pure energy enveloped by an ocean of pure energy manifesting in a million differ-ent ways. Isn't it time that you became proficient at using the basic stuff of the universe?

Exercises Toward Mastery

1: Progressive Relaxation

This is a good prelude to working with energy. Wearing comfortable, loose clothing, and with your shoes off, sit or lie in a comfortable position. Then begin to progressively flex and relax each set of muscles in your body. Your pace should be slow and deliberate; think about what you are doing at each step. Begin with your toes, stretching and wiggling them. Then curl your toes and arch your feet. Move your feet in circles, stretching your ankles. Tighten and relax your calf muscles. Move up through your knees, thighs, buttocks, stomach, chest, shoulders, arms, hands, neck and head, facial muscles, and scalp muscles. Lie still and feel every part of your body. If any part still feels tense or stiff, go back and flex it again, slowly and thoroughly. Then lie still for a few moments, breathing deeply.

2: Energy Cleansing Exercise

With your healer's or physician's approval, fast for one to three days, drinking only distilled water or apple cider (not hard cider). Take a ritual bath by candlelight while burning incense in the room. Then you may wish to cast a circle—how to do this is explained later in the book—while either wearing a thin robe or skyclad. Stand in the center of the circle: breathe in radiant white light and breathe out tension, all negative feelings, and psychic debris. Continue for at least twenty-seven breaths, or for as long as the breathing feels cleansing to you. Return to normal breathing. If a friend is with you, ask them to brush lightly all over your aura with a feather, flicking any toxic energy away from you. If you are by yourself, you can do it. Then wrap yourself in a cocoon of white light, willing it to allow love, air, and positive energy of any kind to flow into you and to repel anything negative. Give thanks and open the circle, then sit quietly and meditate on positive and inspirational thoughts for a while.

3: The Middle Pillar Exercise

Use this exercise to open, balance, and energize the chakras (energy centers of the human body).

The version presented here was created within the Ladywood Tradition of Wicca, modified from the original Qabalistic form, vibrating goddess names rather than the original Hebrew titles of deity. Vibrating means to take a deep breath and intone the name in a loud and resonant manner, for as long as your breath lasts.

We use seven major chakras and seven goddess names as follows:

Crown Chakra: ISIS

Third Eye Chakra: HECATE

Throat Chakra: ARADIA

Heart Chakra: AMATERASU

Solar Plexus Chakra: FREYA

Sacral Chakra: APHRODITE

Root Chakra: GAIA

The original form uses five chakras and Hebrew names for god. If you would like to try it, just leave out the third eye and sexual chakras, and use the god names as follows:

Crown Chakra: EHEIEH (eh-hey-ya)

Throat Chakra: YHVH ELOHIM (yay-ho-vah ay-lo-heem)

Heart Chakra: YHVH ALOAH VA-DAATH (yay-ho-vah ay-lo vay-da-ath)

Solar Plexus Chakra: SHADDAI EL CHAI (sha-di el ki)

Root Chakra: ADONAI HA-ARETZ (ah-do-ni ha-ah-retz)

If you want to get creative, you can substitute the names of any deities or spirits that seem to match the energies of each chakra. Try using your favorite pantheon, or mixing god and goddess names.

1. Wear loose, comfortable clothing, or go skyclad.

2. Find a quiet place where you will not be disturbed.

3. Stand and breathe deeply into your abdomen.

4. Visualize a glowing ball of energy at the top of your head (crown chakra). Take a deep breath and vibrate the name ISIS (Eye´-sis).

5. Follow the channel of energy down to the middle of your forehead, and visualize a glowing ball of energy there (third eye chakra). Still holding the image of the first chakra, take a deep breath and vibrate the name HECATE (Heck´-a-tey).

6. Follow the channel of energy down to your throat, and visualize a glowing ball of energy there (throat chakra). Still holding the image of the first two chakras, vibrate the name ARADIA (Ah-ray´-dee-uh).

7. Follow the channel of energy down to your heart, and visualize a glowing ball of energy there (heart chakra). Still holding the image of the first three chakras, vibrate the name AMATERASU (Ah-mah-ter-ah´-soo).

8. Follow the channel of energy down to your solar plexus, and visualize a glowing ball of energy there (energy chakra). Still holding the image of the first four chakras, vibrate the name FREYA (Fray´-uh).

9. Follow the channel of energy down to a point above your genitals, and visualize a glowing ball of energy there (sexual chakra). Still holding the image of the first five chakras, vibrate the name APHRODITE (A´-fro-dye´-tee).

10. Follow the channel of energy down to the base of your spine, and visualize a glowing ball of energy there (root chakra). Still holding the image of the first six chakras, vibrate the name GAIA (Guy´-uh).

11. Holding the image of all seven chakras, take three deep breaths. As you inhale, pull energy up along your back to your crown chakra. As you exhale, move your awareness down along your front to your root chakra.

12. Still holding the image of all seven chakras, take three more deep breaths. As you inhale, pull energy up along your left side to your crown chakra. As you exhale, move your awareness down along your right side to your root chakra.

13. Still holding the image of all seven chakras, take three pairs of deep breaths. As you inhale, pull energy up to your energy chakra. As you exhale, hold the energy there. As you inhale again, bring the energy from there up through your crown chakra. As you exhale, let it pour down around the outside of your body. Do three sets like this.

14. Beginning at the bottoms of your feet and moving deosil (clockwise), mentally wrap yourself in a band of light, all the way up to your crown chakra: "tie it off" there. Take as many breaths as you need. Think of this wrapping as a semi-permeable membrane that holds in your energy and allows light, life, love, and air to pass freely through and into you.

15. Rest in silence for a while, sensing how your energy feels.

4: Centering

Take a deep breath and focus on your body: what it feels like inside. Close your eyes and imagine a still, quiet point about two inches below your belly button and centered in your abdomen. Feel the solidity and calmness of this point, and imagine that it is the center of your internal universe. Nothing can move you from that point; nothing can touch or disturb you as you remain focused on that point. Take a deep breath and relax into that calm, centered feeling. Now open your eyes, retaining the feeling, and proceed with grounding.

5: Grounding

Sit on the ground, close your eyes, and center. Now visualize energy "roots" moving down into the ground through the root chakra at the base of your spine, as though you are a tree and your backbone is the trunk. Imagine your roots reaching deep into the earth, branching and holding (see illustration on page 88). Feel the roots burrowing through the dirt and around rocks and pebbles. Now inhale and draw Earth energy up through your roots and into every part of your body. Feel Earth's strength, stability, and ancient wisdom filling you. When you are ready, draw your energy roots back into you, sit quietly for a moment, and then proceed with your work.

6: Focusing Breath

This variation on bhramari breathing is from the Hindu breathing disciplines, collectively called pranayama. Begin deep, rhythmic, abdominal breathing. Start to inhale through your mouth and exhale through your nose. Then begin to hum with a long, even note as you exhale. Each time you exhale, make the humming a little steadier and extend it a bit longer. Do at least twenty exhalations, focusing only on that long, steady humming note. (Be careful not to hyperventilate, however. If you start to feel dizzy and light-headed, stop the exercise, put your head down, and breathe normally. The next time you try the exercise, do it for a shorter period and moderate the deep breathing.)

7: Energizing Breath

This form is sometimes called vitalic breathing and gives your body a quick burst of oxygen while clearing your lungs. Sit or stand. Take a deep abdominal breath and expel all the air. Then inhale three times quickly through your nose without exhaling: three deep sniffs. Immediately open your mouth wide and exhale all the air through your mouth, quickly, making a "ha!" sound. Repeat: three quick inhalations through the nose, one explosive exhalation through the mouth. Do five to seven complete breaths, but stop if you become lightheaded. Pause, breathe normally, and internally check your energy level.

8: Playing with an Energy Ball

Here is a classic beginning exercise that will help you learn to handle magickal energy. Sit comfortably, relaxing all over. Begin deep abdominal breathing. With each inhalation, draw in energy from the earth. With each exhalation, send the energy down your arms and into your hands. Feel your hands tingling with the power. If it helps, hum as you bring the energy to your hands. Now cup your hands, still breathing the energy, and form a ball of energy within them. You may see it in your mind's eye as a glowing ball of green, gold, or blue light, or feel it as a warm presence, just a little heavier than air. Play with the ball: expand it, compress it, stretch it, divide it in two. Play with changing its color to red or pink, and back. If a friend is doing the exercise with you, hand the balls back and forth. Put the energy back into your hands, then hold your palms near your friends' and move close and away, feeling the depth and intensity of the energy field. When you are done, "earth" the energy by putting your palms flat on the ground. As with other exercises involving deep breathing, if you begin to hyperventilate and feel dizzy, then stop the exercise and put your head down. The next time you try it, do not breathe so deeply.

9: Raising Energy Different Ways

Think of a positive purpose that you could send energy to: healing, blessing, world peace, prosperity, or whatever. Then experiment with these different ways to raise energy:

+ vitalic breathing
+ drumming
+ dancing, with a very simple step, to lively music
+ chanting a short, simple chant, such as "Healing, healing, come to me; as I will, so mote it be!"
+ visualizing an energy ball

After each power-raising, visualize your goal and send the energy to it, then earth the excess. (Stop if you get too tired or tense.) Compare how the different methods felt, and note the results in your journal.

10: Projecting Energy

For this, you will need the help of a willing friend—preferably one with experience in energy work. Raise power by breathing, chanting, drumming, or your favorite method. Now hold hands with your friend and send the energy into them for blessing or healing (be ready to help them earth the excess, in case you are very successful). After they are normalized, raise power again, but use it to charge a quartz crystal with blessing energy. Earth the excess and do it again, but charge a photograph of a place where people need help (for example, send peace energy to a war zone). Earth the excess and raise power again, but send healing energy into a plant that has been sickly (make sure it has the right amount of water!). Write down your immediate impressions in your journal. After a few hours, check with your friend to see how they are feeling; check the crystal to see if you can still sense energy; and check the plant to see if it looks healthier. Thank them all, and note the results in your journal.

11: Earthing Excess Energy

Raise power by breathing, chanting, drumming, or your favorite method. Send it to a worthy goal, and then release the excess by placing your palms flat on the ground and willing the extra power to flow into the earth. Raise power again, but this time pick up a large stone, sit with it in your lap, and send the extra energy into it. Raise power again, and after you have sent it off, put both hands into running water for a couple of minutes. Raise power again, but this time, don't do anything with the extra. Instead, eat something hearty and solid, such as a cheeseburger, a peanut butter sandwich, or a big helping of potatoes. Now compare how you felt after each method, and record the results in your journal.

Blesséd be.

To follow this path further, read:

Hands of Light: A Guide to Healing Through the Human Energy Field by Barbara Ann Brennan (Bantam Books, 1987)

Wheels of Life: A User's Guide to the Chakra System by Anodea Judith (Llewellyn, 1987)

Your Personality, Your Health: Connecting Personality with the Human Energy System, Chakras, and Wellness by Carol Ritberger (Hay House, 1998)

Magick and Your Health

Physical, mental, and emotional health are necessary for peak performance in the magickal arts, and a strong and sensitive nervous system is also essential. As Isaac Bonewits explains,

> Basically everybody is a walking radio station, broadcasting and receiving—on ultra-long wavelengths of the standard electromagnetic energy spectrum. Anything that will affect the human neural system will modulate the radio waves broadcast and the efficiency of reception for those waves broadcast by others.[1]

Thus anything that debilitates your neural system—or, indeed, any of your systems—weakens your magick. A healthy lifestyle means stronger magick. There are seven key factors that contribute to health. Let's explore them.

Eating Right

For optimum health, eat plenty of organically grown fruits and vegetables, whole grains, nuts, seeds, and legumes. Shop at a whole-foods store if you can, and if you buy food at a standard sort of supermarket, avoid the processed, canned, and packaged items, focusing on fresh produce or frozen foods.

Of course, the ideal would be to set up your own garden. Tending it can be a rich experience that brings you closer to the earth, and you can also be sure that your produce is organic. Harvesting your garden is a delight. Whatever you do not eat right away you can put in the freezer or can. Canning is

---

1   Isaac Bonewits, *Real Magic*, 67.

hard work, but it ensures you a supply of chemical-free veggies and fruit for the winter; if you invite friends over for a canning party, you can make the work seem lighter. Can't do a garden where you live? Maybe there's a seasonal farmer's market in your area.

How you prepare your food is just as important as what you start with. Grains and legumes are at their nutritional best if they are sprouted before grinding or cooking. Your nearest health food store or cooperative may have booklets explaining this simple procedure.

Most foods are best eaten raw, steamed lightly, baked at low temperatures, or heated in a Crock-Pot at the low setting. If you overcook food (and some say that means anything over 200 degrees F), the chemical composition is changed and the food is on its way to becoming pure carbon, which is not very nutritious at all.

A shift toward less meat would be healthful for most people in Western society. Many people avoid vegetarian meals because they have never encountered good ones. The very word "vegetarian" can conjure images of bland heaps of nameless, mushy grains, boiled vegetables identifiable only by their color, or globs of slithery white bean curd floating in an insipid soup.

It does not have to be so, thank Goddess! People "in the know" enjoy such delights as:

- rich, spicy chili accompanied by thick, crusty slices of home-baked, whole-grain bread warm from the oven;
- granola cereal packed with nuts, dates, raisins, and toasted oats, lightly sweetened with wildflower honey and doused with apple cider;
- slightly crisp, savory veggies stir-fried in a savory oriental sauce and heaped over brown rice;
- hearty banana-nut loaves or corn muffins filled with pecans and drizzled with maple syrup; and
- tacos stuffed with beans, onions, guacamole, tomatoes, cheese, leaf lettuce, and spicy sauce.

But what about all you carnivores out there? Am I suggesting that meat and magick don't mix? Not necessarily; but we do need to eat more lightly in order to become healthy, and meat at every meal is not a necessity. When meat is eaten, it is best if from wild or organic sources, lean, and served in small portions or as a minor ingredient in soups, stews, and casseroles. Generally speaking, seafood seems to be the most healthful meat—depending on the source—followed by poultry and, lastly, red meat.

There is an ethical concern here as well as a health issue. Animal-rights activists are helping us to understand that many domestic meat animals are raised and slaughtered in crowded, inhumane conditions. We should ask ourselves whether we want to support such practices by continuing to purchase meat from such sources.

On a less sober note, let us consider seasonings. Many modern folks are used to getting all of their food flavor from salt, sugar, or additives like monosodium glutamate (MSG). Consider retraining your taste buds so that the natural flavors of the food are enough, or use spices like oregano, basil, cayenne, and, of course, garlic and onions. For us former salt addicts, there are tasty herbal substitutes that do not contain sodium chloride.

About beverages—we all know of the undesirable effects of sugar and too much caffeine, and that tap water has become increasingly questionable as the groundwater is polluted. To add insult to injury, some researchers are even suggesting that cow's milk is better designed to feed calves than humans. Fear not! We don't have to give up liquids, but it's safest to drink mostly filtered water, herb teas, and occasionally pure fruit juices or "natural" fructose-sweetened soda pop. No coffee? (Legions of ardent worshippers of Caffeina reach for their torches and pitchforks.) Relax: not "no coffee," just drink it in moderation.

Now, very few people in our supermarket society are going to give up processed foods and drinks altogether. Next time you get behind that big steel cart, however, do stop and read the labels. And think. Your cart doesn't have to look like the one in front of you, filled with processed, sugared, chemicalized products. Before you buy, ask yourself this question: "Would my ancestors recognize this item as food?" Then fill your cart with the freshest, simplest things you can find.

Changing your eating habits can be very difficult, but you don't have to do it all at once. Target the worst offenders in your usual diet and cut back on them one at a time. Don't just remove things from your life—switch to something new, healthful, and delicious. You can do it.

You will feel better physically and emotionally, your family and friends will be glad, and your magick will be more clear and powerful every time you cast the circle.

Clean Air

You may wish to support clean-air legislation and try to avoid areas of factory pollution, heavy vehicle traffic, and gas or chemical fumes. And breathe. Many of us breathe shallowly, using only the upper lungs, due to poor posture, tension, tight clothing, or just bad habits. This starves the brain and body of oxygen. Junk the furniture that makes you sit like a contorted pretzel, stretch out those tight muscles, get a massage or hot bath, throw on some loose clothes, and breathe!

It also helps to practice pranayama, the yogic art of breathing. Various breathing techniques can relax you, energize you, and focus your concentration. A few minutes of practice each day will expand your lungs and make your whole system sing. A couple of examples are given elsewhere in this book—try them!

Regular Exercise

Participate in vigorous aerobic exercise to benefit the lungs and cardiovascular system, and also add a more gentle, stretching/massaging activity for the glands joints, and muscles.

For vigorous activity, you don't have to play linebacker for the Chicago Bears nor run twelve miles a day. Walking, swimming, or playing volleyball or soccer on a local team are all beneficial. Many people have tried jogging but find it too strenuous; an alternative is race-walking, which combines the best of walking and running.

A wonderful stretching activity is hatha yoga. In the past, many people were put off by the Sanskrit terminology and the grainy black-and-white photos of emaciated men in contorted postures: "the instructor demonstrates the reverse spinal twist with his tongue locked around his left ankle." But simplified books and classes are now offered that are more understandable to Westerners. Basically, hatha yoga consists of stretching and toning postures and movements combined with breathing techniques, which may be used in a spiritual context or simply to improve health.

Some of the martial arts' exercises and warm-ups are excellent; I especially recommend exploring tai chi and aikido. In addition, dance classes provide great conditioning, and classes are offered in many areas.

Trying to maintain an exercise program alone, however, can be dull and difficult. If individual self-discipline is a challenge for you, you may need to join a team, gym, or class, or contract with a friend or family member to play, practice, or exercise on a regular basis. With company it's more fun and much easier to stay motivated.

How long should you exercise each day? Most people should start with a modest effort, such as fifteen minutes a day, and work their way up to a half hour or more daily, with longer workouts at least a couple of times each week.

Natural-Fiber Clothing

Choose clothes of cotton, wool, and/or rayon. The skin is the body's largest organ, and it needs to breathe. Mail-order companies such as Lands' End and Deva specialize in natural-fiber clothes. Though they require more care, in some ways, than synthetics, these clothes are worth the effort for the health and comfort they provide. Organic and biodegradable fabrics will someday return to replenish the soil, instead of lingering for millennia as a useless relic of the petroleum industry.

If you choose to wear synthetics, at least save your purchases of them for accessories, special-occasion costumes, and possibly loose outerwear to be worn over inner layers of natural fibers. For everyday wear be kind to your skin, and everything inside it, by using natural material.

And if you are still wearing a smaller size that fit you ten years ago, but you have put on weight—get real, buy clothing in sizes that fit you or are a bit loose. Tight clothing emphasizes that extra weight and makes you look and feel worse. Loosen up your clothes; let your body move and breathe.

Restful Sleep

All of the factors mentioned above will help you sleep better, and don't skimp on the number of hours your body gets to rest each night. Also, consider making time and a comfortable space for short afternoon catnaps, if they will recharge you. I know this is a terrific challenge for most people with busy schedules, but you should seriously consider it. It is a false economy to push yourself too hard when you are too tired to function efficiently.

What if you have trouble sleeping? First, examine your diet. Do you eat late suppers, large snacks, sugary desserts, or caffeinated beverages shortly before bedtime? If so, change to eating your evening meal earlier and keep it fairly light. Switch to fruit for evening snacks; it is easily digested and cleanses the system rather than clogging it.

Is your room stuffy? Did you sit in front of the television all evening? Is your sleepwear made of an uncomfortable synthetic? The remedies are obvious.

Or is there a problem in your personal or professional life that troubles you? Are you tossing and turning because you can't put your worries out of your mind? Make a deal with your Deep Mind: resolve to do something constructive about it, then sleep. Get up and do some magick, or write a letter, or find a counselor in the Yellow Pages and resolve to call for an appointment in the morning. Then let go of it. The Japanese, if they receive an unfavorable divination at the temple, hang it on a "trouble tree" in the temple courtyard for the gods to deal with. You might simply visualize placing the problem in the lap of Goddess (or your deity of choice). She can certainly handle it—meaning that you can—and when you are in harmony with her, the whole universe will help. Having done these things, shift your attention to some unrelated project and work on that until you feel drowsy.

Other remedies for sleeplessness include an evening walk, soothing music, a warm bath, subliminal tapes with appropriate messages, a cup of hot catnip or chamomile tea, getting a massage from a partner or friend, self-hypnosis, Bach flower remedies, making love, progressive relaxation of each set of muscles, or a combination of any of these.

If your bed is ancient, lumpy, too hard or soft, or filled with dust and tiny critters, it's time to start saving for a new one.

If you tend to stay up too late, then when the alarm goes off in the morning, set the alarm again for bedtime. Set it for an hour that will give you eight hours' rest, then adjust it over the next several days until you wake up refreshed in the morning.

Perhaps the greatest help of all, in the long run, is to make sure you have plenty of physical activity and exercise in your life. This will lead to a more relaxed body and a more cheerful and serene emotional outlook.

Natural Light

A daily dose of sunlight helps the body create important vitamins, especially vitamin D, and natural moonlight can help regulate the menstrual cycle. Inside, use incandescent lights or bulbs that reproduce the natural spectrum—never ordinary fluorescents.

Of course it is very possible to overdo sunlight: too much exposure harms sensitive skin and can even lead to skin cancer. The bronzed surfers and beach bunnies of today may pay a terrible price later, especially if the ozone layer continues to be depleted and we are all exposed to more intense solar radiation.

Seek balance and use common sense. During the summer you will probably get plenty of natural light without really trying. If you live in northerly areas with long, dark winters, you may have to make a special effort during the cold season to get enough sunlight. At this time, lack of sunlight may affect your health and emotional balance. Scientists have suggested that the high suicide rate in some northern countries may stem from depression caused by vitamin deficiencies, which are in turn caused by a shortage of natural light; it's called "Seasonal Affective Disorder." So when the winter days are shorter, it becomes important to spend as much time as possible outdoors—at least half an hour a day!

Don't skimp on the indoor lighting, either. If it's cold and dark outside, balance this with a blaze of warm light inside. If the electric bill is a concern, ask yourself whether you would rather sit in the gloom or unplug a few of your gadgets and appliances for the sake of increased light.

As much as light is important, so, sometimes, is real darkness. When you sleep, artificial lights, even tiny nightlights, will affect your natural sleep cycle. Spiritually speaking, making friends with the night counters and heals the crazy moral polarity in our culture, which sells the equation:

GOOD = Light, activity, complexity, masculine qualities, etc.

BAD = darkness, stillness, simplicity, feminine qualities, etc.

There is a saying: "Witches are not afraid of the dark." Well, some are; but most Witches and other magicians face their fear and work with it until they find the beauty and peace that are in the darkness as well as the light.

Love

Study after study has shown that love is a requirement for health, whether it comes from family, friends, lovers, or pets. Creating and maintaining loving relationships is a topic that has filled many books, and we are not going to cover it here in great depth. Nevertheless, here are a few insights that might be helpful.

- Relationships begin with genuine curiosity and openness: cultivate these in yourself. If you genuinely appreciate people—if you understand that every human being has some gemlike quality of the mind, heart, or spirit that you can learn from, and if you reach out—then relationships become inevitable. It begins in little ways:

smile at people, say "hi," make small talk in lines or at work, ask questions. It's not so hard.

* Find pleasure in giving your time, energy, skills, and consideration. Then you can give freely, and create an upward spiral of sharing. If you give grudgingly, and keep an account book in your head to make sure you do not give more than you get, then you will find yourself in a downward spiral of withholding.

* Find pleasure in receiving. Some of us want always to be the Great Provider/Mother/Helper to the world, Daddy Warbucks the powerful philanthropist, and sometimes this is done out of fear and insecurity. Open your heart to the gifts of others; recognize, savor, and appreciate them. This, too, is a gift, to create sharing instead of dependency.

* Don't look for all your needs to be met in one person. Accept and enjoy them for who they are and what they can freely bring to your relationship. What they cannot give, seek in yourself or elsewhere.

* If you are going to love someone, love them for who they are, not who you would like them to become. Encourage, support, and celebrate positive growth and change in your loved ones, but never demand it.

* Show respect. Never criticize or demean your loved ones to others, even "jokingly." Be courteous even in the middle of a fight. All too often people take advantage of the nearness and vulnerability of those they love, and behave towards them in ways they would never dream of inflicting on a stranger. Our families and friends deserve at least as much honor, respect, and courtesy as we show to others.

* Communicate. Explain clearly what you want or need, but without demanding, threatening, or expecting. Never withhold your thoughts or feelings out of fear. Check assumptions, especially negative ones. Talk out problems.

  At the same time, don't ask your friends and family to become your therapists. If you have some ongoing emotional problem, give them a break and get professional help. Of course your loved ones will be there for you in a crisis, but day-by-day you should give them the best and strongest part of yourself, not a basket case of problems.

♦ Never let problems between you linger, unless you are too exhausted, stressed, or distracted to put quality energy into a solution at the moment. Work things out at the earliest possible moment. Folk wisdom says, "Never let the sun set on a quarrel."

♦ Forgive. The people you love, who love you, are human beings, doing the best they can. They will screw up occasionally and act in athoughtless, insensitive, or even cruel manner. These mistakes do not negate their good qualities—the reasons that you love them in the first place. You do not have to "suffer slings and arrows" in silence; point out mistakes, explain their effect on you, tell your needs and preferences—then drop the subject from your mind and heart. Forgive. Refocus on the good stuff.

This is not to say that you should accept ongoing abuse or dangerous behavior; if there is a pattern of harm, get professional help or get out of the relationship. Only you can draw the line between occasional human goofs and a pattern of destructive habits.

♦ Look inside: "If what you seek you find not within yourself, you will never find it without." (This wisdom is from "The Charge of the Goddess.") Work to cherish and respect yourself, and that will be reflected in all your relationships. Helen Reddy sings, "I am a best friend to myself. I'm as nice to me as anyone I know." Make it so.

We all need love, by which I mean caring and emotionally intimate relationships. (Sex is fine as well, but it's not the most essential ingredient.) And we can all find love. If you haven't got enough, give some away and watch it return threefold.

A Word About Addictions

There are many kinds of addictions. It's an addiction if you want it, do it, or buy it all the time, or want too much of it, and if your dependency is harming you or your loved ones. Some people become addicted to substances that are unhealthy in any quantity: tobacco, "hard" drugs, etc. Others rely on things that are fine in moderation, but harmful in large quantities: beer, sugar, chocolate, and so on. Any addiction can interfere with your psychic sensitivity and your ability to communicate with Younger Self and Higher Self (see chapter 5). A wise practitioner once said it this way: "Adepts have the use of everything but are dependent on nothing."

We live in a society where addictions are promoted, marketed, and pushed at us constantly by the advertising power of giant corporations. True, addiction to illegal drugs is discouraged; but addiction to processed food, sugary beverages, big cars, fancy clothing, expensive cosmetics, and a million other consumer products—well, that's the American Way.

We all need to ask ourselves: what are we addicted to? We can be addicted to diet sodas, possessions, sex, high-carb snacks, whining, sleep, food in general, nasty gossip, romance novels, television, movies, or collecting china ducks. If it impairs your health or clarity, or if it ties up large amounts of time, energy, or money that could be put to better use, it's going to hurt your magick and your whole life.

Many of us are kings and queens of denial. The phrases come so easily: "I can quit anytime I want to." "Well, there are habits that are a lot worse!" "Yes, but I'm under so much stress, and it relaxes me." "I've been good today; I'll just reward myself a little." "Well, it's a free country, and I can do what I want."

I've said things like that, too. Yes, it's sad and pathetic.

For once, let us stand up, look in the mirror, and say, "Wow, I'm really overboard on this. I'm addicted, and it's hurting me and my family." Then act. Join a twelve-step program, get medical help, get counseling, take the plunge, make the shift, stop indulging, stop escaping, work magick to release addictions, get back on track with what's really important in life. It might be something you can master in a week or it might be a lifelong struggle. It will demand courage and perseverance, but aren't these the qualities we expect from a magician?

Even magick can become an addiction. The study of magick itself should never become a way to avoid life and its problems. Don't let the fun and mystery of magick become a hidey-hole where you can escape your problems. Instead, use it to confront them.

Magick is tightly interwoven with a life that is healthy and empowered. A healthy lifestyle leads to stronger magick; and magick, in turn, can help create a healthy lifestyle.

Good nutrition, clean air and water, rest, natural light, exercise, natural clothing, and love; these are basics we all need to thrive, and they are a foundation for working magick.

When seeking teachers, lean toward those who work at health. This does not mean that a magickal teacher has to be Mr. Clean Arteries or Miss Slenderbody to communicate something of value; even great magicians are allowed to have personal healing challenges they have to wrestle with. But they should be aware of these matters and working on them, or else there is something wrong.

If your blood sugar bounces all over, you are filled with addictions and cravings, or you are in pain, fatigued, or dehydrated, then you are not in a good position to perceive, catalyze, or channel power. You may still work magick, but you will certainly not be working the best magick of which you are capable. Anything that weakens your neural system weakens your magick.

With a clean, strong, healthy body and a clear mind, you are more psychically sensitive, more attuned to the power currents of nature, and have better judgment in choosing your goals and magickal techniques. This is one reason why Witches are healers. They are first of all self-healers, and this constant focus on their own health and healing makes them more fit, more alert, more capable at *anything* they do—including magick.

Exercises Toward Mastery

You can guess where we are headed next. By the numbers:

1: Improve Your Eating Habits

Track what you eat for one week. Choose one thing that you need to cut out or reduce. Decide what you're going to replace it with so you don't feel deprived. Enlist the help of friends and family to remind you when you start to stray from the plan. And then do it, with courage and grace and humor: no whining. When you have made that one change, then tackle another.

2: Breathe Clean Air

Assignment: if you work or live in a place with bad air (smoky, stuffy, toxic fumes), change it or get out. Talk to the Safety Director at work, or your landlord, or whomever you need to: be demanding, be insistent, be a pain in the butt. It's your lungs and your life! If the battle seems hopeless after a few weeks, leave. Go somewhere that you can breathe.

Alternative assignment: if you are fortunate enough to have clean air—or especially if you aren't—write and call your state and federal representatives: tell them to support clean air legislation.

3: Abdominal Breathing

Loosen your clothing and lie down in a quiet place. After lying still for a few moments, notice how you are breathing. Are your breaths shallow or deep, and when you inhale, does your ribcage move, or your stomach, or both? Now try breathing only from your upper lungs; only your ribcage should move, while your stomach stays still. Next breathe only from your lower lungs: your stomach should lift as the diaphragm muscles push downward, and your chest should be still. Lastly, breathe using all your lung capacity, taking deep breaths, inhaling first in the lower part so your stomach lifts, and then continuing to inhale as your ribcage expands. Exhale deeply, first from the chest, then below, pulling in your stomach. Take several deep, slow, smooth breaths in this way. Then rest and breathe normally again. How do you feel?

4: Up Your Exercise

Nothing fancy, nothing complicated. If you don't already exercise a half hour each day, then start by either (a) taking a fifteen-minute walk daily; or (b) signing up for any kind of exercise, martial arts, dance, or swim class. *Important:* after each walk or class, take a few moments to mentally explore your body and how you feel. Notice and appreciate the changes, and you will become more motivated to continue.

5: Quick Wardrobe Makeover

Throw all your clothes on your bed. Yes, all of them. Pick up one item: if it's too small, or uncomfortable, or made of synthetics (with rare exceptions), stuff it in a bag for a thrift store donation or garage sale. If it's loose, comfortable, and natural, hang it up or put it in your dresser. Repeat until the pile on the bed is gone. Now, if you don't have enough clothes left to get through the week, then buy some that fit your new standards.

6: Adjust Your Sleeping

Choose one strategy from this chapter that will help you sleep better. Put it into effect. If you are sleeping poorly and think there is a medical cause, make an appointment with your doctor, now, to discuss the problem.

7: See the Light

Part 1: Think about your day. Do you get at least one-half hour of exposure to natural sunlight each day? If so, great. If you are among the windowless, cubicle-ized, or graveyard-shift set, and have forgotten what real light looks like, adjust your schedule so that you are outdoors (maybe walking?) for that precious thirty minutes.

Part 2: Check your bedroom for artificial light at night: block light from streetlights, digital clocks, or anything but the moon and stars.

8: Find the Love That's Close at Hand

If you are surrounded by people who love you, well and good—you're doing something very right! If you are lonely, focus first on the love that's within reach, not the great romance or perfect partner of your dreams. In other words, look to yourself. Yes, when you can look in the mirror and truly say to the familiar face "I love you," you will then be in a position to hear that from someone else. Be kind and gentle with yourself, and allow the love to grow. Then look to your friendships; those, too, are loving relationships, just not romantic or sexual ones. What can you do to enhance your present friendships? Next, who is there that you would like as a friend? Invite them for coffee (or tea), and start building that new friendship. Next, is there anyone among your relatives that you like, but have grown apart from? Renew communications with them. Next, do you have an animal companion? That's a wonderful source of unconditional love, and the animal shelters are filled with loving creatures who would like to share your life. (Don't go overboard: you don't want to be the guy with eighteen half-starved dogs or the funny old lady with sixty-seven cats. That would certainly wreck your chances for romance! Quality, not quantity.)

Blesséd be.

To follow this path further, read:

Rituals of Healing: Using Imagery for Health and Wellness by Jeanne Achterberg, et al. (Bantam Books, 1994)

Purify Your Body: Natural Remedies for Detoxing from Fifty Everyday Situations by Nina L. Diamond (Crown Paperbacks, 1996)

Free Your Breath, Free Your Life: How Conscious Breathing Can Relieve Stress, Increase Vitality, and Help You Live More Fully by Dennis Lewis (Shambhala, 2004)

Your Personality, Your Health: Connecting Personality with the Human Energy System, Chakras, and Wellness by Carol Ritberger (Hay House, 1998)

Natural Health, Natural Medicine: A Comprehensive Manual for Wellness and Self-Care by Andrew Weil (Houghton Mifflin, 1998)

Creating the Magickal You

You are the most important element in magick. The crucial tools are your mind, will, and body, not your athame and candles. Few magicians would enter the circle wearing a torn robe and carrying a dirty pentacle, yet many people perform rituals every week with unbalanced personalities and no conscious connection to the divine. You can do better.

We are going to look at some concepts for a kind of personal "makeover": these include balancing the elements in your life, an internal sacred marriage, and connecting more strongly with Spirit. All these will help to develop your magickal persona and will not only lead to stronger magick, but will deepen your whole life.

Balancing the Elements in Yourself

An ongoing task for the beginning magician is to seek balance among the elements within. The pentagram symbol is, among other things, a symbol of balance: five points on the star representing Spirit, Air, Fire, Water, and Earth. In human terms, that would be balance of:

- spirituality (relationship with divinity, living an ethical life),
- mind (intellect, imagination),
- will (passion, direction, focused energy),
- emotion (feelings, intuition), and
- body (health, abundance, other practical matters).

We all know people who do not achieve this balance: highly intelligent people (Air) who don't pay their bills or clean house (no Earth); very goal-directed people (Fire) who seem to lack loving relationships (no Water); practical folks (Earth) who never get passionate about anything (no Fire).

The best magicians—and the most complete humans—are those who develop strength in all these areas.

The Elemental Star

Here is a tool to help you discover how balanced or unbalanced you are, using an elemental model. It is only one model, and there are many others you could use based on the Qabalistic Tree of Life, the major chakras, and so on. But this particular model has proven useful for many students of magick.

Directions

1. Answer each of the following questions by checking the boxes (for "yes" or "mostly") or leaving them blank (for "no" or "usually not"). For your first attempt at the star, do not look for finesse; if a statement is more true than false for you, mark it as a "yes."

2. Once you have finished one section of questions, add up your check marks ("yeses") and put the total in the space at the bottom of that section.

3. When you have all five totals, mark them on the star diagram. Take the total for Air and count out from the center toward the word Air, with the center point being zero. Draw a circle around the point where you land.

4. Do the same with your totals for Fire, Water, Earth, and Spirit.

5. Now connect the dots to form your personal star. Draw a line from the point you circled under Spirit, down and right to the open circle at the junction of two star lines; then to the point you circled for Air, then left to the next open circle clockwise, and all the way around. When you are done, you will probably have a rather lopsided star inside the pentagram in the diagram.

As an example, a person who was very strong in Earth, weak in Fire, and average in the other elements might draw a star like this:

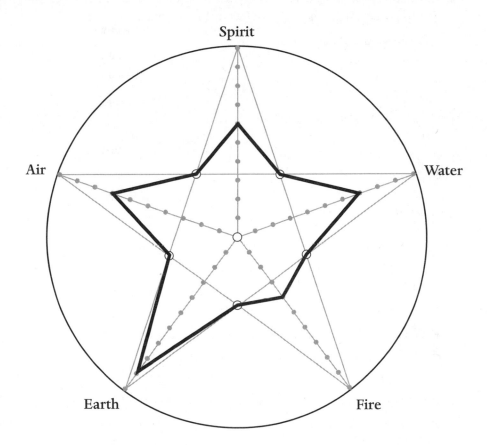

Elemental Star Questions

AIR: Intellect, thought, and imagination

❏ I am curious about life and everything

❏ I pursue ongoing, organized study (in any field)

❏ I have a vivid imagination

❏ I have the ability to think logically

❏ I have the ability to organize information

❏ I can alter my consciousness at will

❏ I have the ability to focus and concentrate

❏ I can easily redirect my thoughts

❏ I use different ways of "knowing"

❏ I usually know where to find information

_____ TOTAL

FIRE: Will, energy, and direction

❏ My life goals are clear

❏ I am effective at achieving my goals

❏ I have a high energy level

❏ I understand will and how to direct it

❏ I exhibit focused passion in my interests

❏ I have strong assertiveness skills

❏ I maintain my chakras and energy body

❏ I am effective at raising power

❏ I am effective at directing power

❏ I am effective at grounding power

_____ TOTAL

WATER: Emotion and intuition

❑ I am in a loving and stable relationship

❑ I am in touch with my emotions

❑ I have a constructive relationship with shadow

❑ I am able to express love and affection

❑ I am able to receive love and affection

❑ I express negative emotions in appropriate ways

❑ I maintain healthy friendships

❑ I trust my intuition or "inner bell"

❑ I have high self-esteem

❑ I control my own emotional state

_____ TOTAL

EARTH: Health, wealth, and material possessions

❑ I usually breathe clean air

❑ I usually drink pure water

❑ I usually eat healthful foods

❑ I usually get sufficient rest

❑ I usually do balanced exercise daily

❑ I work with my physician / healer / dentist as appropriate

❑ My home is clean and attractive

❑ I have steady employment and a sufficient income for my needs

❑ I have a balanced relationship with my possessions

❑ I spend time outdoors with nature

_____ TOTAL

SPIRIT: Relationship with Deity

❏ I perform a daily personal spiritual practice

❏ I have a spiritual support group available

❏ I have the ability to center

❏ I have an array of spiritual tools for coping with stress or crises

❏ I have a relationship with allies or guides

❏ I realize that God/dess is within me

❏ I regularly celebrate or worship

❏ I maintain a relationship with a particular aspect of Deity

❏ I explore and respect other religions

❏ I experience peace and joy

_____ TOTAL

Your Elemental Star

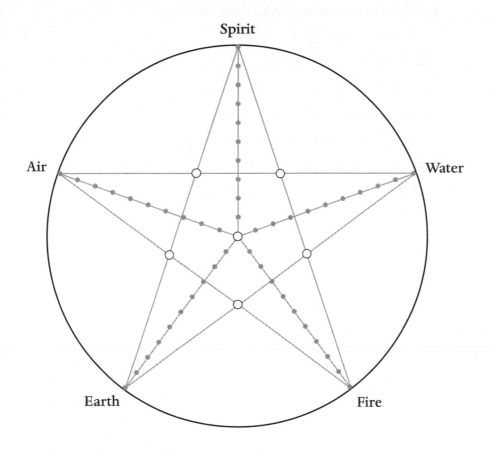

Your Priority Element for Personal Work

Your lowest score, which will appear as the smallest point on the star, is probably the area of your life that needs the most work. Pick one high-priority item from that area and create a plan to fix the problem. (However, an exception would be any Earth issue that threatens your life or health; for example, if you aren't getting enough to eat or have no home. In that case, work on the Earth issue first, no matter how the other areas look.)

Don't be shy about asking for help. If there is a spiritual leader you trust, or family member, counselor, teacher, or simply a good friend, enlist their help to make a plan. You will need to:

+ write down your goal. Be as specific as possible.
+ figure a way to measure your progress; exactly how will you know when you have achieved your goal?
+ write down some very detailed, specific steps to get there. Break them down into small enough chunks so that they seem doable.
+ consider what resources you have already to help you. These can be people, organizations, skills, information, etc.
+ consider what obstacles might interfere and how you can minimize or remove them.
+ add to your list the dates when you expect to complete each step. Remember, "a goal is a dream with a deadline."
+ look at your list daily, and take one action, no matter how small, to move closer to success.
+ celebrate with your helpers when you have achieved the goal!

Then choose another area and begin on that one. Bit by bit, you change your star.

Now, this doesn't mean that you have to wait until your star is perfectly balanced before you can practice magick. Elemental star work can take a lifetime; and sometimes you will take care of one problem area only to realize that another one has slipped and needs some more attention. Keeping your life in balance is like maintaining a really healthy and beautiful garden. A garden needs water, sunlight, weeding, critter control, and more—and all these things have to happen when they're needed and in balance. You can't expect a great garden if you do a great job weeding but never provide any water, and you can't have a wonderful life or do powerful magick if you regularly ignore some of the elements.

If the star is helpful to you, do it at least once or twice a year and compare each one to the previous drawings. That way you can see at a glance whether you are progressing. The ideal is to answer the questions honestly and discover that your star is both large and well balanced. Most people who work at their spirituality and their magick discover, to their delight, that their star grows and becomes more symmetrical and beautiful as the months and years go by.

The Sacred Marriage

The preparation continues. What else must you do to become a magician, an agent of transformation? The alchemists know that you must celebrate the "sacred marriage" within, the hieros gamos. This means the acceptance and union of the yin and yang, lunar and solar, anima and animus, or so-called "feminine" and "masculine" within. "Heraclitus taught that all changes in the world arise from the dynamic and cyclic interplay of opposites, and he saw any pair of opposites as a unity. This unity, which contains and transcends all opposing forces, he called the Logos."[1]

In alchemy this union is symbolized either by the caduceus (a pair of snakes intertwined about a central staff, now used as a symbol of the medical profession and thus, in theory, of healing) or by the Sacred Androgyne, a figure depicted as half female and half male.

In the book *Medicine Woman*, it is symbolized by the "marriage basket" that is the object of Lynn Andrews' quest. Agnes Whistling Elk describes it as follows:

---

1 Heraclitus of Ephesus, Greek philosopher, sixth century BCE, quoted in *The Tao of Physics* by Fritzjof Capra, 6–7.

. . . the marriage basket was conceived by the dreamers to signify the union between the high warrior and high warrioress within your own being. Every woman
seeks after that high warrior, that most magnificent of men, within her. We seek
him all our lives. If we're lucky, we conjure him in our dreams, mate with him, and
become whole. . . . Reach out for that high warrior waiting in the woman's lodge.
Embrace him and be free.[2]

Men, of course, would seek the "high warrioress" within. In either case,
one must understand that this parable relates to an inner emotional/spiritual
experience and not to any kind of "search for Mr. Right" on the material
plane. Intimate relationships are vital to the fulfilled life, but those who seek
fulfillment only in a relationship with another, and not within themselves,
are doomed to disappointment. "The Charge of the Goddess" says, "If that
which you seek you find not within, you will never find it without."

This is where many people go wrong: they externalize an inner quest and
ask another person to fill the void inside. Thus a woman might refuse to seek
her "high warrior" within and look for a man to be that in her life. When
he fails to live up to her dreams and ideal image, the relationship suffers. If
she would first look within and accept/respect/love/express her own "yang"
qualities (strength, boldness, assertiveness, resolute action, etc.), then she
would not need to demand so much of her partner. He would be free to live
out his concept of those qualities and to seek and express the "yin" qualities
within himself.

However, at this point in history men may have a more difficult time with
the sacred marriage than many women. The feminist movement has helped
many women understand and express their "yang" qualities, and there is a
certain amount of social acceptance developing for strong, outspoken wom-
en (it is hardly a tidal wave of admiration, but some encouragement exists).
The men's liberation movement, by contrast, seems to lag years behind.
Most men are still uncomfortable with the sensitive, nurturing, receptive
sides of their natures because such qualities seem "effeminate," even though
they may consciously realize that John Wayne and Rambo are unrealistic
role models. Yet no one can break through the social and emotional barriers

2   Lynn V. Andrews, *Medicine Woman* (HarperSanFrancisco, 1983), 157.

for anyone else: each man must decide whether he is willing to pay the price to become a whole person.

In summary, as long as you confine yourself to the sex roles and stereotypes dictated by society, you will be crippled magickally. When you honor and express all the aspects of yourself that are positive, no matter what the expectations of others, you grow in love, wisdom, and power. It is perhaps no coincidence that many shamans were free of tribal sex roles, and in their dress and behavior expressed the attributes of both sexes.

To be a magickal being, you must first be whole. The sacred marriage within is a giant step toward wholeness.

The Robin Wood Tarot

The Two of Cups tarot image symbolizes this idea perfectly; as you can see from the Robin Wood image above, the intertwined masculine and feminine energies (two serpents) culminate in a creative, transformative Fire (the lion) on a spiritual level (wings). It is important to understand that this occurs within an individual, as well as between a man and a woman on the material plane.

Connecting with Deity

Connecting with Deity is the personal relationship we have with a chosen deity or one who chooses us. It is also our own connection with our own divinity and the divinity in others. All spiritual paths offer this.

This connection is essential to magick. Please understand that I am not pushing any particular religion here—or, indeed, organized religion at all. What you call the "Higher Power," and whether you worship in a grove, mosque, church, synagogue, stupa, temple, or forest, doesn't matter to the energy flow of magick. What does matter is that your Higher Self is included in the linkage and that your Higher Self is nourished by active spirituality.

For convenience, we shall refer to the ultimate creative power as God, Goddess, or Deity/deities. You might refer to it as the Source, the Creator, Providence, Allah, Jehovah, the Divine Mother, Father in Heaven, or the Tao.

Who is Deity, or who are the gods of humanity? Do any of the following descriptions ring true to you?

+ Imaginary beings created by primitive peoples as a way of coping with the unknown.

+ Beings that began as imaginary, but have taken on life and personality because of the psychic energy poured into them by worshippers over generations.

+ Pre-existing supernatural and immortal beings with extraordinary powers.

+ Archetypes—a way of categorizing and personifying the varieties of human experience.

+ Facets or aspects of an original deity who created the universe.

+ Aspects of our own psyches, separated and individualized; imaginary friends on a large scale.

+ Technologically advanced extraterrestrial visitors who were deified by primitive humans.

+ Extraordinary human beings who were exalted and deified by their cultures after their deaths.

- Imaginary beings that were cynically created and fostered by priestly classes as a way of gaining power over others.

- Idols and false beings worshipped by the ignorant in place of the one true creator.

- Unknown and probably unknowable entities who nevertheless fill a need in the human psyche.

- The ultimate organizing principle of the universe; possibly a self-aware unified field theory.

My experience suggests that most people can connect with Deity most easily if it is visualized in human form, with a name, personality, and history. If you are a Christian, you may not truly believe that God always looks like an old man with a flowing white beard; and if you celebrate Goddess, you might not really think that she always appears as either a lovely maiden, kindly mother, or wise crone. But it helps many of us to represent Deity in forms we are familiar with.

To those who say, "There is only one true God," I reply, "Fine; that may be so. But do you believe that God is limited to one form or appearance; and if so, do you know what it is? If not, we are free to visualize God however we please, and probably the Deity won't mind as long as we live good lives and honor Him/Her/It."

Perhaps you have already found your primary deity, or even made a formal dedication to their service. Or perhaps you did not choose, but were chosen; Deity sometimes calls to an individual in unmistakable terms, making "an offer you can't refuse."

If you have no connection to a particular image of Deity, or name, then you are free to choose whatever god or goddess of history will help you in your spiritual journey. There are more than you might dream of: have you ever heard of the Maori Taane-mahuta, the Australian Julunggul, the British Flidais, or the Thracian Zibelthiurdos? Yet these and hundreds more have much to teach us about divinity and the way different cultures understand it.

Janet Farrar and Gavin Bone call the deities "Primary Life Guides"[3] and divide them into three categories:

Primal Deities: Represent forces of nature, such as mountains, the earth, or the rain, as well as principles, such as fertility or truth.

Ancestral Deities: The gods of your nation, culture, or heritage, as well as deities that personify certain skills, such as healing or smithcraft.

Genus Loci: "Spirits of place," or deities who personify or are linked to a specific location: a river, valley, volcano, mountain, etc.

So you might choose a god or goddess of rain, if that power of nature touches your heart, or a deity sacred to your ancestors, or one that inhabits a place that is beloved by you. Or your choice might be related to your life's work or profession: healers may have deities who are healers, such as Brigit, Isis, Apollo, or Hygeia; and so on.

Think carefully about your relationship with the gods. How do you work with them and they with you? How does your connection manifest in your life? What do you need from the gods? What do you expect them to be or provide for you? What can you provide in return? Would you want to dedicate yourself to one deity?

But before you dedicate yourself, do lots of research; learn everything, everything, everything you can about them. Here are some ways you may begin:

+ Read a book or books about your deity
+ Research your deity on the Internet
+ Meditate on your deity
+ Do dreamwork centered on your deity
+ Talk to others who have dedicated themselves to this deity
+ Find or create a statue of your deity
+ Find or create a painting or collage of your deity

---

3   Janet Farrar and Gavin Bone, *Progressive Witchcraft* (Franklin Lakes, NJ: New Page Books, 2004), 197.

After much thought, meditation, and soul-searching, you may choose to make a commitment to a goddess or god. This is not as simple as it sounds. When you dedicate yourself to a god or goddess, you are embracing them in their entirety. You cannot dedicate to Brigit as goddess of healing without also accepting her roles as sovereign, source of inspiration, and smith. Odin is magick and the mystery of the runes, but he is also self-sacrifice. Most goddesses and gods actually represent several facets of Deity; very few are simply one quality personified, such as Love, Honor, or Wisdom.

If your spirit demands that you proceed, then create a dedication ceremony. It can be simple or elaborate, but it should come from the heart. In brief outline, it might include:

+ Preparing yourself by cleansing and fasting
+ Dressing in appropriate costume, robe, or colors
+ Creating an altar special to your goddess or god
+ Creating sacred space
+ Calling the quarters, or elements, as witnesses
+ Inviting your deity to be present
+ Introducing yourself to the deity
+ Speaking your oath or pledge of dedication, in which you explain how you plan to be of service
+ Consecrating a piece of jewelry (one that you will wear always) or a special ritual tool as a constant reminder of your pledge
+ Introducing yourself to the elements in your new role
+ Thanking the quarters and your deity, and opening the circle

Over time, you will discover many ways to serve your chosen god or goddess. You can:

+ Create an altar or shrine for your deity
+ Write a poem about your deity
+ Write and use an invocation to your deity
+ Write a letter to your deity

- Find or make jewelry or a talisman symbolizing your deity
- Teach a class about your deity
- Dance with or for your deity
- Find or create a chant or song for your deity
- Write a story about your deity, and share it with others
- Write a play about your deity, and gather friends to help perform it
- Create a costume of your deity, or a priest/ess outfit, if appropriate
- Create an astral temple for your deity
- Create a complete ritual to honor your deity

You may do the work of the god/goddess in the world by healing, teaching, creating beauty, or whatever your deity is known for. You can simply live your life in a way that honors the particular god or goddess. You may practice deep aspecting (deity assumption) in order to counsel and prophesy to others. You might be an advocate for a particular god or goddess, bringing their special wisdom or energy wherever it is lacking.

Continue to strengthen your relationship. Your first connection to Deity may have happened in an instant, in a flash of insight, or it may have grown slowly over several years. In either case, it may take the rest of your life, or several lives, to really explore the relationship in depth.

The closer you draw to the Divine, the more your life and the lives of those around you will be enriched, the more powerful your magick will be, and the more wisely you will use it.

At first glance, this kind of personal work may seem to have little to do with magick. Yet you cannot become a strong and wise adept unless you first grow as a strong and wise person. Beyond any question of magickal prowess, it is true that such growing will make your life deeper and richer even if you choose never to practice the Art.

Must you achieve perfection before you practice magick? Of course not. Your personal growth, like your magick, is part of a lifelong journey.

Exercises Toward Mastery

1: The Elemental Star

Complete the elemental star exercise as described in this chapter. Make a plan to work on your weakest element. Use the blank star charts in appendix VIII or make a copy and place the completed exercise in your magickal journal or Book of Shadows so that you can compare the results with the next time you do the exercise.

2: The Sacred Marriage

Write down a list of qualities you consider feminine. Now make another list of qualities that you think of as masculine. Looking at each quality, ask yourself whether you know men who exhibit the so-called feminine ones and women who exemplify the masculine ones. Now examine your own character and personality: do you fit neatly into your expected role, or do you follow a middle path that allows you the freedom to explore any facet of your personality? If you have a teacher, ask them to lead you in a guided meditation where you meet your inner Warrior or Warrioress, your inner Hero or Heroine, your inner Sage or Crone.

3: Your Image of the Divine

Write down how you imagine Deity or the Divine. Describe how you imagine its qualities, powers, and appearance. In what ways is this image helpful to you? In what ways does it limit you or draw too narrow a picture of the Divine? Describe a different way in which you could visualize it. What would happen if you were to work with Deity using this different image?

4: Connecting with Deity—Invocation

Use this formula to write an invocation to ask a god/goddess to be present in your life or to help you achieve a goal:

- List three things that your deity represents to you (three attributes, gifts they bring to you, things you associate with them).
- Name one thing you would like them to help you with now.
- Write a short invocation.

Example: "Artemis, goddess of freedom, the open sky, and all outdoors, grant me your aid in finding a new job that allows me more freedom and creativity. For this great gift, I thank you. Blesséd be!"

Use this short prayer/affirmation/invocation often. When you use it, open your root, heart, and crown chakras; give a small offering at your altar; and act in accord.

Alternate goal: ask them to be present in your life and guide you.

5: Connecting with Deity—Journal

Create a god/goddess journal or scrapbook. Look for pictures, stories, images, symbols, and objects that relate to deities you connect with or want to get connected with. To this book, add your personal experiences when invoking deities in ritual.

Blesséd be.

To follow this path further, read:

Toward a Recognition of Androgyny by Carolyn Heilbrun (W. W. Norton & Co., reissued 1993)

The Magical Personality: Identify Strengths and Weaknesses and Improve Your Magick by Mike Leslie (Llewellyn, 2002)

The Way of Four: Create Elemental Balance in Your Life by Deborah Lipp (Llewellyn, 2004)

Androgyny: Toward a New Theory of Sexuality by June Singer (Anchor Press, 1977)

The Varieties of Magick

Not everyone practices magick in the same way. Differ-
ent groups, and individuals, in different locations practice magick differently.
For convenience, we can define and consider here five major styles: nature
magick, intrinsic magick, ceremonial magick, hermetic magick, and kitchen
witch magick. The following chapters will explore the first three of these in
depth.

Styles of Magick

Nature magick is practiced outdoors when possible and emphasizes
attunement with earth and wind and water, with plant devas and
animal spirits, and with the cycles of the moon and the seasons. Its
ritual tools may be rough and simple—a stick for a wand, a handful
of stones for divination, or some herbs for healing cut with a flint
knife at the full moon. Such skills as herbalism, weatherworking,
and shapeshifting can be classified as nature magick.

Intrinsic magick aims at dispensing altogether with material accessories and achieving its results by mental, psychic, and spiritual
development alone. The tools used are the mind, the emotions,
the voice, and the body and its energy field. (The term "intrinsic
magick" evolved from a discussion on the Ardantane Internet list,
when some of us realized that there was no single, universal term
for "propless" magick. We hope this terminology fills a void in

the field.) A subset is called "inner magick," and another, "virtual magick."

Ceremonial magick goes to the other extreme: Stewart Farrar explains that ceremonial magick "involves the extensive use of symbols, colours, perfumes, music, and so on, to put yourself in tune with a particular and precisely defined aspect"[1] of divinity. It is occasionally called "high magick" (though "high magick" usually refers to theurgy or magick performed for the purpose of spiritual development, as opposed to thaumaturgy or "low magick" done for mundane or material goals).

Hermetic magick is a combination of philosophy and magick in which knowledge is seen as the direct link to the divine. This can be practiced with full ceremonial regalia or by using the mind alone.

Kitchen witch magick: There is yet another style that cannot be neatly placed in any of these categories. Sometimes it is called "kitchen witch magick." This does not refer to the little dolls that hang over the stove to keep soup from burning. A kitchen witch uses magick (thaumaturgy) to help handle the details of daily life—for example, to keep a household running smoothly. The ritual tools of this practice are the tools of everyday life: a paring knife for an athame, a carved potato for a healing poppet. Rituals are simple, almost casual, in appearance.

Where does Wiccan magick fit in this spectrum? Though it is mostly sympathetic[2] and nature magick, it can span the whole range of styles and aims. Some Witches are at their best under the sun and moon, in field or forest or herb garden; others experiment with blending ceremonial magick

---

1   Janet and Stewart Farrar, *The Witches' Way: Principles, Rituals and Beliefs of Modern Witchcraft* (London: Robert Hale Ltd., 1984), 198.

2   Sympathetic or imitative magick is based on connection, imitation, or correspondence. It makes use of the principle that anything owned, used, part of, or even touched by a person retains a magickal link to them even when separated from that person (such as a lock of hair on a healing poppet). Imitation involves using models, pictures (such as cave paintings or photographs), or mimicry (as in acting out a successful hunt) to affect people or situations. Correspondence is based on the concept that one can influence something based on its relationship to another thing; for example, I wear red and invoke a lion goddess to strengthen my will.

and sophisticated communications techniques. Still others delve deeply into pathworking, meditation, and trancework, similar to the disciplines of rajah yoga. Some shift from one style to another, depending on circumstances and the nature of the work at hand.

Just to make it more interesting, you can practice any style of magick as a "virtual" or inner working. For a ceremonial ritual, go into your mind and vividly imagine putting on your robe, casting the circle, smelling the incense, and so on. For an inner working, you can still breathe to raise energy, imagine vibrating the names of deity, and see yourself in your mind assuming a sacred posture or whatever you might normally do. For a nature rite, visualize yourself in the forest, feel the moonlight on your skin, hear the wind moving through the trees, call your animal ally mentally. In this way, you can work magick anywhere: riding a crowded subway, sitting at your desk, on an airplane flight.

Of course styles can be blended; there is no special virtue in working "pure" nature (or whatever) magick. If you are drawn to the powers you feel outside under the moon, but you want to take your elegant, artistically crafted athame with you—fine. If you normally like the simple "kitchen witch" magick of hearth and home, but get the occasional urge to dress up and do a really elaborate series of Golden Dawn ceremonies, there is no Board of Magickal Correctness to stop you. Try all the styles, and use the one or the combination that works for you.

What Kind of Magician Are You?
(MSAT: *Magickal Style Aptitude Test*)

No single style of magick is "better" than another, or right for everyone. If you would like to get a preliminary idea of what might suit you, take the little quiz that follows.

1. You prefer to perform magick wearing:

    A. Whatever you have on at the time

    B. Your special magickal robe and cord

    C. Nothing at all

    D. Jeans and a t-shirt, barefoot or in sturdy shoes

2. If you need to cut something during a spell, you are likely to reach for:

   A. A paring knife from the kitchen drawer

   B. Your custom-made bolline with the silver blade

   C. Nothing, since the cutting happens in your mind

   D. A sharp stone or your pocketknife

3. The best lighting for ritual would be:

   A. The electric lights in your house

   B. Your Lamps of Art in the silver candlesticks

   C. No light is really necessary

   D. Sunlight, moonlight, or starlight

4. For magickal help, you might call upon which one first?

   A. The spirits of your home and hearth

   B. A spirit guide, angels, or a discarnate sage or priestess

   C. Your inner archetypes or levels of Self

   D. Animal spirits, allies, or nature devas

5. The best timing for a spell? You would check:

   A. For a time when the kids aren't around

   B. The astrological energies of the planets

   C. Your own biorhythms

   D. The phase of the moon and time of day or night

6. If there is sound in your ritual, it's probably:

   A. You singing as you do household chores

   B. Appropriate recorded music

   C. Your voice vibrating god names or chanting

   D. The wind or the sound of a nearby stream

7. You really enjoy:

    A. A clean, attractive home and your family enjoying health and harmony there

    B. Beautiful costumes, meaningful symbols, and well-crafted ritual tools that lift your thoughts to a higher spiritual realm

    C. The feeling that you can wield your own energies, will, and imagination to shape reality and change the world

    D. Being outdoors, because that's where power and beauty and freedom live

SCORING:

Mostly As? You lean toward the kitchen witch style.

Mostly Bs? You're drawn to ceremonial magick.

Mostly Cs? You're inclined to be an intrinsic magician.

Mostly Ds? You're primarily a nature magician.

Some Magickal Traditions

Throughout millennia and around the world, many cultures have developed systems of magick that reflect their own traditions and one or more of the styles we have discussed. Let's briefly explore some of those systems, concentrating on those that can be studied by Western readers because materials or teachers are available to us.

Shamanism

Varieties of shamanism are practiced among the Native nations of both American continents, by the native peoples of the far north in Europe, and in Asia. In recent years, shamanism has been "discovered" by many New Age folks in the United States, thanks to books by Carlos Castaneda, Michael Harner, and Lynn V. Andrews.

In *The Way of the Shaman*, Harner says that "a shaman is a man or woman who enters an altered state of consciousness—at will—to contact and utilize an ordinarily hidden reality in order to acquire knowledge, power, and to help other persons."[3]

One of the key skills of a shaman is the ability to go into trance and make a journey to another world, usually the "upperworld" or the "lowerworld"; some shamans accomplish this through the use of drumming or drugs, while others rely solely on a mind that is simultaneously disciplined and very free. Once in the otherworld, the shaman might discover (or retrieve) a power animal spirit or do healing work.

The equipment of a shaman might include drums and rattles, which are rhythmically sounded in order to help induce trance, and various medicine objects, such as crystals, shells, and roots, which may be the material-plane homes for various helper spirits.

Wicca

Wicca is a spiritual path that includes reverence for nature, a deep connection with the cycles of the moon and seasons, and celebration of an immanent Goddess and God. Wiccans consider themselves Witches and practice witchcraft, or the magickal traditions of old Europe, though only for benevolent purposes. The primary ethical guideline, the Wiccan Rede, states "An ye harm none, do as ye will." This translates roughly to "As long as you harm no one, including yourself, follow your true will (the divine Spirit within)."

There are many variants or traditions of Wicca throughout Europe, North America, and Australia/New Zealand. These include Gardnerian, Alexandrian, Faery, Georgian, Pagan Way, McFarland Dianic, Re-formed Congregation of the Goddess Dianic, New Reformed Order of the Golden Dawn, Reclaiming, New England Council of Traditionalist Witches, Ladywood, and many more.

The magick of witchcraft probably began with shamanic practices and sympathetic magick focused on survival: successful hunting, good crops, and healthy babies. However, over the years Wiccans and other witches have been exposed to many other systems of magick, and today they use everything from Qabala to tarot to a simplified ceremonial magick.

---

3   Michael Harner, *The Way of the Shaman*, 10th anniversary edition (HarperSanFrancisco, 1990), 20.

Central to much Wiccan magick is the concept of polarity: creation comes from the interaction of Goddess and God, female and male, darkness and light, receptivity and initiation, and so on. The majority of covens are led by a high priestess and a high priest, include members of both sexes, and perform a symbolic Great Rite (union of male and female) within the magick circle. But within many feminist Dianic, all-female covens, the Goddess is seen as incorporating all possibilities and the masculine divine is de-emphasized.

In recent years, however, the focus on male-female balance and fertility has expanded to also emphasize a balance of the polarities within each individual, by cultivating the *hieros gamos* or sacred marriage. It is generally recognized that gay men and lesbian witches can practice polarity magick without having members of the other sex present, though many gay Wiccans mingle happily in covens with their straight brothers and sisters.

Wiccan magick includes reclaimed European folk magick; newly created techniques based on psychology, art, and electronics; and systems borrowed from other cultures (living and dead) around the world. It has been said of the more eclectic Wiccans that they will try any magickal technique that is ethical and doesn't run away.

Norse Magick

It is likely that Norse magick evolved from a shamanic tradition similar to that of the Innuit and the Lapps, and then was influenced by Celtic cultures to the south. In its early form it was nature-oriented and included such skills as weatherworking and partnership with power animals.

Animals important to the Norse included the bear, the wolf, and the raven. Norse adepts apparently knew how to shapeshift, or at least consciousness-shift, into animals; the "berserkers" are the best-known example of this skill. "Berserk" comes from the Norse words *bar sark*, meaning "bear shirt"; the berserkers were warriors clad in bearskins who could enter the consciousness of a bear and fight with all the ferocity of which that animal is capable.

In its later stages, Norse magick and religion included a well-developed bardic tradition. The power of letters was recognized—it is said that Odin voluntarily sacrificed himself, hanging on the world ash tree Yggdrasil for nine days and nights, in order to gain mystical knowledge of the runes. Even today, divination with runes is popular, nearly rivaling the tarot. The Norse oral tradition embraced epic poetry and history (such as the Eddas), and also included spoken charms and incantations. Religious amulets and talismans such as Thor's hammer were also common.

One of the most powerful and moving traditions in the north was the *seidhe,* in which a priestess entered deep trance and then spoke for the gods. Modern Asatru priestesses are reviving this skill.

Huna

On the other side of the planet we find Huna, the traditional psychospiritual system of Hawaii. We owe much of our knowledge of this nearly lost tradition to Max Freedom Long, who arrived in Hawaii as a young teacher in 1917. A student of world religions, Long became fascinated by the mysteries of Huna and eventually discovered many of the keys to its effectiveness.

According to Long's research, there is reason to believe that Huna is extremely ancient, with roots that go back to the ancestral cultures of the Berbers in North Africa. At some point in prehistory, the ancestors of the Hawaiians apparently migrated eastward, first to India and then to the Pacific.

Along the way, the pure magick and spiritual teachings of Huna were subordinated to the trappings of institutionalized religion. When the chief priest learned through his psychic abilities that Christian missionaries were coming to Hawaii, he assumed they were representatives of a faith more pure and powerful than the existing native religion. Figuring that this was a great opportunity (with the aid and example of the new teachers) to re-create the original magick and spirituality of the Hawaiian people, he led a movement to cast down the temples and dismantle the religious bureaucracy.

When the missionaries arrived, they found the native religion in disarray and lost no time in exploiting the situation. By the time the remaining Hawaiian spiritual leaders realized that the missionaries knew nothing of magick and had no interest in the mysteries of the human spirit or psyche, Huna as an organized religion had almost ceased to exist.

When Long came on the scene nearly a century later, he could find no kahuna priests or priestesses who were willing to tell him about their ancient traditions. By using the Hawaiian language as a key, he nonetheless was able to re-create the basic knowledge at the heart of Huna magick.

Without going into great detail, we can say that, according to Long, the kahunas understood the three major aspects of the human spirit in a way that was not even approximated by modern Western philosophers until Freud—and Freud's theories are crude compared to the elegant and practical model on which Huna is based. This understanding allows the kahuna to use spiritual energies to heal (or harm) at a distance, view distant events, telepathically project messages, or "firewalk" on burning lava, among other skills.

Today it appears that Huna may be experiencing a renaissance in the islands, similar to that of Wicca and various Native American religions on the mainland. Whether it is being energetically perpetuated by surviving lineal descendants of traditional kahunas fully trained in the ancient arts, or whether it is being re-created by young Hawaiians with a keen interest in their culture is not entirely clear. But at the very least, some part of this magickal system of great insight and power is still available to serious students of magick.

Alchemy

This ancient art, which combines chemistry, philosophy, and magick, was practiced on many levels, by the most spiritual, high-minded, and well-educated individuals, as well as by charlatans.

For many alchemists, the literal goal was to transmute base metals into precious ones by use of a constructed substance called the Philosopher's Stone, or to create the Elixir of Life, a liquid that might prolong life or even confer immortality. For others, these goals were only symbolic of the true quest: to perfect oneself spiritually. Alchemy was simply a series of principles and processes that could lead toward the goal of purifying the soul and distilling the divine essence from crass humanity. In this sense, alchemy, with its emphasis on the magician's spiritual development, is a form of theurgy or high magick. Some who practiced alchemical techniques, however, were motivated only by greed. They dreamed of unlimited supplies of gold and immortal lives in which to spend it. Others were out-and-out fakers, who had given up serious research but knew enough lore to impress wealthy and gullible patrons into parting with large sums—"just to set up the apparatus and get started, you understand."

Over the centuries, alchemy evolved a vast and colorful vocabulary to describe the elements and processes involved; old manuscripts mysteriously discuss "the green lion," "the silver lady," and "the crow's head of black blacker than black." Though many of these terms refer to rather prosaic materials and chemical operations, others refer to important magickal and spiritual processes. For example, the hieros gamos or "sacred marriage" refers to the harmonious union of the feminine and masculine polarities within a single individual's psyche (see "The Sacred Marriage" in chapter 10).

Alchemy was certainly the parent of modern chemistry, and as a spiritual and philosophical discipline it is still practiced today.

Brujaría (Bruheria, Brujeria)

This is a body of religious and folk magick practices that blends Roman Catholicism and the Aztec goddess faith, and it has been influenced by other traditions, such as spiritism, Santería, and ceremonial magick. It is common throughout Mexico and the United States among the Hispanic population. Practitioners are called *brujas* if female, and *brujos* if male.

Brujaría is centered on the worship of Our Lady of Guadalupe, an aspect of the Virgin Mary who first appeared to an Indian convert in 1531. Though its adherents consider themselves Catholic, there is evidence to suggest that Guadalupe may be a "new" incarnation of Tonantzin, a powerful, beloved Aztec mother goddess. In any case, the faith is very Goddess-oriented and moon-oriented, though Jesus and a variety of saints are also important to it.

Small groups of devotees, usually all women in the U. S. branches, gather at the bruja's home at new and full moons in a room specially prepared as a temple. These *cofradias* generally number thirteen or fewer. The resemblance to Dianic Wicca is not accidental: Brujaría is a living religion, grow-ing, changing, and borrowing constantly.

Magickal techniques in this system include the use of herbs, tarot, candles in many shapes and colors, astrology, prayer and incantation, and blessed medallions depicting saints or Guadalupe in her various aspects.

Qabala (Kaballah, Cabala, Cabbalah, etc.)

Those familiar only with the Orthodox, Conservative, and Reform traditions of Judaism may be surprised to learn that this religion has a fourth branch, which is both more mystical and somewhat more inclusive of the feminine principle than its cousins.

The Qabala is "a medieval and modern system of Jewish theosophy, mys-ticism, and thaumaturgy marked by belief in creation through emanation and a cipher method of interpreting Scripture," according to *Webster's*. In point of fact, its roots go back far earlier than the medieval age, though it did flourish during that era, and oral tradition suggests that Witches and Jewish Qabalists may have helped one another (and shared their magickal systems) during times of persecution.

Of central importance in Qabalistic magick is the Tree of Life (see next page), a symbol that may be likened to a spiritual map of reality. It consists of ten sephiroth, which are aspects of divine manifestation on different lev-els, ranging from Malkuth on the bottom (the material plane) to Kether on the top (the Crown, Supernal Light). Connecting the sephiroth are twenty-two paths; exploring these connections, or "pathworking," is an important exercise for Qabalists.

The names and titles of the Hebrew God, especially the Tetragrammaton (YHVH, later anglicized to Jehovah), are considered extremely significant keys to magickal power and are used extensively in invocations, talismans, and so on. One technique is intoning or vibrating the names of God; for example, one may stimulate the chakras with an exercise called the Middle Pillar (see exercises at the end of chapter 8).

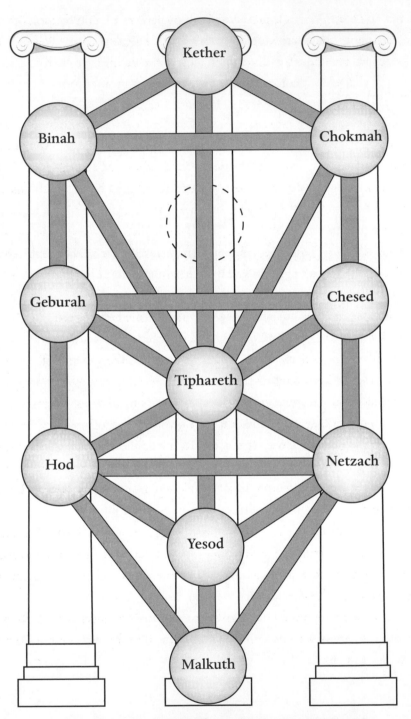

The Tree of Life and its ten sephiroth, twenty-two paths, and three pillars

It is interesting that Qabalistic philosophy accepts feminine aspects of divinity, embodied especially in the Shekinah and in Binah on the Tree of Life, much more than do the mainstream divisions of Judaism.

Voudun (Vodun, Voodoo)

Voudun comes from a word meaning "God" or "spirit" and refers to a religious and magickal tradition that began in Africa, spread to the West Indies and the United States with the importation of slaves, and blended with Catholic Christian beliefs. It is practiced in the southeastern U. S., Cuba, Trinidad, and Brazil, and it is the major religion of the island of Haiti.

The supreme deity is Bon Dieu, the "Good God." There are many other gods and goddesses in the pantheon, such as Ogun, Papa Legba, and Erzulie, in addition to many lesser gods, saints, and spirits, called *loas*—spirits of earth, fire, wind, rain, the jungle, old age, death, and more.

A Voudun priest is called a *houngan*, and a priestess is a *mambo*. With the other worshipers, *hounci*, they meet in a chapel, known as a *hounfor*.

At the rituals, prayers are offered to the gods and spirits; then the houngan or mambo will draw a *veve*, or sacred symbol, belonging to one of the deities. There will be drumming, with certain drum rhythms specific to particular loas, and ecstatic dancing until participants enter a trance and are possessed by the deities or loas. A person so possessed is known as the *cheval* or "horse" of the loa in control. This state may last for a few minutes or several hours, and the incarnate deity may give counsel, heal, sing, and dance during that time.

Voudun practitioners also practice communication with the dead and use spells to protect themselves against negative magick. Like shamans, they may also induce various spirits to take up residence in material objects, which are kept in gourds or jars on the altar.

Voudun has been much maligned in cheap movie thrillers and novels, but for many people it serves as a positive and effective form of religious expression.

Western Ceremonial Magick

The history of Western magick reached a turning point in 1887, when a Rev. Woodford found a mysterious manuscript and shared it with Dr. W. Wescott, a Rosicrucian friend, and with S. L. MacGregor Mathers, a prominent occultist. Enthused about the rituals and lore deciphered from the document, they founded the Hermetic Order of the Golden Dawn, based on Rosicrucian teachings, Qabalistic magick, Egyptian religion, and the creativity of its members, which drew these diverse threads together into a unified whole. During the brief years of its existence, the Golden Dawn included such well-known figures as poet William Butler Yeats, author Algernon Blackwood, and the controversial Aleister Crowley; its influence continues in magickal lodges today.

The aim of the Golden Dawn initiate, as described in the oath of the Adeptus Minor, was to

> apply myself to the Great Work, which is to purify and exalt my Spiritual Nature so that with the Divine Aid I may at length attain to be more than human, and thus gradually raise and unite myself to my Higher and Divine genius, and that in this event I will not abuse the great power entrusted to me.[4]

The Golden Dawn was known for its complex hierarchy: initiates passed through several grades within two orders, earning the titles of Zelator, Theoricus, Practicus, Philosophus, Adeptus Minor, Adeptus Major, Adeptus Exemptus, Magister Templi, and ultimately Ipsissimus. The Third Order was composed of the Secret Chiefs, the legendary adepts who had achieved immortality and magickal powers beyond the comprehension of ordinary folk.

Temples were established in England, Scotland, and Paris; in time, Wescott was elected Supreme Magus of the Societas Rosicruciana in Anglia and left the Golden Dawn. S. L. MacGregor Mathers took control and administered the Order in an increasingly authoritarian manner. Beginning about 1900, the organization began to suffer internal conflict and soon splintered into several factions. The Golden Dawn teachings, however, remain a model for many ceremonial magicians throughout the Western world.

---

4   Oath of the Adeptus Minor, in various works on the Golden Dawn.

Among other skills, the Order taught divination through geomancy, tarot, scrying, and clairvoyance; the use of talismans, sigils, and telesmatic images; Enochian invocations; Qabalistic pathworking; and astral projection, all of which are well beyond the scope of this book.

Other Magickal Traditions

We have touched upon several important magickal traditions in use today, but many others are still practiced, and even more have been lost in the sands of time. What magick might have been known to the shamans of Europe's Ice Age, or to the priestesses of ancient Sumer, or to the magicians of the East African empires? Perhaps someday we shall know—either through archaeological breakthroughs, past-life regression, or a form of trancework or astral travel that transcends time. Until then, we must content ourselves with recent or living traditions.

Such traditions are varied and numerous enough to provide lifetimes of study and practice. In addition to those already discussed, there is Santeria of Cuba and now the United States; Candomble, Xango, and Macumba of Brazil; and Chinese magick (some of it Taoist in origin), including astrology, I Ching divination, and feng shui, which might be defined as the art of aligning human structures in harmony with earth energies.

There is Egyptian and Thelemic Current magick, the arts of the Druids, and the hereditary skills of the Gypsies or Romany peoples. In India, the line between the yogic disciplines and magick is vague indeed, and in Australia the Aborigines still perform their ancient dances and ceremonies. The magick of some Native American nations, such as Seneca stone reading, survive in scattered areas here and there. In a thousand places around this planet, in deserts and rain forests, on islands and on arid mountain plateaus, the religious systems of myriad people still include the magickal arts.

Much has been lost, but much survives, and it requires great self-discipline for the novice to focus on mastering the basics of one tradition before beginning to explore others. Mastery is important; merely dabbling in anything that strikes your fancy will lead to a great collection of lore-fragments, along with very little power or skill. The best approach to magick is to focus on one system until it is second nature to you, and only then enrich your practice with the knowledge and techniques of other systems.

Connecting with the Magick of an Era or Culture

For many, the choice is easy: they want to learn the magick, myths, and traditions of their ancestral culture. For example, Jon says, "I'm Polish, and it's really exciting for me to read about the folk magick of ancient Poland . . . and even the archaeology of that region before Poland existed. It makes me feel connected to my roots, my ancestors."

Wonderful for Jon, but . . .

+ what about someone who is of mixed heritage? If you're part German and part Pawnee . . . or a "Heinz 57" European . . . or Vietnamese-American . . . where does that leave you?

+ what about someone who doesn't have much information about their roots? A lot of African-Americans know, of course, that their ancestors came from Africa, but there is a huge difference between the Yoruban civilization, the Bantu, the Ashanti, and the Dogon, to mention a few out of hundreds!

+ what about someone who knows their cultural heritage, but is emotionally drawn to a completely different culture? What about the Caucasian who feels an affinity to certain Native American traditions, or the black guy who really likes the Norse-Asatru traditions, or the Lakota woman who is attracted to Chinese Taoism?

Once again, we are fortunate: no Magickal Correctness Police in sight! Follow your heart. If you are sincere in your interest, the magickal group or community in question may welcome you as a fellow traveler on that particular path.

However, one cautionary note: if you are interested in learning the traditions of a living culture, don't just copy their ways without training or permission. Go to a respected teacher or elder of that tradition, explain your sincere desire to learn about their magick and/or spirituality, and humbly ask if you may receive their teaching. If they turn you away, keep looking for a qualified teacher of that path; and meanwhile work as a solitary as best you can.

What if there is no living teacher because the culture has long since passed away? The magick and spirituality of ancient Sumer may draw you, but if you go to Sumer (now modern Iraq), you won't find many people following that path today. Still, you can contact the priesthood on the astral planes, and ask for help on your journey; and then do the research to rediscover and re-create what you can of those ways. Through the Internet you may be able to find others who share your interest.

Exercises Toward Mastery

1: Choose a Style of Magick

Take the little quiz earlier in this chapter, and think about the results. Imagine yourself working each different style: nature magick . . . intrinsic magick . . . ceremonial magick . . . kitchen witch magick. Which feels most comfortable to you? Which feels most powerful to you? Which feels most challenging to you?

2: Read About a Tradition of Magick

Of those listed here, which tradition intrigues you the most—Wicca . . . Shamanism . . . Norse magick . . . Huna . . . Alchemy . . . Brujaría . . . Voudun . . . Qabala . . . Western Ceremonial magick? Pick a book from the Recommended Reading list in appendix IV, check it out from your local library (using interlibrary loan if necessary), and read it.

3: Research a Well-Known Magician

Choose one from the list in appendix VII, and do some research on the Internet. Write a short biography. Think about that person's life; what do you admire, and was there anything from their life that you would want to avoid? Was their life a shining example or a cautionary tale?

Blesséd be.

To follow this path further, read:

Shamanism

Shamanism: As a Spiritual Practice for Daily Life by Thomas Dale Cowan (Genealogical Services, 1996)

The Way of the Shaman (10th Anniversary Edition) by Michael Harner (HarperSanFrancisco, 1990)

Book of Shamanic Healing by Kristin Madden (Llewellyn, 2002)

Chosen by the Spirits: Following Your Shamanic Calling by Sarangerel (Destiny Books, 2001)

The Woman in the Shaman's Body: Reclaiming the Feminine in Religion and Medicine by Barbara Tedlock (Bantam, 2005)

Wicca

Earth, Air, Fire & Water by Scott Cunningham (Llewellyn, 2002)

Earth Power: Techniques of Natural Magic by Scott Cunningham (Llewellyn, 2002)

The Witches' Craft by Raven Grimassi (Llewellyn, 2002)

RitualCraft: Creating Rites for Transformation and Celebration by Amber K and Azrael Arynn K (Llewellyn, 2006)

Grimoire for the Green Witch by Ann Moura (Llewellyn, 2003)

Positive Magic: Ancient Metaphysical Techniques for Modern Lives (Revised Edition) by Marion Weinstein (New Page Books, 2002)

Norse Magick

Northern Mysteries & Magick by Freya Aswynn (Llewellyn, 1991)

Völuspá-Seiðr as Wyrd Consciousness by Yngona Desmond (Booksurge Publishing, 2006)

Taking Up the Runes: A Complete Guide to Using Runes in Spells, Rituals, Divination, and Magic by Diana L. Paxson (Weiser, 2005)

Futhark: A Handbook of Rune Magic by Edred Thorsson (Weiser, 1983)

Germanic Magic: A Basic Primer on Galdor, Runes, and Spá by Swain Wodening (Booksurge Publishing, 2006)

Huna

Hawaiian Magic and Spirituality by Scott Cunningham (Llewellyn, 2002)

Huna Magic: Empowers You to Create Health Wealth and Relationships by John Bainbridge and Ronald Peters (Barnhart Press, 1994)

Huna Magic Plus: Adds a New Dimension to the Kahuna Secrets of Ancient Hawaii for Practical Use in Today's High Tech World by John Bainbridge (Barnhart Press, 2004)

Huna: A Beginner's Guide (New Ed edition) by Enid Hoffman (Schiffer Publishing, 1997)

Hawaiian Magic by Clark Wilkerson (Clark & Dei Wilkerson Publishers, 1968)

Alchemy

Alchemist's Handbook: Manual for Practical Laboratory Alchemy by Frater Albertus (Weiser, 1987)

Alchemy Rediscovered and Restored by A. Cockren (Book Tree, 1998)

Sorcerer's Stone: A Beginner's Guide to Alchemy by Dennis William Hauck (Citadel, 2004)

The Practical Handbook of Plant Alchemy: An Herbalist's Guide to Preparing Medicinal Essences, Tinctures, and Elixirs by Manfred M. Junius (Healing Arts Press, 1985)

Brujaría

The Road to Guadalupe: A Modern Pilgrimage to the Virgin of the Americas by Eryk Hanut (Tarcher, 2001)

The Aztec Virgin: The Secret Mystical Tradition of Our Lady of Guadalupe by John Mini (Trans-Hyperborean Institute, 2000)

The Magic and Mysteries of Mexico: The Arcane Secrets and Occult Lore of the Ancient Mexicans by Lewis Spence (Newcastle, 1994)

Healing with Herbs and Rituals: A Mexican Tradition by Eliseo "Cheo" Torres
(University of New Mexico Press, 2006)

Voudun

Divine Horsemen: The Living Gods of Haiti (New Ed edition) by Maya Deren
(McPherson, 1983)

Vodou Visions: An Encounter with Divine Mystery by Sallie Ann Glassman
(Villard, 2000)

The Book of Vodou: Charms and Rituals to Empower Your Life by Leah Gordon
(Barron's Educational Series, 2000)

Secrets of Voodoo by Milo Rigaud (City Lights Publishers, 1985)

Qabala

Simplified Qabala Magic by Ted Andrews (Llewellyn, 2003)

Kabbalah: A Very Short Introduction by Joseph Dan (Oxford University Press,
2005)

Mystical Qabalah by Dion Fortune (Weiser Books, 2000)

Kabbalistic Handbook for the Practicing Magician by Joseph Lisiewski (New
Falcon Publications, 2005)

Climbing the Tree of Life: A Manual of Practical Magickal Qabalah by David
Rankine (Avalonia, 2005)

Western Ceremonial

Essential Golden Dawn by Chic and Sandra Tabatha Cicero (Llewellyn,
2003)

Modern Magic by Donald Michael Kraig (Llewellyn, 2002)

Golden Dawn by Israel Regardie (Llewellyn, 2002)

High Magic by Frater U∴D∴ (Llewellyn, 2005)

Nature Magick

Nature magick involves working closely with the other living things and spirit beings that share the planet with us, both plants and wildlife, and with the elements in their most primal forms: the rocks and soil of Earth, winds of the Air, the Fire of the sun or burning sticks, and the Water of rainfall, streams, lakes, and seas.

Many of us are drawn to the outdoors from our earliest memories. It is there that we find the sacred, and feelings more exalted than we have felt in any church building. It is there we find power, more pure and clean than in bank accounts or boardrooms. It is there we find wisdom that could never be explained in books. And it is there we find healing for the hurts that human civilization has inflicted on our hearts and spirits.

Of course magick is in nature. It was in nature that humankind first discovered magick.

"Nature magick" seems especially powerful for healing and guidance, though it goes beyond these two functions. It takes many forms, and its techniques overlap with intrinsic magick, and even with ceremonial magick. It may involve the use of natural energies to achieve theurgical or thaumaturgical goals, or it may involve the manipulation of natural processes, such as with weatherworking or garden magick. Let's explore.

Hunting Magick

Hunting magick is a very old branch of the Art, possibly even the first one. Paintings thousands of years old show shamans wearing animal skins and masks, and bow-wielding hunters chasing arrow-shot bison. There are hints that the prey animals were respected as sacred beings, almost gods, because they provided food, clothing, shelter, and tools—that is, life—to humans whose survival was precarious.

The magick of the paintings and dances assured that the hunting went well, but may also have propitiated the spirits of the creatures by honoring and thanking them, in much the same way that some tribal cultures do today.

Modern Pagans who hunt do it primarily for food (though other Pagans are vegetarian). There are many books on hunting from a mundane perspective, but little to be found on modern, generalized hunting magick. Some books on indigenous cultures (the Saami of northern Europe, the Inuit of America and Greenland, other Native American nations) include descriptions of how these cultures intertwine hunting, magick, and spirituality.

Herb and Garden Magick

Long and long ago, some clever early human realized that seeds could be planted and nurtured, and plants helped to grow. By eight or ten thousand years ago, the Agricultural Revolution was in full swing and the human world changed. So did magick.

While many tribes were still busy with hunting magick, others figured that magick could also help with this new source of food, medicine, and wealth. Some began to explore how planting and harvesting at certain phases of the moon might help, others adapted the dances to feed energy to the crops, and others made direct contact with the spirits or devas of the plant world.

Some of those who farm or have gardens are said to have a "green thumb"—everything they plant seems to flourish. Many of these people probably have an unconscious connection with the devas, based on their love and respect for plant beings. The living plants sense the energy of these feelings and thrive on it. Other gardeners and herbalists cultivate the relationship quite consciously; they know exactly what they are doing. For a fascinating account of how this can evolve, read the books about the Findhorn Gardens in Scotland. There, a tiny colony of people on a cold and windswept beach planted a garden that should rationally not have survived—but humans and devas cooperated to make a miracle.

Most people are aware of herbalism, but fewer know that there is a field of herb magick that has nothing to do with making teas, tinctures, and poultices. Herbal magick uses the vibrations of the plants, without ingesting them, for amulets and talismans. We can directly absorb the vibrations of living plants, perhaps by changing the crystalline structure of the water in our bodies (see "Water Magick," page 163).

Psychotropic plants are eaten or smoked by some indigenous peoples as part of their religious experience or shamanic journeys. This is not recommended for beginners or for any student of magick unless you are apprenticed to a shaman or spiritual teacher who is experienced in their use—and unless it is legal where you reside.

To follow this path further, read:

A Compendium of Herbal Magick by Paul Beyerl (Phoenix Publishers, 1998)

Encyclopedia of Magical Herbs by Scott Cunningham (Llewellyn, 1993)

Magical Herbalism: The Secret Craft of the Wise, second edition, by Scott Cunningham (Llewellyn, 1983)

Green Magic: Flowers, Plants & Herbs in Lore & Legend by Lesley Gordon (Viking Press, 1977)

The Magical and Ritual Uses of Herbs by Richard Alan Miller (Destiny Books, 1983)

The Secret Life of Plants by Peter Tompkins and Christopher Bird (Harper & Row, 1973)

Divination with Nature

Divination can be performed in a thousand ways using natural materials and phenomena. You may cast stones, bones, or sticks and find meaning in the patterns they form and their relationships with one another. You can watch the shapes of clouds or their shadows on the land, or the movement of flames, or the flight of birds, or the paths of animals.

The fact is that the human mind can discover meaningful patterns any-where if the mind is simultaneously open, alert, relaxed, and attuned to its environment. Within the rich and diverse environments of nature, there is an abundance of colors, shapes, textures, sounds, smells, and kinesthetic stimuli, and any of them can be the signal that awakens us to knowledge that we didn't know we had.

This requires more sensitivity and practice than divination methods like tarot or runestones (which can be approached in a kind of paint-by-numbers way when you are beginning). But one of the benefits of this nature practice is a deeper connection with the beauty and power of the natural world.

Here are a few nature-oriented divination methods listed by their formal names; for more, and slightly more extensive descriptions, see the Gibsons' book listed below.

Aeromancy: Divination by phenomena in the sky: comets, halos, apparitions, etc.

Austromancy: Divination by observation of the winds.

Capnomancy: Divination by the behavior of smoke from sacred fires.

Floromancy: Divination through the study of flowers: size, shape, color, location, etc.

Geomancy: Divination by making marks in the sand, or by casting stones and reading the patterns.

Hydromancy: Divination by water, such as observation of images, currents, ripples in pools, or casting offerings or stones with names into them. **Pegomancy** is a specialized form involving springs and fountains.

Lithomancy: Divination with unusual stones, which change color, inspire visions, or make sounds that can be interpreted.

Nephelopmancy: Divination through the study of clouds.

Onychomancy: Divination by seeing visions or symbols in bright sunlight reflected from one's fingernails.

Ornithomancy: Divination through the movements, songs, and behavior of birds.

Pyromancy: Divination by observation of the behavior of flames, or of objects tossed into a fire.

Selenomancy: Divination by observation of the moon's appearance.

Theriomancy: Divination by the actions of wild animals.

Xylomancy: Divination by interpreting fallen branches or wood litter in the forest, or by the actions of wood in a fire.

To follow this path further, read:

Nature-Speak: Signs, Omens, and Messages in Nature by Ted Andrews (Dragonhawk Publishing, 2004)

The Complete Illustrated Book of Divination & Prophecy by Walter and Litzka Gibson (Doubleday, 1973)

Sun, Moon, and Stars

Darkness has its own magick, but people new to magick often find it easier to work with light energies. Indoors we have candlelight and perhaps the glow of the fireplace, but outdoors, we can choose among sunlight, moonlight, and starlight. To make it even better, each of the three has an infinite number of variations.

Sunlight may be the direct and relentless power of noon in the desert, the fresh and vibrant light of the dawn, the gentle mystery of dusk in a garden, or the seemingly sourceless white light inside mist, fog, or clouds.

Moonlight varies from the near-invisible presence of the dark of the moon to the challenging and hopeful shine of the new crescent, to the full moon's light that illuminates and transforms at the same time. It may be the hard, bright silver dollar of a high winter moon or the heavy, mellow, orange glow of the harvest moon on the horizon.

Starlight changes little, but the stars do shine differently on us in the early evening or the depths of night, and their light shifts from season to season. Starlight is special because it left its sources long ago, and took years to cross the interstellar gulfs and reach our eyes. Some starlight is only five to ten years old, and some starlight is thousands of years old, a window into the ancient past.

Different light for different magick. Natural sunlight keeps us healthy, unless the exposure is too long or too strong, and is great for spells of boldness, reason, and success. Moonlight can help us banish things, grow, fulfill, or divine. And starlight can connect us with the astral and inner planes, the world of Faery, and other worlds barely touched by ours.

Every Witch and many other magicians use light magick, but few specialize in understanding and mastering it.

To follow this path further, read:

Moon Magick: Myth and Magick, Crafts and Recipes, Rituals and Spells by D. J. Conway (Llewellyn, 1995)

The Book of the Sun by Tom Folley & Iain Zaczek (Courage Books/Running Press, 1997)

Light: Medicine of the Future by Jacob Liberman (Bear & Company Publishing, 1991)

Magick and Rituals of the Moon by Edain McCoy (Llewellyn, 2001)

Everyday Moon Magic: Spells and Rituals for Abundance by Dorothy Morrison (Llewellyn, 2004)

Everyday Sun Magic: Spells and Rituals for Radiant Living by Dorothy Morrison (Llewellyn, 2005)

Moon, Moon by Anne Kent Rush (Random House/Moon Books, 1976)

Water Magick

Water is key to life, and we are made up of 70 percent or more water. Our blood is salty, like the ancient seas from which it evolved, and our bloodstreams carry nutrients and wastes just as streams and rivers do on the land.

Some magicians communicate with undines or Water elementals to ask their help in magickal projects. Others use moving water to cleanse negative energies from themselves or their ritual tools, or to block impending evil, which according to tradition cannot cross running water.

The book *Hidden Messages in Water*, featured in the popular movie *What the Bleep*, explains that water crystals change their form to reflect the emotional energies projected into them. This knowledge dovetails well with Bach Flower Remedies, which hold the healing vibrations of certain plants, and East Indian Ayurvedic medicine, in which water is steeped with the energies of gemstones. But of course "wild water" comes with its own vibrations, which can be used magickally. (Note: DO NOT drink water straight from an outside source unless you know it is free of contamination; it may look pure but not be safe at all.)

To follow this path further, read:

The Hidden Messages in Water by Masaru Emoto (Beyond Words Publishing, 2004)

The True Power of Water by Masaru Emoto (Beyond Words Publishing, 2005)

Water Crystal Oracle by Masaru Emoto (Council Oak Books, 2005)

Tree Magick

The Celtic peoples were well known for their connection with trees; the months of their lunar calendar were named for trees (and a few other plants), and the Druids especially honored the sacredness of oak trees. Balefires were kindled from the woods of nine different sacred trees, and each tree was recognized for its magickal energies.

Certain woods were known to be especially appropriate for magickal wands, especially fruitwoods, nutwoods, ash, and hazel. Of course, live wood could only be taken with the permission of the tree. Some magicians carry a "touchwood," or piece of wood that fits comfortably in the palm and still carries the energy of the living tree. With this link, they can tap the tree's energy for healing (willow), strength (oak), imagination (aspen), or whatever quality that species of tree corresponds to.

If you meditate or dream beneath a tree, it may share a message with you to help with some problem or question that besets you. You can ground and center with the help of tree energies, and heal emotional troubles by giving them to the tree, which will transmute the energies into something positive.

You can make difficult decisions using a technique called the Tree Shadow Walk. This works best in winter, because you need to see the shadow of a deciduous tree with large, branching limbs unobscured by leaves. One crisp and sunny autumn day, a tree taught me to use its shadow to make difficult decisions. "Walk along the shadow of my trunk," it said, "and when you reach a fork, know that the two branch-shadows represent your two major choices in any situation, and that hidden in the shade of one of them is yet a third choice, which you did not see at first. Pick a shadow, walk along it, and meditate on the consequences of that choice. When you come to another branching, your original choice has led you to a second point of decision: choose a way and walk it, and see where it leads. When you wish, go back and try another shadow-fork, and learn where that goes. Keep your heart open and your mind quiet, and I will lead you to the right choice for you." Then sit at the base of the tree, make your decision, and thank the tree. (Note: You can also do this as a form of inner magick, if conditions are not right to actually do it outdoors.) So spoke the tree, teaching me a magickal technique of great value.

This is but one example from the very complex and diverse field of tree magick. If you are most at home when among trees, this may become your specialty.

To follow this path further, read:

Celtic Tree Mysteries: Practical Druid Magic and Divination by Steve Blamires (Llewellyn, 1997)

Talks with Trees: A Plant Psychic's Interviews with Vegetables, Flowers and Trees by Leslie Cabarga (Iconoclassics Publishing Co., 1997)

Ogham, Tree-Lore, and the Celtic Tree Oracle by Erynn Darkstar (Preppie Biker Press, 1993)

Tree Medicine, Tree Magic by Ellen Evert Hopman (Phoenix, 1991)

The Celtic Tree Oracle by Liz and Colin Murray (St. Martin's Press, 1988)

Tree Wisdom: The Definitive Guidebook to the Myth, Folklore, and Healing Power of Trees by Jacqueline Memory Paterson (Thorsons, 1996)

Animal Allies

If you receive guidance, protection, and energy from an animal spirit, you are blessed. In most cases, this means the collective spirit of all members of an animal species, such as Tiger Spirit, rather than the spirit of a particular tiger.

An animal ally or personal totem is such a spirit, one that agrees to connect with you personally and that may be called upon in time of need. Such allies are especially good at protecting you and lending you their strengths when you need them: the cleverness of Fox, the vision of Eagle, or the healing energy of Dolphin, for example. Sometimes an animal spirit will come to you and offer an alliance through dreams or signs, or through a messenger—a living representative of that species. It will aid you—not serve you, for it is a partnership of equals—as long as you honor, aid, and protect animals of that species.

A clan totem animal is an ally that has long connections with a clan or family. It supports the people of that bloodline as long as they honor it and observe certain taboos—such as not eating members of that species. Many Native Americans and indigenous peoples of other lands maintain their relationship with a clan totem today. Many Westerners of European and African descent have lost their ties with the clan totem. However, if you have an animal surname such as Fox, Lyon, Wolf, Talbot, or Martin, it may describe what your clan totem was at some point—and possibly you can renew the relationship.

Other animal connections may include familiars, which are living animal companions that assist you with your magick; and Younger-Self animals, which are discussed in chapter 5.

A more advanced magickal technique is that of shapeshifting. A skilled magician can mentally become an animal, share an animal's mind and see through its eyes, or dance the animal and take on its movements and appearance. These are not beginner subjects, however.

To follow this path further, read:

Animal-Speak: The Spiritual & Magical Powers of Creatures Great & Small by Ted Andrews (Llewellyn, 1993)

Animal Minds by Donald R. Griffin (University of Chicago Press, 1992)

Power Animals: How to Connect with Your Animal Spirit Guide by Steven D. Farmer (Hay House, 2004)

Crossing the Borderlines: Guising, Masking & Ritual Animal Disguises in the European Tradition by Nigel Pennick (Capall Bann Publishing, 1998)

Medicine Cards: The Discovery of Power Through the Ways of Animals by Jamie Sams & David Carson (Bear & Company, 1988)

Totems: The Transformative Power of Your Personal Animal Totem by Brad Steiger (HarperSanFrancisco, 1997)

Animal Spirit: Spells, Sorcery, and Symbols from the Wild by Patricia Telesco and Rowan Hall (New Page Books, 2002)

Earth and Stone Magick

You don't have to be born under the sign of Taurus, Capricorn, or Virgo to love Earth magick. If stones come home with you after every hike, and you can feel their different energies when you hold them; or if you can tell that certain places have a current of energy or special feel to them, never mind what they look like or what's built there, this is probably your field to master.

On the macro level, study ley lines and the theory that vast webs of energy run beneath the ground, crossing one another and forming nodes where the power is especially strong and accessible. Hundreds if not thousands of ancient sacred sites, temples, landmarks, and holy wells are situated along these lines. People with dowsing skills can easily locate these power lines (as well as underground water, minerals, etc.). And, of course, the energy can be tapped to perform magick.

On the micro level, work with amulets and talismans of stone and metal. Stones have different energies, depending on their crystalline structure and, to a degree, their color. Others, like holey stones or hagstones, Fairy crosses, and lingams, depend on their shape for their magick. Stones are helpful in healing, purification, attracting, banishing, grounding, changing mood, divination (both scrying and casting), and storing energy.

There are a quarryfull of stone magick books available that will tell you exactly what each kind of stone is "good for," based on various cultural traditions or on the author's personal experience, or information channeled from some entity or other. Read them with a grain of salt, if you will pardon the phrase, and rely more on your own direct experience . . . because sometimes any given stone will affect individuals differently.

There are other kinds of Earth magick, such as work with soils and compost (an art beloved of many Pagan gardeners) or land-forms such as mounds and artificial hills, and the magick of stone monuments, such as circles, menhirs, and dolmens.

To follow this path further, read:

Crystal Enchantment: A Complete Guide to Stones and Their Magical Properties by D. J. Conway (Crossing Press, 2000)

Ley Lines and Earth Energies: An Extraordinary Journey Into the Earth's Natural Energy System by Davis Cowan, Chris Arnold, and David Childress (Adventures Unlimited Press, 2003)

Cunningham's Encyclopedia of Crystal, Gem, and Metal Magic by Scott
Cunningham (Llewellyn, 1987)

The Crystal Bible: A Definitive Guide to Crystals by Judy Hall (Walking Stick
Press, 2003)

Sacred Stones, Sacred Places by Marianna Lines (St. Andrews Press, 1992)

The Sun and the Serpent: An Investigation into Earth Energies by Hamish
Miller and Paul Broadhurst (Pendragon Press, 1994)

Magical and Mystical Sites: Europe and the British Isles by Elizabeth Pepper
and John Wilcock (Phanes Press, 1983)

Ley Lines: The Greatest Landscape Mystery, second edition, by Danny
Sullivan (Green Magic, 2005)

The Old Straight Track: The Classic Book on Ley Lines by Alfred Watkins
(Time-Warner Books UK, 1994)

Weatherworking

As with other magick, some people seem to be born with a gift for influencing the weather. Using the power of their mind, they can nudge cloudbanks
or high and low pressure systems, bring rain or divert it, conjure up snow or
keep the sky clear.

For most of us who can do this work, it requires great concentration and
energy—especially if you are working solitary. I believe I managed a snow-
storm once (to end a winter drought), but my head was tender for days afterward. On the positive side, an experienced group can do it much more
easily: our coven has been successful with rain magick to alleviate drought
on several occasions.

This is a skill that must be used wisely and carefully. There is no such
thing as working "purely local" weather magick; changing moisture patterns
here always affects someplace else. Now, if your "here" is suffering drought
and the "there" is flooding, balancing the weather can be a good thing; at
least in the short term and as far as we can know. But messing with the skies
just so the weather is nice for your coven picnic is a terrible idea. Weather-

working is for emergencies, to avert famine and save lives; it is not for trivial purposes. Whenever you think about doing it, first discuss the need, ethics, and possible effects with a group of wise elders.

Books on weatherworking? There are few to none, unless you count rare treatises on cloud-seeding. However, some general books on nature magick include chapters or short sections on the subject.

The road snakes along the edge of the Valles Caldera of northern New Mexico, the heart of an ancient volcano, now grass-covered and dotted with cattle and elk. I watch clouds within the great bowl, floating across the land, shifting their shapes, sometimes spilling over the road before me . . . wraiths dancing, circling, and spiraling, leaping upward in slow motion or hugging the ground. I know that my watching changes me in subtle ways, and I wonder if it changes them. The mist-dancers teach me that there is power in liminality, the places where the elements touch and change each other: where the Water vapor of clouds meets Earth, and the Air moves the cloud, and the cool Fire of early sunlight illuminates them both. I see a hawk soaring along the edges of the cloud, then skimming the floor of the Valle Grande, enjoying the boundary places. These are places of power and transformation, gateways from one state of being to another. The nature magician knows this and seeks those special places where the elements touch and the world changes . . . and the magician too.

Exercises Toward Mastery

1: Visit Some Herbs

Find an herb garden or plant nursery that you can visit. Spend some quiet time wandering among the plants, feeling their presence. If a plant attracts you or intrigues you, touch it gently and feel its particular energy; greet it, and see whether you receive any impressions, images, or other message in response. When you get home, write your impressions in your journal, and consider how it would feel to plant and care for an herb garden.

2: Explore a New Form of Divination

From the list in the "Divination with Nature" section on page 160, choose one form of divination that you have never tried before. In the appropriate setting or at the proper time of day, experiment with this method: ask an important question, then watch the clouds or stream or bonfire . . . see if any patterns, symbols, or feelings come to you. Be aware that you may get a message that is important but doesn't respond to the same question you had in your conscious mind.

3: Moonlight Vigil

From an astrological calendar, or on the Internet, learn when the next new moon occurs. On that night, go outdoors and spend some quiet time alone with the moon; she will not be visible, but you can still feel her presence. Gently turn off your internal sound when Middle Self jabbers, and simply sense, feel, and breathe. When you go indoors, write your impressions of the moon energy in your journal. Repeat this exercise seven nights later, during the waxing moon; again at the full moon; and about six days later during the waning moon.

4: Sunlight Meditation

On a sunny day, sit outdoors in the shade and watch the sunlight. Do not take it for granted, but see it as a living, changing presence. Observe it and describe its appearance in detail. Listen to it; if it is silent, then open your mind to its subtle vibrations, and listen to the music that it suggests to you. Reach out your hand into the sunlight, and feel not only its warmth, but its texture and intensity. Explore your present mood and how the light affects your emotions. Let it speak to you as a spiritual entity, either sun god, sun goddess, or pure sun spirit, and absorb its message. Afterwards, thank the sun and record your impressions in your journal.

5: Exploring Water

Get a water bottle filled with clean water and a cup or chalice. Find a place near a stream, pond, river, lake, or ocean. Sit and systematically block out all awareness of land, plants, buildings, creatures, light . . . focus all your attention on the water itself. Sense its life, its power, and the specific energy of that water. Greet it, and listen. After a time, shift your perception to the water within you, and do the same things. Later, pour some water from your bottle into the cup, hold it, and send thoughts of love and gratitude into its essence. Slowly, mindfully, appreciatively drink the water. When you are ready, thank the spirit of Water and go home.

6: Ask a Tree for Healing

Choose a tree in your yard, near your home, or in a forest, and visit it. Ask permission to spend some healing time with it, and listen for the response, which may be simple calmness or a slight, welcoming sense of warmth. (If there is no response, or you feel uneasy, leave and choose another tree.) Once you have an accepting tree, sit near its base and ask if it will share healing energy with you. Describe your need—your illness, injury, or problems. Cry if you feel like it. Give the sadness, hurt, and pain to the tree to take into the earth and transmute into nourishment. Then place your hands on the trunk, and draw in healing energy from the earth and sky. A good session will leave you feeling lighter, heart-eased, more whole, with all your senses keener. Thank the tree and give it a gift of water or a silver coin.

7: Connect with an Animal Ally

Think about all the kinds of animals that you like or admire, including birds, fish, reptiles, and so on. Write a list. Next to each species, write the qualities you associate with that animal: perhaps courage for Lion, loyalty for Wolf, cleverness for Fox, patience for Turtle, etc. Now consider whether there is one species whose help might be really valuable at this point in your life. If so, get a picture of that animal, or a little statue, and place it on your altar. Ground, center, and meditate on the image, then on the spirit beyond the image. Greet the animal spirit, and in your own words, ask it for aid and support. Its response may be a picture, sound, or voice in your mind, or a strong feeling of approval or disapproval. If the answer is positive, thank the animal spirit; obtain a talisman (such as a small carved stone image of the animal, strung as a pendant necklace) and wear it often. Talk to the animal spirit frequently to ask for guidance and protection. Bear in mind that it may be appropriate to change animal allies, with thanks, at some point later on.

8: Stone Companions

Find a stone you like, about the size of a golf ball or smaller. It can be one that you find on a walk, pick up in a parking lot, or purchase at a rock and mineral shop. Carry it with you for a week, and occasionally pause to feel it, speak to it, and listen (preferably in a private place, unless you enjoy spooking the folks in a crowded elevator). After a week, describe the stone's energy and personality in a journal. Then do it again for a week with a new stone. In time you will have a collection of stones with very different energies and can choose the one that will best balance your energy during the day, and carry it.

Blesséd be.

To follow this path further, read:

The Deva Handbook: How to Work with Nature's Subtle Energies by Nathaniel Altman (Inner Traditions, 1995)

Earth Power: Techniques of Natural Magic by Scott Cunningham (Llewellyn, 1983)

Earth, Air, Fire, and Water: More Techniques of Natural Magic by Scott Cunningham (Llewellyn, 1991)

Gaia: A New Look at Life on Earth by J. E. Lovelock (Oxford University Press, 1979)

Gaia's Hidden Life: The Unseen Intelligence of Nature by Shirley Nicholson and Brenda Rosen, eds. (Quest Books, 1992)

Intrinsic and Inner Magick

Popular culture conditions us to link magick and ritual tools together. Think of the wizard Gandalf's staff in *Lord of the Rings*, and Frodo's sword, Sting, that glowed when the evil orcs approached, and of course the One Ring itself, so filled with power that the fate of the world rested on it. Or consider Harry Potter and his friends at Hogwarts, relying heavily on their wands, brooms, and invisibility cloaks. Movies and novels are filled with magickal rings, swords, staffs, talismans, amulets, wands, goblets, hats, and all manner of knickknacks. Even in a work of fiction, this can be overdone: "Begone, Frost Demon, lest I smite thee with the Mitten of Power!"

Of course, real magicians do use ritual tools, as covered elsewhere in this book. But an entire branch of magick uses no material tools, costumes, or physical props at all.

In the first edition of *True Magick*, this was covered briefly under the name hermetic magick. Alas, that name means somewhat different things in different traditions and was not the best word to use in a general book on magick. For this edition, I searched for a better term that was universally accepted in the magickal community. Many terms were suggested, from people's personal experience or particular traditions in which they were trained. Very quickly it became clear that there is no universal term for propless magick.

In order to fill this void in the vocabulary of magick, I discussed some possible new terms with some friends who are Witches and magicians. As a result, I propose the term "intrinsic magick," meaning magick where the only tools are the ones that are part of you: your mind, body, voice, will, energy field, and emotions.

As a subcategory, I suggest "inner magick," which is performed entirely in the mind, without even the use of movement or voice.

And for even more precision, "virtual magick" is intrinsic magick that uses tools, props, and costumes, but only visualized ones.

This may seem unnecessarily complicated to some, but do you know what? We are "technicians of the sacred," working with subtle and complex energies in a culture that has little regard and less vocabulary for our Art. We need new terminology because that, too, is a tool.

The Tools of Intrinsic Magick

So if we use no material-plane things to perform an act of magick, what intrinsic tools do we have always with us? Remember the Witches' pyramid? All of its qualities were internal: imagination, will, silence, faith, love, and knowledge. Look at the four qualities of an adept, similar to the pyramid but not identical: to know, to will, to dare, and to keep the silence. Daring is included because it has always been understood that it takes courage to explore the further reaches of reality.

So all these are tools for intrinsic magick (and any other form). Here are some more:

> **Mind:** We can visualize energies moving, events occurring, and symbols influencing the inner and outer worlds. We can imagine possibilities, focus attention, and mentally call on the aid of Younger Self, Higher Self, deities, allies, and guides.

> **Senses:** We can observe the elements of Earth, Air, Fire, and Water in the environment around us. We can see, hear, and feel what energies are most available to us so that our minds can use them. (In New Mexico, we can sometimes smell rain, sunlight, and dust simultaneously; remembering sensations is a wonderful way to connect with the genius loci or Spirits of Place.)

Breathing: By changing the way we breathe, we can calm ourselves, focus our intent, raise energy, or change our emotional states.

Voice: We can call spiritual powers and entities through making the sounds of elements, evocation, invocation, invitation, prayer, and animal calls. We can raise power by chanting, singing, vibrating names, and wordless ululation. We can direct or focus energy by affirmation, incantation, storytelling, the recitation of names, and describing magickal goals as already met. We can change consciousness with trance induction, poetry, and commemoration. Because some of these terms may be new to you, they are defined here:

+ *Sounds of Elements:* The quarters can be called to a circle with imitative magick: with practice, you can make the sound of wind blowing, flame whooshing up a chimney, water chuckling in a brook, or rock grinding against rock.

+ *Evocation:* The calling of "lower powers," such as elemental spirits (sylphs, undines, salamanders, and gnomes) or any entity less evolved than humanity.

+ *Invocation:* The calling of "higher powers," such as angels, archangels, spirit guides, or deities. Invocation is sometimes a prelude to aspecting, drawing down, or assuming the godform, in which a priest or priestess hosts a deity in their body.

+ *Invitation:* A less powerful or commanding form of evocation or invocation, in which a spirit is simply invited to be present.

+ *Prayer:* Communication with Deity, or an aspect of Deity, in which a request or plea is made but no power is raised, unless the emotional content is high.

+ *Animal calls:* Making the characteristic sounds of an animal species, usually when calling a totem animal or ally to your assistance.

+ *Vibrating Names:* Calling the name of a higher power, usually a deity or archangel, in a loud, extended, and resonant voice; either as part of invocation or energy work, such as the Middle Pillar exercise.

+ *Affirmation:* Repetition of a carefully designed sentence with the intent of changing consciousness and / or external reality. For example, "I am filled with strength and confidence, I will run faster than ever in Saturday's race . . ."

+ *Incantation:* Verbal recitation of a charm or spell to produce a magickal effect.

+ *Trance induction:* The use of words and sometimes visual cues to change one's consciousness to a more focused and suggestible state; used in trancework or hypnosis. Example: "You may be feeling relaxed and light, as though floating on a cloud, so peaceful, inhaling serenity with every breath . . ."

+ *Recitation of names:* A calling of names of spirits, gods, or qualities in order to build and focus power. For example, "By Eurus, Notus, Aeolus, and Boreas do I call the power of the winds . . ."

+ *Commemoration:* Another kind of recitation, in which the names of great magicians are called in order to build confidence before a working. For example: "As Hermes Trismegistus has done before me . . ."

Dancing: Many kinds of dance can be used to raise power or enter a different mental state. You can dance freeform as the spirit moves you, dance your power animal, do a circular folk dance, dance in honor of your chosen deity, do a slow and meditative trance dance, raise energy with a belly dance, or just dance joyously and ecstatically to celebrate abundance, health, or love.

Other Movement: You can use walking as a meditation for changing consciousness. Climbing and swimming can be used to raise power. Any of these can symbolize movement toward a goal. Rhythmically clapping or slapping one's body can generate energy. How many ways can you use your body to perform magick?

Mudras and Asanas: Mudras are gestures or positions of the hands and arms that have sacred meaning, and asanas are positions involving the whole body. For example, if you stand with arms outstretched and curved to the sides and up, you become like a chalice receiving the energy of the moon goddess. If you stand with your arms crossed in front of your chest, hands touching your shoulders, you have assumed the Osiris position, which honors the god of death and resurrection.

With Any of the Above: As a more advanced technique, you can set and fire sensory anchors. This is part of the array of techniques in Neuro Linguistic Programming (NLP), which offers psychological and sensory tools for personal change. In brief, anchoring means that you go into a particular mental state (confidence, serenity, etc.) and mark that feeling with a sensory cue: touching the middle finger of your left hand with your right index finger, for example. (The cues of triggers can also be auditory or visual, like a tune or the sight of a certain object.) When you repeat that same action later, firing the trigger, you tend to experience the same mental state. In other words, you can train yourself to recapture a feeling or mental state at will, change consciousness at will, and thus perform magick.

Inner Magick

Inner magick requires your mind and senses, nothing more: just what's in your skull and what you perceive around you. In its pure form, you use no breathing techniques, your voice is silent, and your body is still. It is magick wrought by mind alone.

It will come as no surprise that inner magick is most effective for changing your state of mind, emotional state, or habits of thinking. In all these cases you will work very closely with Younger Self. You can also visit other realms of reality—the astral planes and the underworld—without moving a muscle. Tasks such as shamanic healing and soul retrieval are possible with inner magick alone. Psychic skills like telepathy, precognition, and remote viewing can be developed and used.

Four tools you have in your head are memory, visualization, imagination, and othersight. Each of these can be oriented toward visual, auditory, or kinesthetic sensing.

Memory

Your Younger Self has a vast store of memories from this lifetime and past lives, most of which are not instantly accessible to your conscious mind but can be retrieved with Younger Self's help. They might be visual memories (images), auditory memories (voices and other sounds), or kinesthetic memories (touch, movement, smells, tastes, temperatures). They may be flat and superficial, like watching an old movie, or rich in all the senses, as when you experience past-life regression and vividly relive every sensation.

Jungian psychologists might add that you can tap the "collective unconscious," which holds the memories of our entire species back through time. And according to some adepts, you can also learn to access the Akashic Records, where all knowledge of the entire cosmos is collected.

Memories can be used to re-create a state you have experienced before and (since many memories have an emotional charge attached) to raise power. The wisdom of the collective unconscious and Akashic Records can enhance your magickal understanding and guide you in your workings.

Visualization

This is the ability to imagine something very clearly. The name comes from being able to picture it clearly in the mind's eye, but being able to add the other senses enhances the effect. See it, yes, but also hear it, taste it, feel it, and know what it feels like to be it or be in it. Whatever your magickal goal is, and whatever style of magick you prefer, you must be able to visualize success vividly.

Imagination

With this tool you can create something new on the astral planes, and with the help of Younger Self and Higher Self, charge it with power so that it becomes manifest on the material plane.

As with memory, there is visual, auditory, and kinesthetic imagination. To be effective in astral creation, imagine the thing or state with all your senses, not just the sense with which you are most comfortable.

Remember Robert Kennedy's famous words, "I dream of what never was and ask 'Why not?'" With the focused energy of magick, you can "Dream of what never was" and send power to make it real.

Note that you can remember, you can imagine, or you can blend memory and imagination. For example, you might recall an incident that ended badly, and then replay it with a different, more satisfactory ending, and put energy into the revised memory to influence how you handle such situations in the future.

Othersight

This is the ability to sense realities that are not evident to our normal sight, hearing, or touch.

One of the chief barriers to othersight is the limited consensual reality that we grow up with. We are taught that certain experiences are real, like eating pizza or adding two plus two and getting four. Other experiences, like sensing emotions, seeing dragons, remembering past lives, or hearing trees sing are labeled as "make-believe" or "crazy talk."

The narrow world of consensual reality is relatively predictable and "safe" (or at least the hazards are pretty straightforward and understandable). But it is also false in a way, because it is so restricted that most of "what's out there" (or "in here") is left out. It is like eating an ice cream cone and declaring that only the shape and size are real, and the coldness, flavors, colors, and textures are make-believe.

Scientists usually know a wider reality; at least they can measure invisible radiation, or the spectra of stars, or the movements of one-celled organisms. Their trouble, from a magickal viewpoint, is that they usually have a consensual reality where certain kinds of curiosity, or lines of exploration, are ruled "impossible" from the start: discarnate spirits, psychic talents, and the power of magick are examples.

Well, most people choose to live in very small boxes and pretend that anything beyond the cardboard is unreal. But magickal folk can peek outside, reach out a hand to feel the breeze, and occasionally crawl out of the box altogether. You can experience currents of magickal energy, the colors of auras, the underworld of the shamans, the astral planes, and the worlds of spirit.

Where to begin? Start by remembering what you knew as a child. What was repressed and stuffed away because your experiences didn't fit into the consensual-reality box? Could you see things, hear things, or do things that adults did not believe? Things that you gave up because you wanted to be "normal," to be loved? Perhaps it's time to revisit the wider, more magickal universe you knew as a child.

Secondly, trust your senses. If you cast a circle and can see or feel the energy boundary, assume that what your senses are telling you is real, and go from there. If you call the quarters and sense elemental beings hovering just beyond the circle, act as though they are present and see what happens. If you invite Goddess to your circle and feel a wave of power, love, and joy, believe it—she is with you.

Last but not least, be still. Stop your constant activities, your business, your chatter. Turn off the radio, the television, the computer and cell phone. Get away from crowds and cities and traffic. Be in a solitary and peaceful place: then listen . . . watch . . . feel . . . sense. Then will you discover other worlds.

Energy from Emotions

Your emotions are an inner tool. Some emotions will be linked to memories: the rage you felt when the teacher humiliated you in Potions or chemistry class at school; the joy you felt when you realized you had won your first quidditch or chess match. Imagined events can also evoke strong feelings:

the passion when you visualize a hard-won goal achieved, the joy when you picture your beloved returning to you after a long journey. You can also visualize real events or things you have seen on a newscast, such as natural disasters, and feel a powerful sense of compassion for the victims.

The point is that emotions are powerful, and you can evoke them intentionally, then use their energy to work magick. Indeed, magick done without emotion or passion tends to be feeble and ineffective. Thinking is important, but thought alone will not make magick happen.

Direct Mental Manipulation of Energy

Some magicians have an intuitive, natural affinity for certain kinds of energy and can manipulate them almost instinctively. We have all known potential elemental magicians. These qualities are especially clear in children; some can't keep away from fire and act like budding pyromaniacs, while others are "water babies" from the beginning, fearless in backyard kiddie pool or ocean surf. Some kids are ethereal, intellectual Air types, and others remind us of the Earthy "Pig Pen" from the *Peanuts* comic strip.

You may recognize yourself already. If so, you have a double challenge: first, to develop and focus your natural talent for your favorite element, and second, to explore the others enough so that you maintain a balance in your life and your magick.

Your particular affinity might not be one of the basic four elements. Perhaps you connect deeply with solar or lunar energy, or the stars, or the night, or trees, or something else in nature. Whatever it is, pursue the connection and play or practice with the associated energies until you can actually "touch" them, concentrate them, and use them to influence the world. Once you have some real skill and experience with the energies that come most naturally and easily, then you can challenge yourself by working with others.

Visualization Plus Energy

An inner magick that almost anyone can do from the beginning is to visualize what you would like to happen, then raise energy and pour it into the image. Granted, some people have a much easier time "seeing" things in their minds, just as others can remember music or exactly how a dance step should go. But visualization is a skill that anyone can develop with practice (see the exercises at the end of this chapter). There are three important things to remember when doing this kind of magick:

1. Visualize your desired outcome in great detail, with bright colors and images, and all the auditory and kinesthetic sensations included;

2. Raise energy and put it into the image; and

3. As with all magick, act in accord, taking practical steps to assist the magick in manifesting.

Inner Ceremonial Magick

Inner ceremonial magick is just like outer ceremonial magick, except that all the steps of ritual are performed in your mind.

The more rituals you participate in, the more easily you can create one in your mind. Still, even if you have limited experience in the circle, it will still be useful to rehearse the steps in your mind.

A lovely thing about inner rituals is that you can perform them anywhere in the world (at least within your mental landscape) or outside the world, with all the wonderful decorations and tools you like, and with as many participants as you wish. How about a Fire ritual on the lip of an active volcano, or re-creating the Eleusinian Mysteries in a Greek temple? Would you like twenty-foot banners with dragons embroidered in silk, floating in the breeze overhead? Perhaps a hundred flautists, piping a call-and-response from hidden places in the surrounding hills, would be evocative.

And there's no sweaty hauling of stuff up the side of a hill, or trying to light candles in the wind, or realizing at the last moment that you forgot the chalice.

BUT—remember that a pleasant and colorful visual fantasy is not sufficient to perform magick. You must smell the pungent incense, taste the tang of the wine on the back of your tongue, feel the thunder of the drums vibrating through your whole being, and feel your perspiring body whirling in an ecstatic dance. The ritual must be vivid enough to open your heart and strong enough to raise the cone of power. That takes practice.

Magick with Virtual Tools

One of the pleasures of working magick, for many of us, is collecting, creating, and using the ritual tools. Younger Self really enjoys the taste of a cool wine or juice from a beautifully shaped silver goblet, or the feel of an elegant and well-balanced athame in the hand. There is nothing wrong with appreciating good tools as long as you don't become dependent on them.

So it is useful to learn to do magick without material tools, and then without any traditional tools at all. After all, in an emergency you don't want to tell the other shoppers in the supermarket, "Just one moment! I can handle this, but I need to get my magickal tools out of my car's trunk. Oh, and could you trim these candles so they fit better in the candlesticks?"

Using virtual tools is a great transitional stage between ceremonial magick and intrinsic magick. You can use ritual tools exactly as you would in a normal ceremony, but instead of a material object, you rely on your visual, tactile, and auditory memories of objects that exist on the material plane but are not physically present with you. With as much intensity and detail as possible, visualize your favorite chalice, its color and the way the light moves on its surface . . . remember how it feels in your hand, its weight, its shape, its texture . . . touch it to your mouth, notice its coolness or warmth, how it feels against your lips . . . and so on. A tool used in this way is just as effective as one that takes up physical space on your altar.

You may also use virtual tools that do not exist on the material plane but are created on the astral. You can own and use any ritual tool that you can create in your mind. Want a wand of water-clear diamond, infused with molecules of gold at one end and silver in the other? It's yours. Would you care for an athame with a handle of black Irish bog oak carved by the Sidhe into intricate faery patterns and a blade of alloyed gold and bronze forged by dwarves? Why not? Such a tool costs nothing, and you can have the best one in the world.

Allegorical Inner Magick

An allegory is a story that is not literally true but uses fictional characters, events, and places that resemble or symbolize actual things. Each "made-up" figure or place represents someone or something real in the human psyche and the universe, and when we understand the story, we understand ourselves and our world better. Allegory is related to myth, and one purpose of myth might originally have been to effect inner change by helping us identify with heroic figures who undergo transformative experiences. When we hear about Persephone's descent into the underworld and how she becomes its queen, we identify with her on some level and learn to accept the cycles of life and even the need to descend into the dark places to find our power.

We can create stories that represent our lives and control the action so that the story affects what happens to us. For example, if you are facing major obstacles in your life, you might transform them into mythic boulders that block your way into a fabled land, and call upon Ganesh (the elephant-headed Hindu god known as the "Remover of Obstacles") to help you move them aside. If you are struggling with an addiction, transform the craving into an evil king deep in a cave who tempts you with riches and comforts that will enslave you to his will. If you would have prosperity, ask yourself what qualities, skills, or actions would bring you wealth; then create a story in which you are the pure-hearted pilgrim who must find each of several magickal objects on a difficult journey in order to discover the dragon's treasure hoard.

By creating your own allegory and putting energy into it on both magickal and mundane levels, you can make it come true.

Symbolic Inner Magick

Most challenging, in some ways, is the inner magick of the manipulation of symbols. The most common symbols we use are words, either written or spoken. Since we are discussing inner magick, we refer only to words seen or heard in the mind, not spoken aloud or physically written out.

Words are symbols because they are only a shorthand way to evoke or reference a thing, not the thing itself. Nonetheless, they can trigger strong emotion and move people to accomplish great things. To the degree they transform our consciousness and thus the world, all words are words of power.

Perhaps, in the real world, two armies face each other, fear and anger in their hearts, death in their hands. In your mind, a third "army" of ordinary people—children, women, and men of all ages—moves between them, chanting the word "Peace." Could this visualization make a difference? It might. Billions of people believe that prayer is effective, and what is prayer but strings of words offered with heartfelt intention?

We can also use such magickal symbols as the tattvas (Hindu elements) and other elemental symbols, alchemical signs, runes and bindrunes (combinations of basic runes), the Tree of Life, I Ching hexagrams, and tarot pictures. Of course these are only useful for inner magick if you have memorized the symbols and their meanings.

All this can be difficult for Younger Self, which relates very little to abstract symbols unless they are closely connected with powerful memories or with strong sensory impressions. For example, a red equilateral triangle, point up, is one symbol for the element of Fire. If you have used this in a ritual that involved a huge bonfire, then Younger Self might have a strong association between this shape, the color red, and the physical embodiment of Fire. Otherwise the symbol might mean nothing to Younger Self; it has no more relation to "Fire" than a purple hippopotamus would. So you must be careful when using symbolic magick that you are not just performing a sterile, intellectual exercise: there must be feelings, juice, power, mojo attached to them.

Many symbols are strictly personal and have power or emotional impact only because they were important in our individual lives. Remember our earlier discussion of personal correspondences? Perhaps when you were small, your mother held you on her lap at bedtime and read to you from a book with a picture of a teddy bear on the cover. Ever after, that picture is a symbol of love and nurturing for you. You can work such symbols into your inner magick workings.

How does one use symbols in magick? If you have trained yourself, simply visualizing the symbol may trigger a certain kind of energy flow: you need extra strength, you picture the Strength card from the tarot major arcana, and suddenly you are more powerful. Alternatively, you can charge a symbol with energy, so that what it represents will manifest in your life. You can manipulate the energies behind the symbols by changing their size, color, or brightness in your mental picture. You can combine energies by visualizing two symbols connected or merging, such as combining the runes for "wealth" and "growth" into one bindrune. You can change your reality by "morphing" one symbol into another; for example, transforming a Saturn symbol into the sign for Mercury if your life is "stuck" and you want more travel and freedom.

One Goal, Five Inner Methods

As examples, let us look at five very different ways to do weatherworking with inner magick. Suppose you live in an area suffering a prolonged drought, while other parts of the country are flooding. After careful thought and discussion, your magickal group decides that it will be appropriate to bring some rain to your region. However, it would be difficult to gather for a ritual just now, so you will all do inner magick at the same time, each in your own home or workplace. How might you structure this work?

Direct Manipulation

You can pull the moisture in the air toward you, "calling the wet." Remember how it feels to stand in a rainstorm: the cool wetness, the veils of swiftly sheeting water in the gray light, the sound of constant, myriad drops pattering on the ground. Your experience and memory of moisture allows your kinesthetic-psychic sense to reach out and detect a kindred state far away, and then attract like with like.

Visualization

You can visualize the clouds coming to you, picturing their great gray shapes looming over the horizon, spreading across the sky, blocking out the sun, filling the sky overhead. Raise power with a mental chant and pour it into the image. As an example, adapted from another chant:

> *Weave, weave, weave us the storm clouds,*
>
> *Bring us the falling rain;*
>
> *Weave us the hope of a new tomorrow*
>
> *The land will bloom again!*

Ceremonial

In your mind, create a temple with hangings of silver, blue, and green, and a statue of a rain or water deity (such as Tiamat, Tefnut, Zeus, Ganymede, or Thor) on the altar. Include a fountain with crystal-clear water cascading from a high place. Then perform a complete mental ceremony: asperge with water alone, cast the circle, and call the quarters as Water of Air, Water of Fire, Water of Water, and Water of Earth. Invoke the rain god or goddess, state your need, and raise power with thunderous drumming; since this is in your mind, you can have a corps of a thousand drummers of you wish, pounding on really huge drums, such as the Japanese *kodo*. Release the energy to its intended purpose, give thanks for the coming rains, and close out the ritual as you normally would.

For a simpler approach, you can visualize a virtual wand, either your own or the perfect weatherworking wand (perhaps wrought of lodestone and crystal in the eye of a hurricane); then focus your will, powerfully drawing the clouds closer and closer.

Allegorical

Visualize the spirit of the land around you, the genius loci, as a lovely queen in her beautiful castle. Her responsibilities keep her from venturing far from the palace. One day she discovers that the castle cisterns are dry and the fountains have failed; her people begin to suffer. She dons her robes of magick and climbs to the highest tower; there, she creates a shining beacon to call the elemental sylphs and undines, spirits of Air and Water who can bring the rains.

Symbolic

You can visualize the tattvic symbol "Water of Air" (a silver crescent superimposed on a sky blue disc). Make it into a gateway for cloud and mist, an irresistible funnel that draws similar energies, then expand it and reach through it to the distant rain clouds, drawing a filament of energy to connect clouds with the gate.

Intrinsic Magick, Pluses and Minuses

There are some obvious advantages to using intrinsic magick, at least at certain times and places. You do not have to carry props and tools, nor do you need to be in a natural environment. And the more work you do, the more confidence you develop in your own powers.

A potential disadvantage is that workings have less allure for Younger Self, since there are no colorful costumes, wonderful smells, or pretty tools on the material plane. And you need Younger Self to complete the circuit, so you may have to work extra hard on movement and a vivid imagination to keep it interested.

A second possible disadvantage is that you may lack skills in dance, singing, or other intrinsic sorts of tools. Yet this has its positive side, in that you are motivated to "push your boundaries" and improve your skills if you want to use intrinsic magick effectively.

To the extent that modern, well-educated, sophisticated people are willing to believe in magick at all, they find it easier to believe in magick with tools and props than in mind magick. Perhaps we are such dedicated tool-users, ever since the time that *homo erectus* broke a rock to get a sharp edge, that we have trouble imagining anything worthwhile happening without tools—whether they are stone hand axes, nuclear accelerators, or magick wands.

Yet amazing things, miraculous things, happen all the time with no tools at all. People have ideas that blossom into a Bach oratorio or the Declaration of Independence. People discover new ways to look at the world, perhaps seeing commonalities or connections and love instead of differences, alienation, and fear. People roam around inside their heads and hearts, and they discover beauty, courage, forgiveness, and the strength to continue.

So it is true that, with nothing but the resources within us, we can change ourselves and the world. It's hard to do. Swinging a hammer or diagramming DNA chains on a computer is so much easier. But when you perform magick with your body and voice and heart and mind, not only do you get the desired effect, but you also have evolved inside; your intrinsic and inner tools have acquired a little more strength, and you have greater skill and understanding.

Exercises Toward Mastery

1: Breathing Varieties

Try breathing in a way that fills you with energy and makes you vibrate. Now try breathing so that the energy gently flows into the earth. Now breathe in a way that calms and relaxes you, almost to a trancelike state.

2: Voices You Didn't Know You Had

Find a poem you like. Read it aloud in an Earthy voice; then Fiery, Watery, and Airy. Do it again, but speak for a longer time in each voice. Speak in a commanding, godlike voice and a compassionate, goddessy voice. Now speak in a compassionate, godlike voice and a commanding, goddessy voice. Speak in a voice of thunder and a voice of gentle breezes. Suck a cough drop.

3: Dancing Free

Put on loose, comfy clothing. Find a space where you can be alone and have lots of space to move. Do some warm-up stretches. Now dance all the same elements and deity energies that were listed in the previous exercise.

4: Make Mudras

Find a ritual gesture or posture that represents your favorite aspect of deity. Assume the posture or make the mudra. Now do it again, but visualize yourself as that deity; do it with depth and feeling and intensity. Make another, different posture/gesture to represent a sun deity, a moon deity, a warrior, a sea deity, a deity of abundance, a deity of love.

5: Imagination Calisthenics

As vividly as possible, imagine yourself as a truck driver. Now a Buddhist monk. A fisherman in a storm. A Russian ballerina. A Baptist preacher. A nun in a cloistered convent. A cowboy. A singer in a Las Vegas lounge.

6: Othersight Experience

Look at the world around you, allowing yourself to see what others will not, using other senses as well. Keep looking, off and on, for a week if necessary, until you see/sense something that is not part of consensual reality. It might be a human aura . . . a nature spirit . . . a ghost . . . an elemental spirit . . . a Sidhe . . . an energy charge in a talisman . . . a magick circle . . . or something else.

7: Sensing and Feeling Energy—One Kind

Choose one form of energy that you feel you have an affinity for and would like to explore further: Earth, Air, Fire, Water, Oaks, Stones, Chamomile, Rain, or whatever. Spend a full hour in the presence of that energy, discovering everything you can about it through observation and mental exploration alone.

8: Visualization of Your Future

In your mind, create yourself ten years from now, living the best life you can possibly visualize. Include all aspects: home, work, family, friends, activities, and so forth. Make it detailed and include all sensory modes.

9: A Virtual Tool Masterpiece

In your mind, create the most stunningly beautiful and powerful athame ever imagined. Do the same for a chalice, a wand, and a pentacle.

10: Intrinsic and Inner Ritual

Perform all the steps of ritual (attunement, cleansing the space, casting the circle, calling the quarters, etc.; see chapter 15) using intrinsic magick. Now do the same using inner magick.

11: Your Own Allegory

Describe your life in terms suitable for a myth, a fairy tale, an epic, or a heroic poem. Think of three directions the story could go from the present.

12: Magickal Symbol Systems

Choose a symbolic system and read one book about it or discuss it with your magickal teacher. It might be about the Qabalistic Tree of Life, runes, tarot cards, astrological symbols, alchemical signs, or anything that intrigues you.

Blessèd be.

To follow this path further, read:

Frogs Into Princes: Neuro Linguistic Programming by Richard Bandler and John Grinder (Real People Press, 1979)

Magic in Action by Richard Bandler (Meta Publications, 1992)

NLP: The New Technology by NLP Comprehensive (Harper Paperbacks, 1996)

The Structure of Magic: A Book About Language and Therapy (Book 1) by Richard Bandler (Science & Behavior Books, 1975)

The Structure of Magic: A Book About Communication and Change (Book 2) by Richard Bandler (Science & Behavior Books, 1975)

Trance-Formations: Neuro Linguistic Programming and the Structure of Hypnosis by Richard Bandler and John Grinder (Real People Press, 1981)

Getting Ready for Ritual

bviously, preparing yourself to work magick is no light task. In truth, this kind of preparation never ends. Yet at some point you will need to proceed with the work itself, knowing you are not fully prepared— for no magician on this plane is ever a "finished" magickal being. You will continue to grow as you prepare each working, and what you learn from the work will, in turn, help you grow.

Knowing Your Purpose

The first step in the actual practice of magick is to define the purpose of your working. This is not as simple as it might seem. Let us take an example from the realm of thaumaturgy: suppose it occurs to you to work magick in order to obtain a car. Your job is at a great distance from your home, and public transportation and ride-sharing seem inconvenient.

But wait—is it really a car you need? You could as easily do magick for a job closer to your house, or to help you accept and enjoy car-pooling, or to obtain a bicycle or motor-scooter. Perhaps you have considered carefully and are quite sure you need a car. What kind of car? An inexpensive used Chrysler, you say? So you work the spell, and three days later you run across an inexpensive used Chrysler. A brown Chrysler. You hate brown. So you start over and specify blue. Soon a blue inexpensive used Chrysler crosses your path, and you buy it. The next day the transmission falls out. So you start over and specify that it must be an inexpensive used blue Chrysler in sound mechanical condition . . .

This can go on and on *ad nauseam*. When you work for *form*, specifying how you want the magick to manifest, every detail had better be right. With magick, you get what you ask for. Not necessarily more than you asked for (like a good transmission in that pretty blue car), and not necessarily what is appropriate, or useful, or what you need—just what you ask for.

So knowing what to ask for (or "call into your life") is half the secret. The simplest way to avoid all the hazards illustrated in the example is to work for *essence*, rather than form. In the case above, you would work a spell for "the most perfectly appropriate form of transportation for me at this time" or for "the best car for me at this period in my life." Then you trust your Higher Self to work out the details. If you say "transportation," you might wind up with a motorcycle or a horse, but it would work out very well for you. If you specify a "car," it might be any color, make, and model—but again, it would turn out to be just what you need.

Turning to theurgy, you can also work for essence, if you wish: "I call into my life whatever experiences are most appropriate to help me grow spiritually." However, in the field of personal growth there is much to be said for working for form as well as for essence. For one thing, it forces you to take good, long looks at yourself and thus to understand yourself better. You can't specify a change unless you know what you want to change. The resulting insights are valuable, and you become an active partner in your own growth and transformation (that is to say, Talking Self does).

When you work for form in theurgy, once again it does not pay to be vague or sloppy. Magick to "become comfortable in crowds," for example, could be hazardous. Some people achieve a certain comfort level by becoming drunken boors. Others fall asleep. Still others—well, drive past a crowded urban cemetery: everyone there is comfortable.

In this case, you would explore yourself until you find out what makes you uncomfortable: what feeling of fear, or inadequacy, or what gap in your knowledge is at the root of the situation. Then you can work on that issue with intelligence and precision.

Thus ritual's first step involves clarifying your purpose. You may simply need to meditate or talk it over with Younger Self. You may want to do some of the "values clarification" exercises that were popular in the sixties and seventies in order to better understand your values and goals. Of course, you should also consider divination. Use of the pendulum, tarot, scrying, astrology, I Ching, runestones, lithomancy, and other such techniques can be illuminating. Exploration of these topics is too broad a subject for this book, but it is worth your while to browse among them, choose one that feels especially attractive, and seek teaching from a skilled practitioner.

Your Ritual Tools

Though ritual tools are not absolutely necessary in magick, many people find them helpful as tangible symbols of the processes initiated by the magician. Younger Self in particular enjoys the use of tools, and with time will become so familiar with magickal procedures that simply picking up a given tool will signal it to begin channeling a certain kind of energy or moving into a certain mental state.

There is a great deal of nonsense written about ritual tools in fantasy literature that gives the impression that magickal power resides in the tool, to be released by anyone who happens to come into possession of it. In point of fact, the magick is in the magician, and the tool is merely a symbol or at most a channel for the power. The only time that substantial power is vested in a tool occurs when you charge it (as with a talisman); even then the power is transient.

The traditional tools used by most Wiccans and other magicians include the athame, pentacle, wand, and cup or chalice, each of which symbolizes an element. Most altars also include candles, an incense burner, bowls for salt and water, and a Book of Shadows. These basic tools, as well as some other fairly common ones, are described below:

Asperger (or aspergillum): A device used to sprinkle water for purification at the beginning of rituals. Some are constructed of brass or silver, but a spray of evergreen, a pine cone, or your own fingers will do as well.

Athame: A black-handled, double-edged, knifelike tool used by Witches to channel energy, as in casting the circle, but not used to cut anything material. It is marked with the owner's name in runes and with other symbols, including the pentagram, and may symbolize either Fire or Air elements (different traditions vary on this point).

Bell: A bell or gong can be used early in the ritual to "alert the quarters," that is, to prepare Younger Self to operate in the modes of Earth, Air, Fire, and Water.

Bolline: A white-handled knife used by Witches for cutting, carving, or inscribing things in the course of a ritual—candles, talismans, cords, etc. It is usually single-edged and sometimes has a sickle-shaped blade that is handy for harvesting herbs.

Book of Shadows: A magickal journal kept by each Wiccan initiate, in which spells, invocations, ritual notes, herbal recipes, dreams, divination results, and material from the coven book can be recorded. Some people write it in Theban script or in other alphabets. Some use a "Disk of Shadows" or "CD of Shadows."

Candles: These are used by some magicians in spells. The oils they are anointed with and their colors, as well as the shapes and inscriptions carved on them, all have a symbolic purpose. *See also* Lamps of Art.

Chalice: A goblet or cup, usually holding wine, that is shared around the circle in Wiccan ritual. It is both a female and a Water symbol, and it can be used for scrying.

Charcoal: Often incense is burned on a charcoal briquet, placed in a thurible or on a stone. "Self-igniting" charcoal disks are sold in occult supply stores and are very convenient to use.

Cord: A "cord" can be either a heavy string used in binding and releasing magick, or it can refer to the piece of apparel circling the magician's waist (also called a "girdle" or "cingulum"). In many covens and magickal lodges, the color of the cord indicates the wearer's degree of attainment.

Incense: This comes in sticks, cones, powders, resinous chunks, and herbal or floral mixtures, and can be purchased or made. The incense burned depends on the purpose of the ritual and on the energies being invoked, but frankincense and sandalwood are two all-purpose favorites that can be used for almost any ritual.

Lamps of Art: These are two candles on the altar that provide illumination and may also symbolize Goddess and God. They are made preferably of beeswax, although paraffin will do. Choose natural color or white, or use colors based on the season or on the nature of the magick being done.

Pen of Art: A special pen reserved only for entries into the Book of Shadows or for other ritual uses. This can be an old-fashioned dip pen or quill pen, but any writing implement may be assigned this role.

Pentacle: This is a disk of metal, ceramic, or wood with a pentagram and other symbols inscribed on it. It is a symbol of the element Earth; sometimes salt or cakes are placed upon it, though it was originally designed to be used in rituals of protection as a magickal shield.

Salt Bowl: Rock salt symbolizes Earth and is mixed with water and sprinkled over things to purify them. *See* "Asperger."

Sword: A special sword can be used to cast the circle for a group and is considered a symbol of either Air or Fire, depending on your tradition.

Thurible: A metal censer, dish, or burner to hold charcoal and incense. It can either stand on the altar or swing from a chain, and it is often considered to be an Air symbol.

Wand: A stick about eighteen inches long, or "from elbow to finger-tips," carved from one of the traditional sacred woods and used to channel power and represent Air or Fire, according to various traditions. It may be carved and decorated, with a phallic shape (acorn or crystal) on one end and a yoni on the other. Also called a *baculum*.

Water Bowl: Water mixed with salt may be used to purify; the bowl (or large shell) containing it is kept on the altar.

Other tools or symbolic apparati include the cauldron, scourge, staff, broom, stang, herbs, oils, stones, and an astrological calendar. In addition, there are divinatory tools such as tarot cards, the magick mirror, showstones, pendulums, casting stones, yarrow stalks or coins for the I Ching, and rune-stones or rune sticks.

Tools can be obtained in several ways. Often it is best to make them yourself, so that they are well attuned to you. They can be as simple or as elaborate as your tastes and skills dictate. For a wand, you can simply cut a length of ash wood, or you can carve coiling serpents and complex runes on ebony and set rubies or sapphires into the wood. Mold the cup of river clay and bake it in the coals of a sabbat fire, or turn it on a potter's wheel and glaze it with vivid colors. If you feel the need to have an elaborate tool but do not have the skills to make it, commission a craftsperson to create one to your design.

Sometimes a family heirloom from a favorite relative can be adapted as a tool, or a friend will offer one as a gift. Whatever the source, you may want to personalize it by painting or engraving your magickal name on it in runes. Some tools can be purchased at antique shops, occult supply shops, import shops, or estate sales. Never haggle over the price: the perfect tool is invaluable. And never buy something "pretty good" because the price is right—it must feel just right, either "as is" or with modifications you can accomplish.

Any purchased tool should be ritually cleansed before use. The simplest ways are immersing it in running water (in a stream under a rock, for example) or burying it in the earth from full to new moon.

When you have a new tool, consecrate it at the full moon. Purify and bless it with Earth (salt), Air (incense), Fire (flame) and Water (or wine), as well as Spirit (ritual oil). Present it to the four quarters, then to your favorite aspect of Deity or a deity appropriate to the element your tool represents.

You may wish to say something like this: "Lady Aphrodite, goddess of love and emotions deep as the sea, I present to you this chalice, ritual tool of Water and the west, of all emotions and intuition. Grant that I may use it in your favor and power, with harm toward none and for the greatest good of all." Then immediately use the tool for its intended function—in this example, by sipping wine from it, by mixing a healing herbal drink, or by scrying.

Keep your tools safely stored when not in use, wrapped in natural-fiber cloth and placed in a special box, pouch, or basket. Keep them clean and (if metal) polished; wooden tools may require an occasional application of tung oil so they won't dry and crack. At least once a year, ritually cleanse and reconsecrate them. The sabbat of Imbolg (also called Oimelc, Brigit, or Candlemas) on February second, is an appropriate time for this. Remember that, traditionally, no one should touch your ritual tools without your permission; nor should you handle the ritual tools of another without their consent.

Your Altar

Outdoors or in, you will need an altar or at least a place to put your tools while working. It can be any shape or size, as long as there is room for your materials. Some people simply spread a special cloth on the ground or in the center of the floor. Traditionally the altar is in the east (dawn and new beginnings) or the north (wisdom and spirit).

One possible altar layout is shown below in the accompanying diagram. The incense is in the east as a symbol of Air; a red candle is placed in the south as a Fire symbol; the chalice is in the west to denote Water; and the pentacle sits to the north as a symbol of Earth. Other working tools or supplies are placed wherever they are handy.

A: Candles/Lamps of Art

B: God/dess statues

C: Pentacle

D: Incense burner

E: Wand

F: Athame

G: Red candle

H: Salt bowl

I: Water bowl

J: Chalice

K: Book of Shadows

This is simply a suggestion; there is no One Correct Way to set up an altar, and your altar will probably change tools and placement for every magickal working. Sometimes the altar may be in the east, but you could just as well place it in the center of the room, or have four elemental altars at the cardinal directions, or hang it in a tree, or even have it in a pond floating around on a piece of wood.

The Timing of Ritual

It is possible and helpful to fine-tune the timing of magickal work, choosing a date and time when the season, astrological configurations, day of the week, phase of the moon, and planetary hour are all favorable to the specific spell you wish to cast.

For those new to magick, however, it is sufficient (and far simpler) to consider only two factors: the phase of the moon and the day of the week. Let's consider lunar phases first.

> **Diana's Bow**, when the first slender crescent is visible, is an excellent time to do magick for beginnings or the conception and initiation of new projects. This occurs two or three days after the new moon.
>
> The **waxing moon** is appropriate for spells involving growth, healing, or increase.
>
> The **full moon** represents culmination, climax, fulfillment, or abundance. It is the high tide of psychic power.
>
> The **waning moon** is the best phase for cleansing, banishing, or completion.
>
> The **dark of the moon** or **new moon**, though no longer visible to the naked eye, is the most useful time for divination of all kinds: scrying, tarot, I Ching, casting the runes, etc.

Every two or three days, on the average, the moon will be "void of course" for a few hours, or essentially "between signs." Do not begin a ritual (or any new project) during these periods, because the lunar energy will be unfocused if not chaotic, and your plans are likely to go awry. An astrological calendar will show voids-of-course.

Each cycle of the waxing and waning moon spans several days, and within such a span you may wonder which day is best for the magick you plan. These hints may help:

☽   **Monday** is devoted to the moon and relates to psychic sensitivity, women's mysteries, tides, water, and emotional issues.

♂   **Tuesday** is connected to Mars/Tiw and action, vitality, assertiveness, courage, and battle.

☿   **Wednesday** is special to Mercury/Woden and communications, travel, business, and money matters.

♃   **Thursday** is linked with Jupiter/Thor and leadership, public activity, power, success, and wealth.

♀   **Friday** is related to Venus/Freya and love, sex, friendship, beauty, and the arts.

♄   **Saturday** is dedicated to Saturn and knowledge, authority, limitations, boundaries, time, and death.

☉   **Sunday** is special to the sun and growth, healing, advancement, enlightenment, rational thought, and friendship.

Understanding Correspondences: The Language of Ritual

In planning a ritual, you must understand clearly that much of ritual magick involves the manipulation of symbols or symbolic objects, because sometimes these communicate more powerfully and vividly with Younger Self than do mere words. For most practical purposes, the Younger Self is nonverbal; but like a pre-verbal child, it responds to colors, shapes, rhythms, smells, movement, and other sensory stimuli. We include speech in the ritual (invocations, poetry, song lyrics, chants, and words of power) because it can evoke feelings and images that Younger Self responds to, and because words are an important avenue of participation for Talking/Middle Self.

One of the creative and enjoyable parts of ritual design involves choosing the symbols to be used—that is, translating the aim of the ritual from abstract ideas or words into music, colors, scents, images, objects, dance movements, and so on. Choosing and arranging the symbolic elements of ritual is as much of an art form as choreography or sculpture.

We call the symbolic relationships "correspondences" because in magick one thing corresponds to another, and both belong to an open-ended set of interconnected elements. Thus Fire, the color red, cinnamon, the quality of courage, the direction south, and the goddess Vesta all correspond to one another in many magickal traditions, along with salamanders, red peppers, fire opals, and lions.

A coven or other magickal group should agree on the basic correspondences, so that they all "speak the same language" in ritual together. When you work by yourself, you have more flexibility because you can draw on your personal experiences. Perhaps seagulls correspond to Fire qualities for you, because as a child you always saw them in bright sunlight while walking on hot sand; or maybe popcorn is a Fire symbol for you, because on holidays your family popped corn with an old-fashioned popper in a blazing fireplace.

In a group ritual to boost your courage and energy, then, everyone could invoke Vesta in the south, roar like lions to raise power, and channel it to you in the form of red light. They might also "witness" aloud to situations where they have seen you display these qualities. Later, at home, you might make and charge a talisman bag of red cloth, placing inside peppers, a few kernels of popcorn, and a little model of a seagull. Thus you make use of your personal correspondences as well as those familiar to the group.

Every culture having a magickal tradition has its own set of recognized correspondences. A concise table of correspondences used by many Wiccans is included in appendix II. For a more extensive (and partly cross-indexed) set, see *The Spiral Dance* by Starhawk.

Exercises Toward Mastery

1: Setting the Goal

Choose a goal that you might like to do ritual magick to achieve. Now answer these questions:

a. Is it something that could actually be accomplished by some other means than ritual? If so, what are the advantages and disadvantages to doing it with magick?

b. Is it something that will not harm you or others, as far as you can tell?

c. When you think about achieving this goal, how do you feel? Any mixed feelings?

d. What are the positive things that might occur if you do not achieve this goal?

e. If you have any divination skills (pendulum, tarot, runes, etc.), what does your divination say about this goal?

f. Is the goal clear and measurable? How will you know when it is achieved?

g. Do you still want to do magick for this goal?

h. If so, what are three ways you could "act in accord" to support the magick on the material plane?

2: Physical Setup—The Altar

Think about how you would set up an altar for a prosperity ritual. If it helps, get a pen or pencil and some blank paper to jot notes or make sketches. What colors, tools, symbols, plants, props, or other things would you use? Now do the same for an altar for a healing ritual, to help you recover from an illness. Now do the same for an altar for a shadow work ritual, where you will confront and transform something negative about yourself.

3: Assemble a Basic Set of Tools

To get started, make, find, or buy the following basic ritual tools:

Athame: a double-edged dagger with a black handle.

Chalice: a stemmed cup or goblet.

Wand: a stick or shaft, from elbow to fingertips in length.

Pentacle: a disk, usually wood or metal, from four to eight inches across, with a pentagram inscribed or cut into it.

Review the magickal uses of each one.

4: Personal Correspondences

Make a list of images, sounds, smells, or tastes that you associate with each of the following qualities:

a. Feeling safe

b. Abundance or prosperity

c. Sheer happiness

d. Meeting difficult challenges

e. Success

f. Healing

Blesséd be.

To follow this path further, read:

Wheel of the Year: Living the Magical Life by Pauline and Dan Campanelli (Llewellyn, 1997)

The Ritual Use of Magical Tools by Chic Cicero (Llewellyn, 1951; out of print)

Complete Book of Incenses, Oils & Brews by Scott Cunningham (Llewellyn, 2002)

Cunningham's Encyclopedia of Crystal, Gem, & Metal Magic by Scott Cunningham (Llewellyn, 2002)

Spell Crafts: Creating Magical Objects by Scott Cunningham and David
Harrington (Llewellyn, 2002)

Crafting & Use of Ritual Tools by Eleanor Harris (Llewellyn, 2002)

Altars: Bringing Sacred Shrines into Your Everyday Life by Denise Linn
(Wellspring/Ballantine, 1999)

*The Magick Toolbox: The Ultimate Compendium for Choosing and Using Ritual
Implements and Magickal Tools* by Carl Neal (Weiser Books, 2004)

Witch Crafts: 101 Projects for Creative Pagans by Willow Polson (Citadel
Press, 2002)

Creating and Performing Ritual

Y̧ou have prepared yourself and your temple, defined your purpose, gathered your tools, chosen the date and the moon phase, and considered the correspondences you will use. Now it remains to finalize your ritual plan and work the magick.

The Steps of Magickal Ritual

A ritual outline follows. You will fill in the content according to your own style and beliefs—but know that each step has its purpose, and to omit any one may lead to failure. Here is a list of the steps, followed by explanations of each:

1. Advance preparation

2. Physical set-up

3. Self-preparation

4. Attunement

5. Asperging the area

6. Casting the circle

7. Alerting the quarters

8. Calling the quarters

9. Invoking the god

10. Invoking the goddess

11. Stating the purpose

12. Raising power

13. Channeling power

14. Earthing excess power

15. Cakes and wine

16. Thanks and farewells

17. Opening the circle

18. Acting in accord

1. **Advance preparation** may include such tasks as obtaining special herbs or candles, making a ritual tool, researching an appropriate deity for the invocation, and planning the details of the ritual.

2. **Physical set-up** covers the preparation of the temple or outdoor ritual area, laying out tools, putting up special hangings on the walls or symbols on the altar, and so on.

3. **Self-preparation** immediately before the work might include a ritual purification bath with candles and incense, a period of meditation, an aura-cleansing or energy-channeling exercise, and other activities to cleanse and focus.

4. **Group attunement** is important if anyone will be working with you, whether or not they are physically present. Chanting or singing together will psychically harmonize a group; but guided meditation, play, or work together on some task of preparation (such as decorating the temple or creating a circle of stones) are alternatives. It's a good idea to do this even if you are practicing alone; it's a chance to collect yourself into the moment, ground and center in preparation for your work. Read a poem aloud, sing a song or chant, or breathe consciously for a few minutes.

5. **Asperging the area**, ritually cleansing it of inappropriate or negative influences, is often done with salt and water. You may begin by tracing a pentagram over the salt: visualize it glowing with

white light beneath the athame or wand as you say: "I exorcise thee, O spirit of salt, casting out all impurities that lie within." Do the same over the bowl of water, visualizing it boiling and bubbling: "I exorcise thee, O spirit of water, casting out all impurities that lie within." Add three measures of salt to the water, stir deosil (clockwise) three times, then walk deosil around the outside of the circle area, sprinkling the salt water lightly over everything with an asperger or your fingers.

Having asperged with Water and Earth, you may also purify with Air and Fire by taking a censer or smudge stick (such as a bundle of burning sage) around the circle area, stopping to salute the quarters.

6. **Casting the circle** creates a boundary around the sacred space of your ritual, both to protect those within from outside influences or distractions and to contain and concentrate the power raised until it is channeled to its goal. Walk deosil from the altar, pointing your athame or sword at the ground. Visualize a line of blue flame or light rising from the ground as you say, in a slow and powerful voice:

    "I conjure thee, O circle of power, that thou shalt be a boundary between the world of humanity and the realms of the mighty ones, a guardian and protection to preserve and contain the power we (or I) shall raise within; wherefore do we (or I) bless and consecrate thee!"

    If you are working with a group, use "we" and have everyone join in on the last line: "wherefore . . . " Restore the athame or sword to its place.

7. **Alerting the quarters** is the next step. The term "quarters" is verbal shorthand for the powers of Earth, Air, Fire, and Water. These correspond in part to:

    Earth: body, foundations, the material plane

    Air: mind, intellect, imagination

Fire: vitality, will, purpose

Water: emotion, intuition

These qualities or aspects of reality are sometimes represented as guardians or archangels.

By "alerting" these, we are really preparing Younger Self to experience the ritual in all of these modes: physically, mentally, with our energy fields, and emotionally.

Walk deosil (clockwise) around the circle from the altar (or starting in the east), carrying a bell, gong, or chimes. Pause and ring at each of the cardinal points. Add a fifth soft chime when you return to the altar or east.

8. **Calling the quarters** follows. Face the east and draw an Air-invoking pentagram with your athame. See the symbol glowing in the air, and behind it you may visualize the personified power of that element; for example, a spirit robed in light blue and white, with wind moving its robes and hair.

Air: invoking

Water: invoking

Fire: invoking

Earth: invoking

Face the south, west, and north in turn, draw the appropriate pentagrams and visualize the elemental spirits. If a group is present, this is done in unison. After the pentagram is drawn each time, the group may intone the name of the corresponding spirit or archangel (Air = Raphael, Fire = Michael, Water = Gabriel, Earth = Uriel). As an alternative, one person may step forth, lead the signing of the pentagram, and speak an invocation. For example:

"Spirit of Fire, Guardian of the Watchtower of the South, Red Lion of the Burning Desert, come to our circle this night and grant us the will and energy to achieve our aims. So mote it be!"

9. **Invoking the god** activates the masculine aspect of divine creative power within the ritualist. He may simply be referred to as God, or a particular aspect (Pan, Cernunnos, Thoth, etc.) may be invoked who is appropriate to the work at hand. In any group working with men present, a male usually invokes the god. (In Wiccan tradition a priestess may invoke the god into the high priest, if the god is to be aspected or channeled, or into herself, if no male is present or able. However, aspecting is an advanced magico-spiritual skill that should be learned firsthand from an experienced priestess or priest; it will not be covered here.)

   Stand before the altar, raise your arms, and speak appropriate words of welcome; for example:

   "Great Cernunnos, hornéd god of the wilderness and the beasts which dwell within, bring your power, vitality, and blessings to the circle this night. Hornéd one, wild king of the forest, welcome to our circle!"

10. **Invoking the goddess** follows the same pattern, but is usually done by a woman. Again, a specific and appropriate aspect (Diana, Cerridwen, Ma'at, etc.) may be invoked, or simply Lady or Great Goddess. A sample invocation might begin:

    "Great Diana, moon goddess, we invoke and call upon you as the full moon rises. As you fill the night with your silver radiance, fill us too with your power and love, and grant your continued blessings . . ."

11. **Stating the purpose** is important for clarity and to make sure that all present are in accord. You might say, "We are here to celebrate the new moon, the Maiden and Youth within, and to work magick for growth and healing in the days ahead," or "We meet to work magick for the purification, blessing, and protection of this house, our sister Thea's new home," or whatever is appropriate to the purpose for gathering. If anyone has doubts about the need, strategy, ethics, or timing of the suggested work, this is the last chance to express them before the work begins.

12. **Raising power** may be done in any of several ways, as mentioned earlier. Chanting a simple couplet is a common method—such as the following, for a man feeling apprehensive about an upcoming confrontation: "Mighty Mars, this boon we crave: help Jack feel both strong and brave!" It can be the veriest doggerel: Younger Self is not a poetry critic. The important things are that it be simple and vivid. A chant can be combined with a simple circle dance, or with drumming or clapping, or these can be done without a chant.

    Other ways to raise power include singing, breathing techniques, or even pounding stones in unison. It must be simple to do, repetitive, rhythmic, and continue long enough for intense energy to be felt by everyone in the circle.

13. **Channeling power** toward the goal occurs the moment the energy peaks. This may be done simply by visualizing the goal as achieved, or the energy may be sent through a "witness" or "object link," as explained before. This may be an image (such as a photo), something associated with the recipient (a ring belonging to a person requesting prosperity magick, for example), or an actual part of the object (like a flake of paint from a house you wish to buy). Of course, if you are doing work for an individual and they are present, then the beneficiary can simply stand in the center of the circle and receive the power directly.

14. **Earthing excess power** or "grounding" is a necessary part of ritual hygiene. We have discussed this briefly before, but it is worth expanding on. Assuming you have raised any significant amount of power, you will feel a strong physical sensation—a tingling, vibrating, or thrumming throughout your body. Ordinarily not all of this new energy will be perfectly channeled to the goal, so a residual vibration will be felt. Ignoring this can lead to hyperactivity, tension, restlessness, irritability, and/or insomnia until your energy field or aura gradually rebalances. It is best to channel the excess into the earth immediately after you have sent all you can to the goal. Often it is enough to place your palms flat on the ground (or floor) for a minute or two. You can also put a fairly large rock in your lap and place your hands on it. Or you can lie full-length on the ground, on your belly. You must be sensitive to your energy field and to your body to know when this process is completed.

15. **Cakes and wine**—that is, sharing food and drink following the work—is an enjoyable and valuable part of many traditions. Of course, it need not literally be cakes and wine; fruit juice or chips and dip would do as well, but a ritual tradition of serving little crescent-shaped cakes and homemade herbal wine or the like adds an extra measure of magick to the proceedings. In any case, refreshments remind us to be grateful for Earth's bounty, help ground us further, and provide an opportunity to socialize and share one another's company. It is a congenial transition from a magickal state of consciousness to ordinary "reality."

16. **Thanks and farewells** follow. Face the altar and first thank Goddess for her presence. In some traditions, she is bid "farewell" on the theory that she will recede to a deeper layer of being, away from our waking consciousness or Talking Self. I prefer not to say goodbye, since she is always with us and within us, and I want to keep her close to conscious awareness.

A similar process is followed for God, by whatever name he was invoked.

Air: banishing

Water: banishing

Fire: banishing

Earth: banishing

Next, thank the guardians (or spirits) of the quarters, and say "farewell." Some books speak of "dismissing" or "banishing" them, but I prefer to work in terms of cooperation rather than domination. Starting in the east, draw an Air-banishing (or "Farewell to Air") pentagram with your athame, and say:

"Mighty ones of the east, we thank thee for attending . . . and if go ye must, we say hail (kiss athame and salute with it) and farewell."

Do likewise for south, west, and north. Feel free to adapt the wording. Instead of "Mighty ones of the south," you might say "Spirit of Fire" or "Red Lion of the Desert" or "Lady Brigit, Keeper of the Flame," and so on.

17. **Opening the circle:** walk widdershins (counterclockwise) with your athame pointed at the line you traced earlier, and visualize the

flames or light fading or being drawn back into your athame. You have returned to ordinary space and time and may confirm this by saying: "The circle is open but unbroken—blesséd be!"

18. **Acting in accord** means taking action on the material plane, or in "mundane reality," to support the magick done within the circle and on other planes. Do not just sit back and wait for results to drop into your lap. Magick is an adjunct to the rest of your life, not a replacement for it. If you did magick to physically heal yourself, support it with herbal medicines, proper nutrition, rest, sunlight, and so on. If you did magick to express yourself more clearly and assertively, then place yourself in situations where such abilities will be demanded, and practice what you will say beforehand. If the magick was to strengthen your relationship with the natural world, then go camping, learn to identify birds, or photograph animals in the wild. Younger Self and Higher Self will help in any worthy endeavor, but they can't be expected to do all the work. You are still the channel through which the magick manifests.

A Sample Ritual

Let us suppose that you are wrestling with a problem such as addiction to alcohol (though the following material could easily be adapted to any addiction or excess—food, candy, tobacco, caffeine, etc.). You ask for counsel through the tarot, and both the Magician and Temperance cards come up. It seems clear that magick can help you, so you design a ritual for abstention.

During a waning moon, prepare a Saturnian talisman. Saturn is the god (and planet) of discipline, limitation, and learning. In a small square of black cloth, place a piece of black jade, black onyx, or obsidian. Add any combination of Saturnian herbs, such as cypress, balm of Gilead, comfrey, fern, henbane, High John the Conquerer, ivy, mullein, pansy, slippery elm, Solomon's seal, or even asafoetida (if you can stand the odor). Stitch the planetary sigil or astrological symbol of Saturn (♄) in violet thread on the bag; gather and tie with the same kind of thread.

Obtain an amethyst in a silver mounting as a pendant that can be worn on a cord or silver chain. It need not be an expensive cabochon or faceted jewel; a rough amethyst or a baroque polished one will do as well, though it should have a deep purple color.

If you will be working indoors, decorate your altar and temple in black, with purple or violet candles. Outdoors, use a black altar cloth or a flat stone on the ground. In addition to your usual tools, place your talisman, the pendant, and an inverted wine glass or shot glass on the altar.

At the dark of the moon, asperge the area and cast the circle. Alert and call the quarters. Invoke the goddess Hecate, "Wise Crone, Mistress of Magick, Lady of the Dark Moon, Guardian of the Crossroads, that she may be present and lend her power at this crossroads in my life." Then invoke Saturn, "God of Boundaries, Limits, and Discipline, Lord of Higher Learning, that he may teach me wisdom and restraint."

Tell them why you have invoked them. Sit. Ground, center, and clear. Meditate on the ways you have permitted alcohol (or whatever) to change your life and on what your life could be like without the addiction.

Raise power by drumming and chanting. In low but intense tones, say:

"By fallen leaf and powers fey,
I call the name of Hecate:
Make strong my will, make true my aim,
As I from [alcohol] abstain!"

You may wear the pendant and hold the talisman in your lap as you chant and drum. When the power peaks, pick up the talisman and channel the energy into it, by visualizing or with hands or wand.

Earth the excess energy. Then meditate on a time when you were able to abstain, hold back, and resist temptation to drink, and when something else seemed so important to you that you successfully focused your attention on that rather than on drinking. Relive the experience vividly; reexperience the feelings strongly. When they are clear and powerful, grip the amethyst pendant in a strong, firm grasp. Repeat this sequence nine times, and each time work for greater vividness and depth.

Rest a while and imagine your new future free of your addiction. Plan the ways in which you will enlist the help of family, friends, and organizations—that is, the ways you will "act in accord" with the magick you have performed.

Thank Saturn and Hecate, and the powers of the quarters, and release the circle. Place the talisman under your pillow. Wear the amethyst all day each day; if you are tempted, reach up and grasp it in exactly the same way you did at the ritual. Say in your mind, "In Hecate's name, NO!" Then instantly turn your mind to something else, preferably something absorbing, demanding, or challenging. Later you may take a moment to reflect on how well the magick worked and to congratulate yourself on passing temptation by.

It should be noted that I selected deities to invoke who will be effective for modern Pagans, that is, adherents of nature-oriented religions. Readers of other faiths could perform this magick by substituting their own names and images of Deity, preferably those aspects that focus on wisdom and self-control.

Remember that the ritual alone is not sufficient: you should also consider changing your diet to low-sugar forms of nutrition (an "anti-yeast" diet), changing your recreation and social patterns, and probably joining a support group. Hypnotic suggestion by a trained professional may also be helpful. Remember, the magick must not end with the ritual: you must act in accord and provide a vehicle for it to manifest in the everyday world.

Analysis

So what has really happened here in successful ritual magick, beyond the outer events and trappings, the candles, robes, and chanting?

First, your conscious mind has chosen a goal, hopefully in consultation with Younger Self and Higher Self, through divination, meditation, trancework, dreamcraft, or other communications techniques. You have clearly communicated the desired outcome to Younger Self through the language of ritual: chants, colors, incense, symbolic objects or actions, and so on. But nothing can be accomplished without energy, so you have raised power—

that is, Talking Self initiated the process and Younger Self raised the power from outside sources in nature. Younger Self then channeled the energy to the goal through Higher Self, which had the wisdom and knowledge to use it to manifest changes inside you or on the material plane. (In the case of magick for someone else—say, a healing—the energy is channeled to the Higher Self of the recipient.) Then your Talking Self returned from the altered state necessary for participation in magick to ordinary consciousness.

Thus ritual is a theater for the Younger Self, whereby you communicate concepts that words alone cannot convey. Magick is also a team effort among various aspects of your Self to direct energy into transforming reality.

The important thing to understand is the process, but the precise forms of ritual vary from group to group and tradition to tradition. Here, for example, we have assembled the group (if not working solitary) and cast the circle around them. But in many Wiccan traditions, the high priestess (assisted by the high priest) casts the circle, then invites the coven members to enter through a created gateway or portal. The important thing is that the circle was cast to contain and focus the power and keep out distractions. Precisely how it was done is not as important as the intent. Should you research other traditions of magick from various cultures around the world, look for the common elements in all of them. These are the foundations of magick.

Exercises Toward Mastery

1: Self-Preparation—Purification Bath

Take a bath, but design it so that it prepares you for important magickal work. Include candles, music, perhaps incense, and whatever bath oils seem appropriate. Afterward, if you have no other magickal work planned, do a simple self-blessing ritual.

2: Attunement

Name six techniques you could use to get a small group attuned and in harmony prior to working magick together. If you are part of such a group, choose the most unusual method and ask to lead it at your next ritual.

3: Asperging Alternatives

Try three different ways of cleansing a ritual space: sprinkling salt and water, smudging with a smoldering sage bundle, and sweeping with a ritual broom (you can make a simple one just by binding a bundle of twigs to a stick). Which do you like better? Why? Then make up three more ways, and analyze them.

4: Casting the Circle

Try casting a circle, as explained in this book or in the way taught by your tradition. Now stop and just look at the circle with your othersight. What do you see? If you see nothing, dim the lights and look again; imagine it is visible, if necessary: visualize a ring of glowing blue flame. Once you have an image, check the circle for weak and strong places. Uncast or open the circle, drawing the energy back into your blade. Cast it again, putting more energy into it, and again check the intensity and consistency, until you are satisfied with its strength.

5: Calling the Quarters

From within a cast circle, invite each of the elements to your circle in three different ways. First, invite them very quietly and politely. Pay attention to the result; what do you feel or sense? Second, command them very loudly to appear; again, check the result. (Apologize afterward, explaining that this was just a training exercise.) Lastly, call them in a way that is strong and firm, yet very respectful. How does that feel?

6: Invoking Deity

Think of a reason why you might like to talk with Deity: to give thanks, request help for yourself or another, or ask an important question. Within a magick circle, stand and invite a deity aspect to join you in the circle. If you are not experienced with this, just use simple language; if you want to be more creative, write something as poetic and beautiful as you can. Once you have finished speaking, become utterly silent and still, and scan the circle with your psychic antennae. Do you sense a presence that you did not feel before? If so, welcome the deity and say what is on your mind. When you are done, thank the deity for being present. Write your impressions of this experience in your magickal journal.

7: Raising and Channeling Power

See the exercises in chapter 8, "The Energies of Magick."

8: Earthing Excess Power

See the exercises in chapter 8.

9: Cakes and Wine

Obtain a nice goblet or chalice, and fill it with pure water, wine, or natural fruit juice. Also get a piece of really good bread. Sit in a quiet place, and bless the beverage and bread. Now eat and drink very slowly and mindfully; notice every detail of texture and flavor. Also consider where the ingredients came from, and how many people put energy into growing, harvesting, and preparing them. Remind yourself that Deity provided the original plants as a gift of nourishment and abundance to us, and thank whatever aspects of deity seem appropriate (such as Demeter and Dionysus, for example). Sit a while and meditate on the experience and how it differs from your usual meals.

10: Releasing Deity and the Quarters

Do the opposite of whatever you did to invoke them, and let them go with thanks and a benediction.

11: Design Rituals

Design rituals for the following purposes, taking into account the purpose (not too broad, not too narrow), the phase of the moon and day of the week, and basic elemental correspondences:

   a. Finding the right pet

   b. Excelling in a class or course

   c. Learning to be at peace when you are alone

   d. Increasing your business income

   e. Communicating with your deceased grandmother

   f. Protecting your home from negative influences

12: Act in Accord

Do the practical things that will bring your desire to fruition, and "fake it till you make it"—act as if the result has already happened.

Blesséd be.

To follow this path further, read:

The Art of Ritual: A Guide to Creating and Performing Your Own Ceremonies for Growth and Change by Renee Beck and Sydney Barbara Metrick (Celestial Arts, 1990)

The Spell of Making by Blacksun (Eschaton Productions, 1995)

Castings: The Creation of Sacred Space by Ivo Domínguez, Jr. (Sapfire Productions, 1996)

RitualCraft by Amber K and Azrael Arynn K (Llewellyn, 2006)

Spellcraft:
The Techniques of Magick

At the heart of each ritual, unless it is a ritual of celebration such as a sabbat, is a spell—a magickal working directed toward a specific goal. A spell may be extremely elaborate or bare-bones simple, solemn or light-hearted, lengthy or quick. It may involve candles or herbs, crystals or parchment talismans, words of power or silent meditation, runes or cord magick, dancing or drumming, singing or chanting, or quiet breathing exercises. To an observer, it might look like a dazzling theater production, full of music, special lighting, and choreographed dance and colorful costumes; or it might look like a person sitting in an empty room doing nothing. Yet all spells are aimed at vivid and accurate communication with Younger Self, whether they are ceremonial or intrinsic in style, whether nature-oriented or kitchen witch magick.

The spells that follow are samples for you to consider; they can be worked "as is," but will be more effective if you adapt them to your own style. All of them should be performed in the context of a fully cast circle, with asperging and quarters and all the trimmings, at least until you are more experienced and have a clear sense of when the circle is necessary and when it may be dispensed with.

The more emotional and psychic intensity you can build, and the more clearly you focus on your goal, the more effective your magick will be. Remember always to consider the ethics of a spell before it is cast. If there is any possibility that it will manipulate or affect another individual without their express, informed permission, then discard the spell and design a better one. You should, of course, spend as much time and energy planning how you will "act in accord" as you do planning the ritual.

With these guidelines in mind, let us look at a few sample spells.

A Spell to Become Calm and Centered

Equipment

A very smooth, rounded stone, smaller than your fist, and some soothing recorded music.

The Spell

Cast your circle. Sit while holding the stone and listening to the music at home, or in the outdoors if the weather is nice. Breathe deeply and rhythmically. Begin inhaling through your mouth, then exhaling through your mouth with a long, steady humming note. With each exhalation, make the note smoother and draw it out longer. Breathe your tension and anxiety into the stone. When you feel calm and centered, put the stone on the ground, open the circle, and walk away. The stone will dissipate the tension into the earth to be transmuted; if you wish, you can retrieve the stone in a day or two for later use.

Acting in Accord

Be sure you are eating well (no sugar or nasty chemicals, please!) and getting plenty of rest and exercise. Meditate on the causes of your upset, and either find ways to eliminate them from your life or to transform your attitude and perceptions so that they become positive for you.

A Spell for Easing Grief or Sadness

Equipment

Any memorabilia that tend to powerfully evoke the sadness: letters, pictures, gifts, etc.; an object that reminds you of some upcoming event that is likely to bring you pleasure (it can be an upcoming holiday or a gathering of your group, for example); and blankets and pillows.

The Spell

Cast your circle. Sit while holding the memorabilia, and allow the feelings to come freely. Say aloud why you are sad. It's okay to cry, yell, or pound. Find a key phrase that expresses your grief and say it out loud, over and over. Now visualize yourself being held closely in the arms of the Mother Goddess, who rocks and comforts you. Swathe yourself in the blankets and pillows, and rock gently back and forth as you feel her warm embrace.

After a while, look at the memorabilia again, and recall that in the circle, all time is now. What you once had, you always have in your heart, as long as you don't shut it out. What you were given was real and helped mold your life, and can never be taken away as long as you remember and cherish it. Remember the good times, and when you are ready, thank the Lady that you had them.

Now bring out the object that reminds you of the coming event: a visit to a favorite friend or relative, a special holiday, or a conference that should be exciting. Remind yourself that life goes on, that there is still much to look forward to: this is only a tiny sample of the good times ahead for you. Ask the Mother Goddess to heal your pain. Open the circle, and go visit a friend.

Acting in Accord

After you have visited the friend, sit down and rethink your goals in life. Do not rush out to find or recapture what you miss or have lost, but focus a while on matters like your health, your career, and learning new skills. Be gentle with yourself, but not indulgent. Spend special time often with a variety of tried and true friends, or in a congenial group.

A Spell for Employment

Equipment

A lodestone, or a small but powerful magnet from a hardware store.

The Spell

Cast your circle. Holding the stone or magnet, imagine vividly the kind of job you want and the feelings you will have while working there. Do not imagine names, the appearance of the workplace, or other details that might limit your choices. Speak aloud the qualifications you have for holding such a job, and ask aloud that you find it within a certain number of days. Raise power and charge the stone by dancing or breathing. Ground the energy and open the circle. The following day, have the stone or magnet with you as you make six job contacts, and make precisely six contacts a day until you have the job you desire.

Acting in Accord

In making the job contacts, be sure you have a well-written résumé and appear at interviews neatly dressed, confident, and relaxed. Do not limit your possibilities to the classified ads; tell everyone you know that you are looking for employment, and ask them if they know of openings or leads. Also, call companies or organizations that you admire, where you believe you would enjoy working. Ask to speak to the personnel director about future possibilities with them, even if nothing is available right now. Call back at intervals. Consider jobs that fall outside the narrow field you've trained for; stay open, be curious—ask, ask, ask.

A Spell for a House Blessing

Equipment

Bells, light blue candles, ritual oil, a large quartz crystal, several pieces of onyx or obsidian, a few pieces of rose quartz (two for each door into the house), salt water, rosemary, magickal friends.

Before the Spell

"Weed" your belongings and give any excess away to charity, throw out the junk. Clean your yard, and make the house inviting to those you wish to welcome.

The Spell

This consists of three steps: cleansing, blessing, and sealing (protection). Assemble your group and attune, but do not cast the circle right away. Beginning at the heart of the house, where you have placed the large crystal, proceed deosil through every room and level, ringing the bells and asperging with salt water. At the heart, attune again; then go through the house a second time, this time with the candles, and sprinkle rosemary in every room. You may want to sing or chant a blessing rhyme, such as "Goddess, bless this house below; Hornéd God, bless this house above; keep it safe by day and night, fill it with your power and love." Then return to the heart, attune, and cast the circle. Seated, with linked hands, chant wordlessly (or use "Evohe" or "Mm"), and with a swelling, powerful circle of sound, expand the magick circle until it encloses all the house and grounds. Then proceed one last time, with ritual oil and stones. The large crystal stays at the heart of the house, where it has been charged by the chanting. An onyx or obsidian ward is placed over each door, and a Spirit-invoking pentagram is drawn with oil over every opening—door and window, fireplace or vent. Two rose quartz pieces are placed on either side of each door into the house. The group returns to the heart for singing and refreshments. Leave the circle up and expand it into the outer walls of the house.

Once the initial cleansing is done, merriment and humor are not out of place at a house blessing: they can set the tone for many happy times to come. If you want a chant or poem on the light side, then use this at some point in the process:

> "This home be safe from tigers wild,
> Here only tame things domiciled;
> No boggle, troll, nor grinch allowed,
> Nor motley mob nor creeping crowd.

Bless everything within these walls,

No matter if it sits or crawls.

Let mild weather be inside,

For those who 'neath this rooftree bide;

And too, if not enlightenment

Then pizza, love, and merriment.

And if these lines seem slightly odd,

Be glad at least they mostly rhyme."

Acting in Accord

Lock your house when you leave, keep your kitchen clean and your bed made, and burn incense once a week to purify your home. Repeat this spell as often as you need to.

A Spell for Love

Equipment

Two candles, one white, one in your favorite color; two candleholders; a rose-colored altar cloth; a piece of red chalk.

The Spell

Cast your circle. In the circle, ground and center. Meditate on all the preconceived ideas you have about the perfect partner. Maybe you have a particular candidate in mind for romance. Release the thought of that person (it would be most unethical to work magick to make a certain person love you; this would violate their free will and put you in jeopardy by the Law of Return). Release all notions of what your perfect lover will look like, or do for a career, or even sound like. These are externals, and if you cling to them, then you run the risk of overlooking your ideal mate simply because your conscious mind was focused on superficialities.

When your mind is clear and open, hold the candle of your favorite color: this represents you. Meditate, then speak aloud all the qualities and energies you are willing to bring to an intimate relationship, such as: "Honesty, daily expression of affection, good humor even in difficult times, and the ability to listen carefully and sensitively," and so on.

Replace that candle on the altar, and pick up the white one. This represents your ideal partner, whoever she or he may be. Speak aloud the essential qualities you desire in a mate, and ask Aphrodite to bring you together in this lifetime.

Then place the two candles in their holders at opposite ends of the altar. Draw a heart on the center with the red chalk, large enough for both candle holders. Each day thereafter, meditate on the perfect loving relationship for a few minutes, and move the two candles an inch closer together. If you started on the new moon, then by the full moon the candles should be touching in the center of the heart. When they meet, draw two more hearts around the first one, raise energy by singing your favorite love song (or singing along with a recording), and charge the candles. Keep the circle up throughout, letting yourself in and out by cutting a "gate" with your athame, and only take the circle down after the whole ritual is complete.

Acting in Accord

Keep your antennae out during the days this ritual continues. Mingle a lot, and open yourself to be more attentive, perceptive, and receptive than you normally are. Extend yourself to others with compliments, friendly conversation, and little kindnesses. Look at old friends and acquaintances with new eyes, and see whether dropping your preconceptions might allow old affections to blossom into a greater love.

A Spell for Prosperity

Equipment

Some money and/or pictures of cash, checks, and jewels to place on the altar (assuming you are working for material prosperity); drums.

The Spell

Please note that doing magick for wealth is not wrong or irreverent, always assuming that you use the wealth in positive ways. The money is placed on the altar not as an object of worship, but as a symbol to your Deep Mind of what you intend to obtain. You may wish to place a Goddess statue or other religious symbol behind the symbolic wealth as a reminder that money is not, after all, the ultimate in value.

Then proceed. Cast your circle. While standing up, drum and chant to raise power. Your chant can be something as simple as, "Wealth, wealth, come to me, I deserve prosperity." As the power moves toward its peak, imagine a huge transparent funnel over you and huge amounts of cash, checks, and other forms of wealth cascading down through it to pile up around you (or, at least, enough for your needs plus some to donate to worthy causes). Give thanks for the wealth you know to be headed your way, and open the circle.

Acting in Accord

Now is the time to seek a job if you don't have one, or ask for a raise, or a promotion, or look for a better-paying position. Consider new ventures, call in old debts, ask the counsel of friends and acquaintances who are financially successful. Open yourself to prosperity gained "with harm toward none, and for the greatest good of all." When prosperity begins to arrive, give some of it freely to worthy causes such as environmental organizations or charities, and invest some in solid enterprises that will multiply your investment. Always give thanks, and more than thanks.

A Spell for Safe Travel

Equipment

A piece of malachite or malachite jewelry and a map showing the route to your destination.

The Spell

Cast your circle. Invoke Mercury, god of travel, and Iris, the rainbow-messenger goddess, and ask them to guard you as you go. Sing or breathe to raise power, and charge the malachite. Then trace it along the route on the map, visualizing yourself traveling in comfort and safety; if you intend to stop along the way, pause there when the stone reaches that spot on the map. Otherwise, move it in a smooth, uninterrupted line. Carry the stone with you when you go, or place it in the vehicle. And as you travel, visualize a huge pentagram of white light, encircled, surrounding the car, plane, train, or ship in which you travel.

Acting in Accord

If you are driving, be sure your car is checked for safety before you leave. Get plenty of rest the night before, and stop occasionally along the way to stretch. Do not drive if you begin to get drowsy, and do not rely on candy, pop, or coffee to keep you going—they may perk you up temporarily, but the following plunge in your blood-sugar level can be dangerous.

A Spell for Self-Blessing

Equipment

A chalice of wine or pure water, a candle (white or pale blue), a little salt, and a beautiful, fresh rose.

The Spell

Cast your circle. This is adapted from one in *A Book of Pagan Rituals* by Herman Slater. Once the circle is cast and your favorite deities are invoked, sprinkle the salt on the floor or ground, and stand, skyclad, on it. Hold the candle for a few moments, feeling its warmth and comfort. Then take up the chalice, breathe deeply, and lift the chalice to the image of Goddess as you visualize her before you. Say the following aloud:

"Bless me, Mother, for I am your child."

Dip your fingers into the chalice and anoint your eyes, saying:

"Blessed be my eyes, that I may clearly see thy path before me."

Anoint your lips, saying:

"Blessed be my lips, that I may speak thy truth."

Anoint your breast, saying:

"Blessed be my breast, that I may love well and feel thy love for me."

Anoint your loins, saying:

"Blessed be my loins, which bring forth life and pleasure, as thou hast brought forth all creation to please thee."

Anoint your hands, saying:

"Blessed be my hands, that I may do thy work with strength and skill."

Anoint your feet, saying:

"Blessed be my feet, that I may ever walk in thy ways."

Present yourself with the rose, knowing that it is her gift of love and blessing to you.

Holding the rose, meditate quietly for a while, playing a CD of beautiful music if you wish. Close the circle quietly, with gratitude.

Acting in Accord

Take care of yourself, giving yourself as much respect and attention as you would your best friend. Allow yourself proper nutrition and enough rest and recreation. Dress more elegantly and carefully than usual, in some of your favorite clothes. Give yourself a special treat: a night out with friends, a small present, a trip to someplace you have always enjoyed. Consider whether there are parts of your life that make you bored or unhappy, and plan now to change them.

A Spell for Self-Confidence

Equipment

Four objects connected with your skills or successes (anything from bowling trophies to woodcarving tools to cookie cutters); red cloths for wall hangings and the altar; brass candlesticks with red candles; a large golden sun symbol, if you can make or find one; and red clothing for yourself.

The Spell

After the circle is cast, the quarters called and Deity invoked (almost any deities will do, but solar goddesses [Amaterasu Omikami, Bast, Arinna] and gods [Ra, Helios, Apollo] are especially appropriate), pick up the first of your success objects and face the east. Display it to the guardians of that quarter, and explain what it is and how it represents a success in your life. Say aloud, "I am confident!" Visualize the energy before you and inhale deeply, saying in a strong voice, "I have the power of Air!" Repeat the process in the south (Fire), the west (Water), and the north (Earth). Then stand in the center of the circle, surrounded by your power objects, and meditate on all that you have achieved in your life: the obstacles you have overcome, the goals you have attained. If you wish, play stirring music while you do this. Then lift your arms and say in a mighty voice, "I am Spirit!" Close the circle, giving thanks to the deities for their gift of confidence. Wear something red on your person for the next six days.

Acting in Accord

For several days, focus your energies on those areas where you already are successful and confident, and spend extra time with people who admire your competence. When you tackle a new project in an unfamiliar field, ask yourself what skills, knowledge, and techniques you bring to it from other areas in which you have already proven yourself.

A Spell for Self-Healing

Equipment

A cord to tie about your waist, a pair of scissors, and a large chalice of pure, cool water.

The Spell

Once the circle is cast, invoke a healer god (such as Aesclepius or Apollo) and a healer goddess (such as Brigit or Hygeia). Meditate for a while on the feelings you have about your illness or injury. Are you frustrated? Angry? Afraid? Concentrate all the negative feelings into the cord you are wearing about your waist. Whisper to yourself, "Peace and love and healing wait without." Then cut the cord and all it contains, and cast it away from you, shouting "I release all anger, fear, and frustration!" Sit quietly for several moments, inhaling peace and relaxation.

Then begin to remember how it felt to be healthy and strong. Keep breathing deeply. Cup your hands, and fill them with a ball of glowing rose-colored light, with all the health and strength you recall poured into it. Keep breathing health and healing into the ball until you can feel it tangibly in your hands. Slowly place the ball into the water in the chalice. Lift the chalice, saying: "Great God and Goddess, I release my illness (injury) and accept the blessings of healing you offer me." Drink all the water, feeling its energy pouring through every cell of your body. Open the circle and wash the scissors and chalice.

Acting in Accord

Get plenty of rest, pure water, natural foods, sunlight, and whatever mild exercise you can handle. Spend time with good friends and loved ones. Follow the counsel of a trusted healer or physician. Repeat the chalice spell, but during the rest of the time, focus your attention on creative projects that intrigue you. Think about the lessons you might have to learn from this experience, but do not dwell on them constantly. Trust your body and Younger Self to heal as soon as the time is right.

Techniques

The spells shown here include a smattering of various magickal techniques, but there are many more to choose from. Every magician eventually finds particular tools or specialties that become favorites. Each of these deserves a book to itself, and most of them have been dealt with at length by various authors. Here, I can simply list them and advise you to seek instruction from a reputable and experienced practitioner.

+ Words of power (affirmations, charms, incantations)
+ Candle magick
+ Trancework
+ Cord magick
+ Symbols, sigils, and images
+ Herbal magick
+ Thoughtforms
+ Auras and chakra work
+ Pathworking on the Tree of Life (Qabala)
+ Power animals, totems, and familiars
+ Gem and stone magick
+ Amulets and talismans
+ Runecraft
+ Tree lore and magick

- Dreamwork
- Oils and incenses
- Drumming
- Earth currents, ley lines, and dowsing
- Mudras or sacred gestures
- Sacred dance

Of course, the magickal systems of different cultures each have their own specialties.

You may be drawn to the tree magick of the Celts, Jungian-Senoi dreamwork, the Jivaro approach to power animals, Chinese feng shui (knowledge of Earth's power currents, directions, and spatial relationships), Norse runecraft, Zuni fetishes, or the Seneca method of stone divination.

Be careful, however, about mixing techniques from various systems: this is a challenge best suited to those who have a solid knowledge of the fundamentals and a strong magico-religious framework in which to fit the pieces. Most practitioners of magick begin by learning the skills special to their religious tradition, and after a few years' training begin to include or adapt compatible techniques from other systems.

To simply grab bits and pieces here and there, without understanding their origins or relating them to an overall model of reality or system of ethics, is to act like a crow snatching up any little shiny thing it encounters; at best you would have a jumble of odds and ends that you would not know how to use effectively. So it is worthwhile investing a great deal of time and effort in establishing a foundation before you reach too far afield for additional material.

There are many books full of spell "recipes," and these can be fun to explore. But when you read someone else's spell, even the ones above, always ask yourself three questions:

"Is it ethical?"

"Do I understand how it is meant to work, why it is organized as it is, and why it includes the things it does?"

"How could I adapt it to work better for me?"

Remember always that the magick is in the magician, not the spell. A well-constructed spell is a tool, period. When someone asks me whether a given spell is effective, my immediate response is: "For whom, in what circumstances?"

Exercises Toward Mastery

1: Practicing One Priority Spell

Choose three of the spells in this chapter that address your needs. Then pick the one that focuses on your greatest need, and perform the spell as written here. Make notes in your magickal journal afterward.

2: Adapting the Spell

Now go over the spell bit by bit, and recall how it felt. Rewrite the spell with changes, emphasizing the parts that felt powerful and dropping or replacing anything that did not feel powerful. Perform your new version of the spell, and again make notes in your magickal journal.

3: And Again

After you have the results you wish, choose another spell from this chapter that feels relevant to you. Perform it, make notes, revise it, and do the new version.

4: Your Own Spell Three Times

Now meditate on any changes you would like to make in yourself: your character, personality, habits, way of thinking, etc. Craft a spell from scratch to accomplish the desired change. Perform it and make your notes. Revise it and do it again. Improve it once more and perform it for a third time.

Blesséd be.

To follow this path further, read:

Spells and How They Work by Janet and Stewart Farrar (Robert Hale Ltd., 1990)

The Witches' Way: Principles, Rituals and Beliefs of Modern Witchcraft by Janet and Stewart Farrar (Robert Hale Ltd., 1984)

Everyday Magick and Daily Spiritual Practices

Is magick so special and wonderful, or so hazardous in the wrong hands, that it should be reserved for times of overwhelming need? Or is it all right to bring magick into everyday life and use it wherever it makes life a little easier? There are differing views on the appropriate uses of magick: some believe the Art is best saved for theurgy ("high" magick or spiritual work) or at least for formal ritual on special occasions. Others see no barrier to doing daily thaumaturgy ("low" or practical magick) for any purpose that does not cause harm to another.

I would support the latter view, partly because I think magick is the birthright of every human being, and partly because daily practice with magick, in small things, makes one that much more confident and skilled when it's time for a life-changing act of high magick. So here are some "little (but not necessarily trivial) magicks" for everyday use.

Daily Spiritual Practice

Many people set aside a little time each day to do something that helps them feel spiritually connected, more serene, or express appreciation for the blessings of their lives. Possibly your spiritual tradition has some customs, such as prayer; here are a few more ideas.

Ground and Center Each Morning

Begin and/or end your day by connecting with the earth that sustains us. You might take a short, quiet walk and just absorb the peace of nature, lose yourself in a photograph of a beautiful place you have visited, or hold a stone in both hands and feel its ancient strength.

Pick a Tarot Card/Animal Card/Goddess Card/Runestone

To get some idea of the "energies of the day," choose a single card or symbol-stone and meditate on it for a minute. Many tarot decks are available, and you should have no trouble finding one with art that appeals to you. You might prefer a deck with images of various goddesses, animals, trees, or flowers. You also could use stones with Norse runes or other magickal symbols carved or painted on them. You might be surprised how accurate these methods can be; look at the same card or stone at the end of the day, and you will usually be able to see how that energy was present.

Meditation

Meditation comes in many varieties, from focusing completely on one image, word, or chant to going on "journeys of the mind," such as Qabalistic pathworking meditations. Some are great for achieving calmness and others may lead to spiritual learning.

Visit Your Astral Temple

You can build a personal temple on the astral plane using visualization and focused energy. It can be small and simple, with a single room; or sprawling, complex, and diverse, with libraries, chapels, sanctuaries, and ceremonial chambers, plus gardens, fountains, pathways, and sacred groves. Visit it daily for healing, renewal, learning, to talk to deities or spirit guides, or just to be in a safe place.

Appreciation

Choose one person in your life, sit quietly, and visualize them. Mentally review everything that you like or admire about this person, send them some loving energy, and express your gratitude to your deity or simply to the universe for bringing that person into your life. Of course you can also give thanks for your home, career, health, or any other blessing you enjoy.

Grounding and Centering

Centering with Mass

When you are feeling scattered, jittery, and unfocused, take a walk outdoors and focus your attention on any large and massive object: a big tree, a building, a mountain. Inhale and take the object's mass into yourself through your eyes and breath. (However, if it is a building, be sure to take in only its mass and not the various human energies permeating it.) You will soon feel more calm and stable.

Instant Vacation

Another way to find tranquility is to sit in a quiet place where you won't be disturbed for a few minutes, and in your mind, visit a favorite spot that holds fond memories for you. This might be a lakeshore, a clearing in the forest where you once enjoyed a picnic, or a charming bed-and-breakfast where you stayed on your honeymoon. Re-create the experience of that place in as much detail as possible, and then inhale its energy with slow, deep breaths. Return when you are ready.

Your Secret Room

Visualize your life as a large house with many rooms: your home life, your work, your clubs or organizations, and so on. Now imagine a small, hidden room at the very heart of the house; no one knows that it exists, except you. It may be furnished with your favorite chair, your bed, and all the little things you need for a comfortable getaway: good books, a favorite game, whatever you want. As with the Instant Vacation, go to the room in your mind whenever you need a break.

Your Secret Garden

If you are a gardening type, or wish you were, imagine a nineteenth-century country estate with an ivy-covered wall behind the house. A big iron key is hidden nearby, and only you know where it is. It unlocks the old wooden door concealed behind the ivy, and on the other side lies a beautiful garden, half-wild, with all your favorite flowers. Enjoy this peaceful, lovely place.

Adding to Your Astral Temple

Expand this temple of your own on the astral plane (see above). Add a new room, garden, or pathway. Visit the temple for more extended meditations when you need healing or spiritual renewal.

Protective Spells

Caim of Brigit

Caim is an old Irish word for "charm" or "spell," and Brigit is (depending on your faith) either a Catholic saint or a Celtic goddess, who wore a magick cloak (mantle) of healing and protection. If you find yourself in a threatening situation, act quickly to move to a safer place, then visualize a ring of light around you and say: "Brigit spread above my head your mantle bright to guard me." Visualize her mantle protecting you.

Setting Wards

Wards are magickally charged objects that discourage people (or at least those with ill intent) from approaching the area. Stones, crystals, or crossed twigs are easy to find and work well; however, you could make a ward of your office door, a wastebasket, or almost anything else. Focus your desire onto the object (such as "Stop!" or "Turn aside!"), and then energize it with breathing, a chant, or any other means of raising power. It will need to be recharged occasionally, especially if it is organic (like wood or a plant).

"Invisibility"

While I don't know any magick that can make a person transparent, other magicks have the same practical effect. If you practice with your body's energy field, you can learn to draw your aura in close to your skin so you are not "radiating." (Most people subconsciously become aware of your energy field before they see your body.) For another approach, stand right next to a tree, touching it, then let your aura merge with the tree's energy field and allow your mind to go blank. You will seem like part of the tree to a casual passer-by.

"Slow Glass" Spell

Occasionally I run across an interesting idea in a work of fiction and find that a trained mind can use it as a magickal spell. This was adapted from a science fiction story. If you are approached by someone who is angry or difficult, visualize a sheet of "slow glass" between you. This is a transparent material that allows energy to pass through it, but very slowly. When the person begins to yell at you, make unreasonable demands, or whatever, you can see them normally but their energy does not hit you immediately. Their negativity trickles through slowly, giving you time to stay calm and come up with the best possible response. Better still, time is affected so that the other individual doesn't notice any important delay in your reaction. Take all the time you need, safe behind the glass, and then respond like a hero to handle the situation.

Quick Divination

Pendulum

You can train yourself to use radiesthesia (a divinatory technique that uses a pendulum) to answer "yes/no" questions. You can buy a pendulum at a metaphysical shop, or make your own from a fairly heavy bead and a piece of heavy thread or fine jewelry chain about eight inches long. Hold the thread about five inches from the bead; you may have to adjust up or down a little to get the best swing. Tell the pendulum, "Show me yes," and hold the thread lightly. After a moment, the bead should move, either deosil (clockwise), widdershins (counterclockwise), or in a straight line. Now ask the pendulum, "Show me no," and notice how it moves. With practice, you will be able to read its replies to your questions—and the replies will be amazingly accurate, if your questions are worded precisely.

Tarot Card Visualization

Ask a question: for example, "What kind of energies or situations am I likely to encounter today?" Now visualize yourself shuffling a tarot deck, with the different cards flipping rapidly past your gaze. In your mind, stop the deck, turn a card face up, and focus on the card that shows. This works best, of course, if you are very familiar with at least one tarot deck. For beginners, I suggest a fairly traditional deck such as the Rider-Waite, Morgan-Greer, Aquarian, Universal, or Yeager decks.

Rune Visualization

This is a similar technique, except that you visualize pulling a single rune-stone from a pouch. Again, you need to be familiar with all the runes in a particular system.

Travel Magick

Safety Check

If you carry a pendulum with you, it is possible to find out in advance whether your planned trip will work out safely. You can ask "yes/no" questions about the weather, driving conditions, or whether an airplane will reach its destination without any problems.

Circle of Protection

When you climb in your car, take a moment to say a little charm such as this: "Goddess (or the name of your deity), bless and protect all the parts of this vehicle that they work well and smoothly, give me a clear path as I travel, and grant that I may safely reach my destination. Circle of protection, one, two, three (visualize a clockwise circle of white light around the car three times), so mote it be!"

Stretching Gasoline

Occasionally you may find yourself driving along, miles from any service station, and suddenly realize that there's very little gasoline left in the tank. Don't panic—you can use mental magick to extend what's left and reach a service station easily. This does take concentration, but at the same time you must stay relaxed. Visualize your vehicle gliding along the highway with very little help from the engine, under perfect control but almost sliding without friction. Repeat some little mantra to yourself, such as "smooth and easy, floating, gliding . . ." Before you know it, you'll be at your destination or a service station with fuel to spare.

Dancing Deer Spell

A Faery friend once shared this custom. When you see a traffic sign that looks like a gold diamond with a leaping deer on it, point two fingers down and do a little can-can dance with them, imagining a row of deer doing the same. Hum can-can music: "DAH dah dah, dah dah dah dah DAH DAH . . . " You can do this with a serious purpose: to keep deer off the highway in front of your car. Broadcast a flashing beam of mental energy ahead of you as your fingers do the can-can, and visualize the deer dancing off the road and into the woods or fields. (I can't promise this works, but the only time we ever hit a deer—actually an elk, and no one was hurt much, the elk bounded away into the woods—we had not done the dancing deer spell beforehand.) Act in accord by installing deer whistles on your car, aligning your headlights, and driving safely.

Daily Theurgy

Listening to Your Intuition

Marion Weinstein calls it the "inner bell . . . the inner sense of truth . . . the inner knowing which exists deep within all of us."[1] It is knowledge and guidance that you already own subconsciously, but it only rises to the conscious level if you open your mind to it. I received a gentle lesson in this many

---

1   Marion Weinstein, *Positive Magic: Occult Self-Help* (Custer, WA: Phoenix Publishing, 1991), 11.

years ago, when I visited Churchill Downs racetrack in Kentucky. I am not a gambler, but wanted to place one bet just for the experience. I had a feeling that one particular horse might win, but I didn't have much confidence in my hunch and so I bet on the horse to "show" (come in either first, second, or third). Well, the horse won easily and I won $2—instead of the $11 that I might have, if I had honored my feeling and bet the animal to win. The horse's name was "Intuition."

Begin now to pay attention to your hunches, feelings, intuition, inner bell. At first it may not be easy to tell the difference between a genuine intuitive flash and, say, wishful thinking or groundless fears, but you can always check it with a pendulum or other form of divination. In time you will learn to trust the bell and rely on that guidance from deep inside you. In the beginning this will have very practical uses, like warning you to avoid a dangerous situation or take advantage of an opportunity. As you build trust in yourself, you will find your spiritual growth enhanced as well.

A Gift of Energy to Higher Self

Our Higher Selves do so much for us that we scarcely acknowledge: they offer guidance, protection, even help in making our dreams come true (if they are wise and beneficial dreams). They are like guardian angels, only more intimately part of us. From time to time, raise some energy and just send it to your Higher Self as a gift. No strings, no begging for anything, just a gift. You can dance, drum, chant, or just take a few deep breaths—then, asking Younger Self to help, picture Higher Self (perhaps as a glowing, angelic couple floating above you) and lovingly channel the power to them. Who knows—it may return, magnified, in a wonderful new form.

Help Is At Hand

The next time you find yourself in a stressful, difficult, or even dangerous situation, simply visualize your animal spirit or ally, spirit guide, or favorite archangel (or any other spirit being who seems appropriate) standing behind you, glowing with power. That should give you an extra boost of confidence for handling the situation.

Deity at Your Back

If you pursue your spiritual studies in a certain direction, in time you will be able to host a god or goddess aspect within you; it is much like channeling a spirit guide, but with Deity it is called aspecting, assuming the godform, or Drawing Down the Moon. However, you don't have to master that advanced form of theurgy in order to get some divine help. If you find yourself in the kind of challenging situation mentioned above, visualize your favorite deity behind you (instead of an animal ally or angel), about ten feet tall, ready to support you.

Magick to Sacralize the World

Random Blessings

What if you were to write short blessings on bits of attractive paper, roll them, tie a colored ribbon around each, and carry them with you? What if, whenever you saw someone who seemed worried, tense, or sad, you handed them one, with a smile? Or what if you simply left one in a restaurant or public library to be found by whomever needs it?

Roadside Altars

If you find a beautiful spot by the side of the road or hiking trail, you might create a small altar using natural materials: pretty stones, a simple arrangement of dried weeds and wildflowers, a pattern of pebbles or pine cones. This says to spirits of the place and other travelers, "I was here and shared the beauty of this place."

Animal Souls

When my partner and I see animals on the road that have been killed by traffic, we scoop up their spirits and offer them to Goddess, saying: "Goddess, please take to yourself the soul of this creature; bless it, protect it, love and heal it, and keep it with you in Summerland until it is time to be reborn." Along with the words, we visualize the creature whole and well on the higher plane, being welcomed by Deity. For safety, if you are driving, wait until the road is clear or you are out of heavy traffic before you do this.

A Gift of Serenity

If you have any skill at energy work, and you see a friend who looks frazzled, offer to "comb out" their aura. If they agree, then calm and smooth their energy field, healing any weak spots and removing negative energy that doesn't belong there. If you can carry a tune, hum or sing as you work.

Energy for Plant and Animal Companions

Draw a little energy up from the earth, and share it with an animal friend or a plant in your home or garden. Gentle touching or stroking is the best way to transfer the energy.

Odds and Ends

Psychic Shield

Remember that pain, exhaustion, hunger, thirst, negative emotions, and drugs can all weaken your energy field. A psychic shield will only help temporarily if you are suffering from any of these, so take care of your physical and emotional needs as soon as possible.

Meanwhile, you can protect yourself from negative or distracting energies by psychically reinforcing your overall energy field. Inhaling deeply, draw energy down from the sky and up from the earth simultaneously. Allow the energies to meet at your solar plexus (right under your rib cage), and then flow out to your energy field. Visualize the field as a glowing layer all around your body; as new energy enters it from within you, see it strengthening and expanding. If it initially feels as though it is only a thin layer over your skin, see it thickening and moving outward as it grows stronger and brighter.

Now visualize the surface of your energy field becoming a silvery mirror that reflects anything you would not wish to enter your space. However, know that it is a semi-permeable membrane; light, love, and any positive energy can pass easily through it, into your body.

If you wish, you may also call upon your special deity, animal ally, guardian angel, or spirit guide to lend their protection and remind you when your energy field needs another boost.

Elemental Sweep

Once you are familiar with the energies of Earth, Air, Fire, and Water, you can do a mental scan of each one—in yourself, in a group that you are part of, or in your surroundings (home, workplace, public places). If you are un-balanced, breathe in more of the element you need and exhale excess energy you don't want right now. If it is your group that is off-balance, you can evoke the element needed silently or by carefully slanting your words, tone of voice, and body language. (Of course, in a coven or magickal group you need not be subtle; just say, "Hey! Anyone notice that we need some Fire energy?") At home, if the energies are out of whack, some feng shui work may be called for. In public, you may just put up a psychic shield so that the imbalance doesn't affect you.

Condensing and Stretching Time

We have all had the experience of time changing its pace, either crawling slowly during a dull day at work or flying by too quickly when we're having fun. Well, you can intentionally change the pace of time with mind magick. If you want time to speed up, you can focus your attention inward; for exam-ple, by creating a poem or organizing a project in your head. An outer focus that is very narrow, such as creating artwork or a finicky craft project, will also work well. To slow time, focus outside your mind and broadly. Watch the landscape, people-watch, gaze at the stars. If you think of your mind as a camera lens and practice focusing out and in, wide and narrow, you can change time rather dramatically.

Money Magick

There is nothing wrong in wanting, having, or spending money, as long as it's for a worthy purpose and doesn't harm others or yourself—so do that wealth magick. A sample prosperity spell is provided in the previous chap-ter, but you can do a quick visualization at any time. In your mind's eye, see yourself glowing with energy, a magnetic force that is drawing wealth to you; see smiling people handing you cash, checks arriving in the mail, your retirement fund blossoming, and so on. Always end with a spoken condition, such as: "With harm toward none and for the greatest good of all, so mote it be!"

Raising Energy Quickly

Sometimes you need power fast in an emergency. You can train yourself to boost your accessible energy in seconds. The Air energy all around us is usually the easiest to tap quickly, though there is some individual variation. Certain people may be able to tap Fire rapidly, especially if the sun is shining, and a few can access Water best, particularly if there is a lake, stream, or ocean nearby. For Air, say to yourself, "Powers of Air, sudden winds, come to my call!" At the same time, visualize a shining swirl of energy flowing toward you and coalescing around you. Now inhale deeply with an abdominal breath, and pull the power in through your solar plexus. Repeat until you feel yourself filled with vibrant power (but pause if you start to become lightheaded). Use the energy as needed, and immediately afterward earth the excess energy very carefully, rest, and eat if you haven't recently. Earth energy is usually slower and calming, so is not often called on for this purpose.

Appreciation (of Objects)

Here's another one from a fiction novel. Sometimes an inanimate object doesn't cooperate, like the lid of a jar that seems to be waiting for Godzilla to open it, or a key that jams in your front door or car ignition. Don't get mad, get . . . appreciative. Contemplate the gizmo fondly. Speak to it softly. Thank it for doing its job so well, and quietly explain that it has fulfilled that half of its mission and the other half is to release or open, so it may now relax, release, let go (or whatever). Take a deep breath, smile, and try again. When the lid opens easily or the key works smoothly, thank it one more time. This can also work for starting cars that seem dead.

Tree Shadow Decision-Making

Use this technique (described on page 164) to help in making particularly difficult decisions.

Portable Ritual Tools

You can carry all sorts of simple ritual tools with you, either by wearing them or carrying them in a pocket, purse, or glove compartment. Here's a starting list:

Magickal Jewelry

All your jewelry can have spiritual or magickal significance. The material (specific metals or gemstones, for example) can represent certain qualities and be charged to serve as a talisman or amulet. For example, an amethyst ring or pendant traditionally will help you with issues of moderation or abstinence, especially if charged in a ritual. To most observers, it's just attractive jewelry, but for you, it's a ritual tool.

Traveling Pendulum

Many people like to carry their favorite pendulum in a small cloth or leather pouch. You can also use a pendant on a thin chain or a ring on a thread as a pendulum.

Pocket Stone

You might carry a stone for its special energy in your pocket, purse, fanny pack, or book bag. I like pyrite or petrified wood for grounding, amber or carnelian for most healing, tiger iron for stamina, amethyst for self-control, turquoise for cheer and happiness, rose quartz for blessing, jade for wisdom and being centered, and black onyx for serious protection.

Healing Crystals

If you are an energy healer or are training to be one, you may want to carry a quartz crystal point with you for use in diagnosis or energy channeling.

Small Wand

Although traditional wands are fairly long, one that is about six inches long will fit in most purses, or an even longer one will fit in a briefcase or backpack. However, most magicians find it more useful to use a virtual wand in public, if one is needed at all.

Piece of Cord

A nice cord about one-eighth inch in diameter and eighteen inches long will serve for most knot magick or simple binding spells.

Mini Tarot Deck

A few decks, notably the Rider-Waite, are manufactured in very small sizes (two inches tall or less); some are small enough to fit on a key ring.

Pouch of Runestones

Though actual stones can be awkward to carry, you can make a lighter set by inscribing a set of runes on small wooden plaques or chips by using paint or a wood-burning tool. Cross-sections of a small, dead tree branch will work.

Spell Serpent

This is our tradition's name for a sort of Pagan rosary that has beads of different sizes, shapes, and colors to represent the steps of spells or meditations. The beads can stand for the triple goddess, the five elements, the seven main chakras, the sephiroth of the Qabalistic Tree of Life, the deities in your favorite pantheon, the tarot major arcana, or whatever you wish.

Travel Altar

If you like having a complete altar when you journey away from home, you can easily assemble a set of small ritual tools in a compact box to carry in your vehicle, suitcase, or backpack. You might want an altar cloth, such as a silk scarf; tiny candles and holders; a miniature pentacle; a cordial glass or tiny goblet to serve as a chalice; a smallish wand; a short-bladed athame; little statues of your patron deities . . . and any other tools you use often.

Many people wall off their magick (and sometimes their spirituality) into little compartments of their lives. For them, magick is for scheduled rituals at certain phases of the moon or for cases of extreme need. Religion is dusted off at regular weekly services or on set holy days.

I have never been comfortable with that approach to life. It seems to me that magick and Spirit permeate the universe everywhere, all the time, and that we are either attuned to that or resisting it. Being spiritually aware part-time, or being an occasional magician, seems to me like deciding that you will be healthy only when you visit the gym or happy only during scheduled recreation time. Health and happiness are not events but lifestyles, and if you want to be adept at magick, there is no better way to grow in skill than to make it your lifestyle as well.

So why not make magick a way of life, intertwined with spirituality and everything you do? That means finding magickal ways to see or do as many of the normal activities of life as possible; and if that makes you a kitchen witch, maybe you will find that's a very fulfilling way to live.

Exercises Toward Mastery

1: One at a Time

Pick just one magickal technique from this chapter, and try it every day for one week. That should be enough of a trial run to tell whether you like it and find it useful. Then either add it to your daily practice or file it away in your mind in case it is helpful someday. Choose another technique and try that for a week.

2: The Butterfly Approach

If that feels too slow and stodgy to you, then do one of the techniques every day until you have tried them all. Keep your magickal journal on hand, and make notes about each one: did it work, was it easy or difficult, did it feel potentially powerful or not, would it serve you better with a change of some kind? After you've sampled them all, go back and practice more with your favorites or those that felt like they had the most potential.

3: Carry One Tool

Choose one portable tool from the list near the end of the chapter; carry it with you for a month and use it as often as it occurs to you. If it comes in handy a few times, either continue to carry it or experiment with using the virtual version of the same tool in your mind. If you never use it, choose another tool and try that.

Blesséd be.

To follow this path further, read:

Wheel of the Year: Living the Magical Life by Pauline and Dan Campanelli (Llewellyn Publications, 1989)

Cunningham's Encyclopedia of Crystal, Gem, & Metal Magic by Scott Cunningham (Llewellyn Publications, 1988)

Magickal Herbalism by Scott Cunningham (Llewellyn Publications, 1982)

The Magickal Household: Empower Your Home With Love, Protection, Health, and Happiness by Scott Cunningham and David Harrington (Llewellyn Publications, 1983)

Natural Gardening: A Nature Company Guide by Jim Knopf (Time-Life Books, 1995)

Sacred Space: Clearing and Enhancing the Energy of Your Home by Denise Linn (Random House, 1995)

Essential Feng Shui: A Step-by-Step Guide to Enhancing Your Relationships, Health, and Prosperity by Lillian Too (Rider, 1998)

A Charmed Life: Celebrating Wicca Every Day by Patricia Telesco (New Page Books, 2000)

A Witch's Beverages and Brews: Magick Potions Made Easy by Patricia Telesco (New Page Books, 2001)

Your Magickal Education Continues

$\mathscr{P}$erhaps you are already receiving guidance in your magickal studies, and this book is simply a supplement to your work. If so, excellent! Perhaps, however, you are working by yourself and have no contact with teachers or teaching groups near you. Of course, it is possible to develop some skill in magick on your own, especially if you are careful and diligent. But if you work with an ethical and experienced teacher, and especially within a group, your progress will be swifter and more sure.

How can you find a teacher, assuming you want to continue in magick at all? You might begin with a ritual: ask your deities or spirit guides for help, meditate on the qualities you seek in a teacher, and charge a lodestone or talisman to draw the appropriate one into your life.

Contact Points

Then, act in accord on the material plane by reaching out. Here are some potential contact points:

Spiritual/Religious Networks

For those interested in Wicca, there is the Covenant of the Goddess (www. cog.org or Box 1226, Berkeley, CA 94704), which can offer referrals to covens in many areas, including some outside the United States.

An international organization of Goddess-oriented folk is the Fellowship of Isis (Clonegal Castle, Enniscorthy, Eire, or P. O. Box 19152, Tucson, AZ 85731; the website is at www.fellowshipofisis.com).

For Pagans, there is the Pagan Spirit Alliance (c/o Circle, Box 219, Mt. Horeb, WI 53572).

And for Pagan women, write to Of A Like Mind (c/o R. C. G., Box 6021, Madison, WI 53716).

Newsletters and Periodicals

Many of these are oriented toward Pagans and other magickal folk. In them, you may read about groups or individuals near you, especially in the classified ad or "contact" sections. Or you may want to place an ad, such as:

> "NEW TO MAGICK, seek instruction from an ethical and experienced teacher or group in the area; especially interested in [Wicca, herbal magick, shamanism, whatever]. Please contact Sue, Box xx, this city, state, zip."

Many newsletters are listed in the *Guide to Pagan Resources*, published by Circle (see address last section), which also publishes *Circle Network News* quarterly.

Festivals

Every summer, in most regions of the United States and in some other countries, Pagans gather to share, network, celebrate, and learn. Most of these events include workshops in which you can check out various teachers and topics, as well as rituals, the barter and sale of magickally oriented crafts, drumming and dancing around a fire, and more. Most newsletters or magazines published for Pagans include a calendar of events that lists the major festivals; also look for information at metaphysical bookstores and at the Witchvox website online (www.witchvox.com). Though designed mainly for those of nature-oriented religions, most festivals are open to folk of other spiritual paths, so long as they are friendly and courteous.

Bookstores

Many cities have bookstores or supply shops that can be characterized as "metaphysical," "occult," "New Age," or "alternative spirituality." Watch their bulletin boards for notices of classes, workshops, or organizational contacts. If you sense that it is appropriate, ask the owners or clerks if they can refer you to teachers.

Internet Contacts

There are thousands, if not millions, of resources on the worldwide web: magickal lodges, covens, metaphysical schools, religious associations, and authors of magickal books all have websites. For those seeking Wiccan or Pagan teachers, Witchvox is a great place to start: it lists groups, festivals, and other resources state-by-state. If you have a specific interest, such as Christian magick, runes, or Golden Dawn teachings, you will need to do a search and keep narrowing or refining it until you have some likely possibilities.

Schools That Teach Magick

Spiritual/Metaphysical Schools and Seminaries

Programs exist that teach magick face-to-face, usually as part of training for the priesthood in various spiritual traditions. Most have occasional weekend seminars geared for the schedules of busy adults with jobs; some are a mixture of independent study with a mentor and occasional seminars at a main campus or satellite center. Some of the more prominent Pagan institutions include:

> **Ardantane:** A school for all positive Pagan traditions, with weekend intensives and certificate programs in Magickal Arts, Shamanic Studies, Healing Arts, Witchcraft, Pagan Leadership, and Sacred Living. Most programs are on-campus, though faculty can travel to present weekend programs for groups nationwide. Ardantane, P. O. Box 307, Jemez Springs, NM 87025. Website www.ardantane.org. E-mail Registrar@ardantane.org. No correspondence or Internet courses (yet).

Cherry Hill Seminary: Professional Pagan ministry education, with programs in Public Ministry and Pagan Pastoral Counseling. Mostly online classes, with some intensives required at the campus. Cherry Hill Seminary, 307 Christian Hill Road, Bethel, VT 05032. Tel. 802-234-6420. Website www.cherryhillseminary.org. E-mail dean@cherryhillseminary.org.

Circle Sanctuary: Circle Ministers' Training Program and study circles (Shamanic, Craftway, Goddess), primarily at the sanctuary. Circle Sanctuary, P. O. Box 9, Barneveld, WI 53507. Tel. 608-924-2216. Website www.circlesanctuary.org. E-mail events@circlesanctuary.org.

Grey School of Wizardry: An online school of wizardry and magickal teachings at an apprenticeship level, designed primarily for ages 11–18 (middle through high school), though many adults enjoy the program. The school focuses on magic rather than spirituality, and has sixteen departments, each with its own dean, professors, and classes. Website www.GreySchool.com.

Women's Thealogical Institute: Affiliated with Re-formed Congregation of the Goddess. Cella priestess training, Crone (women over 53) and Guardian (Amazon spirituality) programs. Classes at main center and seven regional centers. WTI/RCG-1, P. O. Box 6677, Madison, WI 53716. Tel. 608-226-9998. Website www.rcgi.org. E-mail rcgi@rcgi.org.

Woolston-Steen Theological School: Affiliated with Aquarian Tabernacle Church. Degrees in Wiccan ministry, primarily ATC Tradition, but open to other Pagans and Wiccans. Woolston-Steen, P. O. Box 409, Index, WA 98256-0409. Tel. 360-793-1945. Website www.wiccanseminary.edu. E-mail Seminary@AquaTabCh.org.

Correspondence Schools

Several individuals and organizations offer instruction by mail in magick, Wicca, or Goddess spirituality. While learning by mail is far from ideal, it can be a helpful method for those living in small towns or rural areas with no groups nearby, or for anyone who has not found instruction locally in a particular specialized field.

Most correspondence teachers make a sincere effort, organize their programs carefully, and follow ethical paths. A few have serious shortcomings: for example, it is wise to avoid schools which advertise their subject as a means to wealth, romance, and the domination of others. Some even misuse the words "Wicca" or "Witchcraft" and teach hexes, curses, and manipulative magick rather than an ethical spiritual path or magickal system.

Others are not as morally flawed, but teach general information available in books everywhere. In these cases you are paying for the accessibility of the teacher in answering written questions that come up as you work. If the teacher is responsive and knowledgeable, the course may be worthwhile even if the printed lessons are lackluster.

One excellent correspondence course is offered by the College of the Crossroads, www.collegeofthecrossroads.org.

Internet Educational Programs

Web-based classes are appearing more and more frequently, such as those offered by Cherry Hill Seminary or the Grey School of Wizardry. Some of the others are sincere and well-organized programs, others are amateurish but free, and a few are in it just for the money. Do not sign up for anything that charges hefty fees unless you can find some very good references vouching for the program's value.

Evaluating Teachers

There are teachers, and then there are teachers. Some are ignorant, greedy, or corrupt. Others are highly evolved magickal beings full of wisdom, love, and power. Most are somewhere in between, having the common flaws of humanity but doing their best to teach what they know.

How can you tell whether a teacher is worth studying with? Begin by letting go of preconceptions of age, sex, race, or mannerisms. Thanks to the conditioning of fantasy novels, motion pictures, and the patriarchy, most of us carry around a stereotype of a magickal adept as an old man with a flowing white beard, a sonorous voice, and rune-covered robes; usually he is also tall, thin, and white (think Albus Dumbledore).

In fact, competent magickal teachers come in both sexes and many colors, shapes, and sizes. Occasionally they are quite young in years, but have recovered much knowledge and wisdom from earlier lifetimes as an adept. But I wish particularly to emphasize how many women today are magickal and spiritual teachers in America and in some other continents. We are a strong majority in Wicca, for example, and our psychic and magickal heritage is blossoming again after centuries of suppression.

You may wish to look for a teacher who:

- approaches magick from an ethical and spiritual perspective (possibly a priestess or priest in a religion you find compatible with your own beliefs);
- encourages the use of magick for healing and self-knowledge;
- is filled with serenity, joy, and love much of the time;
- is attentive to the special needs and strengths of each student;
- honors each student, respecting their dignity, worth, and experience;
- encourages hard questions and free discussion;
- insists on experiential exercises and constant practice, and mastering skills instead of merely wading in theory;
- freely networks and shares with others outside the group, and encourages students to do likewise; and
- has a great deal of knowledge and experience, and can refer students to resources in fields outside their expertise.

Are there certain kinds of teachers to avoid? Most of us would not wish to study with an individual who:

- uses magick to dominate, manipulate, or curse others;
- emphasizes wealth, luxury, and material possessions over spiritual growth and harmony;

- treats students as servants or inferiors to boost an inflated ego;
- demands control of students' personal lives, sexual favors, or exorbitant amounts of money in return for teaching;
- is unable or unwilling to interact freely with other practitioners of magick;
- is filled with anger, pain, hatred, bitterness, or cynicism;
- seems more willing to discuss their own powers and exploits than to actually help students develop their own strengths;
- insists that the use of addictive drugs is an appropriate path to power or fulfillment; or
- becomes impatient or obscure when faced with hard questions.

Unfortunately, there are a few unscrupulous occult "teachers" who project an air of mystery and power, and draw naive seekers into their orbit to be used and fleeced. If you ever encounter such a one, get away as fast as you can and sever all contact. If they try to force you to stay or return by threatening magickal curses against you, do not give in: you can shield yourself from magickal attack, and if they try it, then they will suffer the consequences of the Law of Return. Stay away, surround yourself with white light, and focus on developing your own spiritual strength.

The Question of Fees

Should you expect to pay for instruction in magick? If Wicca is the spiritual path you are exploring and you begin training with a coven, you should not expect to pay for teaching (minimal dues for ritual supplies or photocopies of handouts are another matter). On the other hand, if you sign up for a correspondence course or perhaps a workshop on tarot that is open to the public, you will generally pay a modest fee.

Sometimes it is difficult to say what is appropriate, because there are questions of motivation and accessibility. If a teacher teaches so as to get rich rather than to impart knowledge, the teaching will be tainted. And if a fee is so high that some people are excluded, say, from learning about the spiritual aspects of magick, that is not right. If a fee is charged and you are unsure whether it is appropriate, talk it over with the teacher—then follow your inner guidance.

If no fee is charged, yet your teacher generously shares knowledge with you, then consider making a free-will donation. Even magicians and priestesses usually need to eat.

Learning Magick from Books

Books are an important resource, if carefully chosen. A list of recommended works is included in appendix IV. Most of them are currently in print, so any bookstore should be able to order them for you, or your library can obtain them through interlibrary loan. Also, mail-order suppliers of occult books frequently advertise in the major Pagan periodicals. Write and ask them for their catalogs.

In shopping for books, avoid anything full of hexes, curses, or spells to compel others. Nor should you invest much in magickal "recipe books," which imply that you can get great results simply by burying three beans and reciting a couplet at the new moon. Books that explain how magick works and give exercises to help you develop new skills and disciplines are far more valuable than those that imply magick is supernatural or easy.

In building your magickal library, it might be wise to focus at first on really good books about one system or path: shamanism, Western ceremonial magick, the Qabala, Wicca and nature magick, Huna, or whatever approach strikes a deep chord within you. The alternative—picking up a variety of books on every conceivable facet of magick as you run across them—is tempting but can get very confusing. Focus on one aspect or system until you are well grounded in it, then move on.

When you are considering any given book, learn as much as possible about the author. Have they had extensive experience in the field covered, or is this a popular writer or hack journalist doing some superficial or sensational reporting? To take "Witchcraft" books as an example—I have read some written by crusading clergymen who knew nothing about the Craft but had a theological axe to grind, and others written by non-Wiccans who breathlessly promise to "reveal the secrets of witchcraft" and gain the reader instant wealth, power, and love. Others merely seek to titillate readers with an unrelated hodge-podge of magickal spells, medieval tortures, demons, devil worshipers, and hints of naked orgies. Such books are not worth the time of any serious seeker. Look for books by respected priestesses, priests, and magicians who have some stature in the magickal community, or classics which have stood the test of time.

Learning from Nature

Perhaps the greatest teacher of all is nature, the source of all magickal power. A day outdoors puts things in perspective, sorts the true from the false and the important from the trivial, and cleanses the spirit. Without the counsel of nature, a magician may turn fanatic, "redoubling his efforts when he has forgotten his aim." With it, we remember who we are and what magick is for.

So give yourself a gift of contact with nature often. Walk in the woods; closely observe the different herbs and trees and the signs of animals. Stroll on the beach or lakeshore, and see what treasures the tide has swept up at your feet. Seek out caves and experience their silent mystery. Climb a rugged cliff and watch hawks soar over the roof of the world. Explore the life of the marshes, meditate on an Indian mound, touch the tiny wildflowers on a mountain meadow.

Such activities are not to be rushed: they are not "time away from" your important tasks. They are important in themselves: important to your growth as a magician and as a human being living on this planet. And though you may come back from your expeditions with nothing more tangible to show than a dried wildflower or an agate pebble, what you carry in your heart will be a far greater treasure than anything you carry in your hands. In fact, when I think of the most magickal moments of my life so far, few occurred at indoor rituals. My most magickal experiences were where the spirits of nature taught me what I could never have learned within walls.

Among the first I remember: I was eight or nine years old and lived in a big house with several great old oaks around it. These were more than "just trees," they were Strength, and Solidity, and they held in their wood a hundred summer suns and winter snowstorms. The house stood in front of one especially vast Grandfather of Oaks, whose branches shaded the entire back yard, as well as my bedroom window on the second floor. At night the moon goddess rose and shone through his vast crown of dark and rustling leaves, creating patterns of light and shadow on the walls of my room. I felt a holy presence then: I knew that at night the theologies of men were tucked away and the church doors safely locked, but the powers of nature lived and moved in the darkness still.

My favorite tree was a huge and ancient Great Grandmother of Willows. In size she rivaled the oaks of Sherwood Forest that I encountered years later, where Robin Hood could hide his whole band in a single tree. The lane before our house twisted agilely to miss the tree (who had claimed her place generations before the old lane came to be) and passed inches from her trunk. A child could, with a boost, shinny through a crevice where two of her mighty limbs crossed and nestle in a large cup surrounded by them. Occasionally a car wound along the lane and passed below, its driver oblivious to the hidden, watching child overhead. There I began to absorb some of the peace and long perspective of the willow, who was immersed in the experience of being—her rugged roots drinking cool water from the rich, moist soil, her enormous crown of withies soaring to dizzying, windswept heights in the sun-filled sky. My endless summer hours in her branches were just a flicker in the venerable story of her existence, yet I felt more a part of her than kin to the drivers in their closed machines beneath us.

Years later, I walked the beach of Puget Sound at a Pagan festival in the state of Washington. The sky was gray, the waters rough and choppy, and a fine, cool mist hid the farther shore. I watched the dark heads of seals bobbing and could feel the cold water sliding over me, the dark depths beneath, the stormy skies above; the wildness in my soul. The sensations spoke to the Dolphin Spirit within me, and I knew the kinship of the ocean mammals. When I returned to the beach, I discovered wonderful stones at my feet: some pale green, some the milky white of foam, and some patched black and white, which I named "orca stones" after the whales that range these waters. The power of the sea and shore was in the stones, and some returned home with me. They are the bones of our Sea Mother.

Once I sought bones of another kind on the hills and high plateaus of Colorado, in the Morrison Formation. Two hundred million years ago and more, dinosaurs walked here, and their bones encrust these dry slopes. I dug for their bones, but most that I found were black, rotten and crumbling—more like charcoal than ivory. Squatting there in the sun in those bleak hills, what was I really digging for? I had no need of bones. No, I was seeking a talisman of sorts, a magickal link that could enable me to reach across eons and understand a creature very different from my species—yet perhaps ancestral to it in a sense. I could not stretch that far that day; I found more magick in the wind and sun and solitude than I ever did in the fragments of bone.

Sometimes there is more mystery in the ancient places of humankind than in the immeasurably older relics of an extinct species. There is a mesa in the mountains of northern New Mexico, only minutes' walk from a tract of modern homes. There is one trail onto the mesa, along a steep and narrow spine of rock; the path has been worn three feet deep in places by the sandals of the Ancestral Puebloan peoples who once lived a mile or two away. Their potshards litter the valley floor; their dwellings pock the cliff faces not far from here—but on the mesa are no shards, no petroglyphs, no single stone set upon another as a sign that this place was known and used. Only the deep grooves in solid rock, worn by thousands and thousands of feet passing over many generations. A ritual site perhaps, but one that demanded neither altar nor temple. Here I found a glimpse of the magick of living lightly on the earth, strange to a daughter of a race of engineers and city-builders. The Ancestral Puebloans are not so distant from us as measured by the span of Earth's life, and perhaps their hopes and fears were not so different from ours, yet they created a wholly other way of life . . . and if we could but see the world through their eyes, that magick might spell survival for our species.

That silent mesa in the Jemez Mountains may have been a special place of power for the ancient Puebloans; Greywethers in England certainly is a place of power even today. I visited Dartmoor, where Greywethers is located, because of its wild and lonely beauty, and because a Bronze Age culture had flourished here four thousand years ago. I had been hitchhiking through Europe with a friend, who chose to spend several days in London. I preferred to walk the moors. Dartmoor is a rolling, heathery land, inhabited now by a few wild ponies and the stone remains of long ago. Here a stone "clapper bridge" crosses the River Dart; there a beehive-shaped hut has endured long past its memories and drowses empty in the summer's warmth. No one knows much of the people who lived here, not their legends nor songs nor the names of their gods. But we know that they understood the energies and currents of the earth, and apparently could shape and direct them in ways we no longer know. Greywethers consists of a pair of large stone circles that intersect or touch at one point; the stones are evenly spaced several feet apart, but they are not as tall as the great stones of Stonehenge, nor are they shaped. I first saw them as I trudged up a long slope; as they came into view at the top of a ridge, they, rather than I, seemed to be marching and bobbing rhythmically over the rise in time with my steps. As they appeared and I drew close, thunderheads swept in from the sea, and the sky grew dark. Thunder rolled; I kept walking. As I set foot between the stones, the clouds opened and a deluge engulfed the moors. I had miles to go before I could expect to find shelter, so I kept moving, across the first ring and then the second. About me was a sense of limitless power, concentrated and shaped and well-nigh eternal. As I stepped from the second circle on the far side, the rain abruptly stopped; and as I swung away down the side of the ridge, the clouds moved off and the sun reappeared.

There is power on the earth and in it. You can feel it in caves, the wombs of the Mother from which are born silence and patience. With my coven I have climbed and crawled into a long and rough and wet tunnel, and found a deep chamber lined with clay. We sat in the dimness of our lights and fashioned earth goddesses, speaking softly and sometimes chanting low songs to her, there at the end of a long journey. Or was it the end? There was a place back there . . . and just around there . . . through which one might just slither further into the darkness, if one had strength enough and courage. Cave tunnels twist and turn, stop suddenly and then offer an unexpected crevice meandering off in another direction. They are as surprising and unpredictable as life is, but with an underlying logic and pattern that speleologists are just beginning to appreciate. And often, beauty. We can look and murmur at cave formations, at towering columns and creamy stalactites, at sheets of sparkling flowstone and delicate gypsum flowers; our glimpses are snapshots of a process that has been happening for echoing millennia. I have seen the looming pinnacles of cave onyx, but I have also seen incredibly tiny crystals of calcite forming within a single drop of water—the crystals that built that magnificence. She is so patient to build such enduring beauty from such tiny tools; one drop of water, one fragile crystal at a time over the ages. We can learn from this magick.

Practice and Experimentation

Whether you learn from human teachers or from nature, from books or past-life memories of magick worked long ago, effectiveness will come with repeated practice and careful experimentation.

If you are working with a group under the guidance of an experienced teacher, then you will doubtless build a foundation of basic skills and then move on to more unusual and challenging magick. One day you might find yourself investigating the effects of ritual drumming patterns on the human nervous system, or working to contact cetacean intelligences, or searching out past-life connections in ancient civilizations, or exploring the astrological energies of the outer planets, or redesigning the tarot as a transformational and healing tool.

If you are working basically alone, or perhaps trading ideas and experiences with a magickal pen pal, then you should proceed slowly and focus on foundational skills: grounding and centering, concentration, casting the circle, raising power by various methods, and spellcasting. In addition, divination provides a huge and fascinating field of study: look into tarot, I Ching, runes, astrology, and so on, and choose one to explore more fully.

There are other forms of magick and psychic activity that are best avoided by the beginner, at least until you have the support of friends and teachers as well as some experience in the basics. Do not attempt advanced forms of raising power (such as kundalini yoga) that are likely to have a major impact on your energy field or heartbeat; indeed, do not try to tamper with any of your natural physiological rhythms unless you have training and supervision from an experienced teacher. Do not do out-of-body work, such as astral travel or shamanic journeys to the underworld, without teaching and support. Do not attempt to do major healing work on anyone else without responsible supervision and, of course, the permission of the recipient. Also, if you seek direct contact with astral intelligences or otherworld entities, have a trusted companion, experienced in magick, at your side.

How can you obtain a broad and thorough magickal education? Many people have read the Harry Potter books and dreamed of attending Hogwarts School of Witchcraft and Wizardry. What fun to register for Potions 101, Ritual Drumming 206, Runecraft 118, and a seminar on the Care and Feeding of Magickal Creatures!

The good news is that the various schools and seminaries mentioned earlier offer courses in the magickal arts now. Thanks to the re-emergence of the nature-based spiritual paths such as Druidry and Wicca, new research into ancient cultures, and technologies such as the Internet, there is more to teach every day and more opportunities to learn it.

But for many, learning is more likely to come in bits and pieces, from many different teachers over a span of many years. Much of the world's magickal knowledge is lost or fragmented, and while we have wonderful communications networks through which we can share what is known, it is still the task of a lifetime to even begin to learn the field.

But whether you aspire to become an adept or simply want to master a few simple skills to help you through the rough places in life, you will probably find magick one of the most intriguing and enjoyable subjects you have ever explored.

Exercises Toward Mastery

1: Metaphysical Bookstore

Find a metaphysical bookstore within traveling range, preferably one you have never visited before, and go there when you have a couple of hours to spend. Browse a while, and tell the staff about your interest in magick. Find out what books they recommend, and ask them if there is any well-respected organization in the area that offers classes. If they have a bulletin board, look it over and see what other resources there are in the community.

2: Internet Quest

Go online (use a public library computer if you don't have one at home), and start doing searches on the topics that interest you most. For example, if you are drawn to Norse runes, do a search on that. Then narrow it down: try "runes + classes" and the name of your town or city. Or search for "runes + recommended books + beginners." Choose one book, organization, class, or whatever, and follow up on it.

3: Internet Quest—Schools of Magick

Another time, go online and visit the websites of the major schools that offer magickal training. Check out Ardantane . . . Cherry Hill Seminary . . . Circle . . . Woolston-Steen . . . College of the Crossroads . . . Women's Thealogical Institute . . . the Grey School of Wizardry . . . and any others you run across. Consider whether you might get involved in any of these programs.

4: Nature as Your Teacher

Think of a place outdoors, within fairly easy travel distance, that you consider remarkable. A mountain . . . a beach . . . a waterfall . . . a desert . . . it can be any kind of environment, as long as it intrigues you. Plan an expedition to that place, and figure to spend a day there (and either take a friend or at least let someone know exactly where you're going and when you expect to return). If it is a rugged or wilderness area, take all other necessary safety precautions: water, warm clothing, cell phone, first aid kit, etc. Once you get there, spend most of your time opening yourself to the spirit of that place;

ask what magick it has to share with you. Take a notebook or your magickal journal, and discover what you can.

Blesséd be.

To follow this path further, read:

The Well-Read Witch by Carl McColman (New Page Books, 2002)

Change, Death, and Magick

I
t should be clear by now that the practice of magick changes both the magician and the outer environment. You cannot affect the one without influencing the other. We have discussed the truth that self-transformation is a little death, a dying of the old persona as the magickal being blossoms. It follows that your feelings about death/change have a powerful influence on the effectiveness of your magick.

We can be partners in the process of expecting, guiding, and savoring change, or we can fear it and cling hopelessly to the past as it slides through our fingers. If you fear change and death, your mind will throw up obstacle after obstacle as you attempt magickal work, especially work directed upon yourself. Daring is a quality necessary to the true adept; you must have the courage to confront your fear and heal it.

All too many people fear death, perhaps because we have the capacity for imagination and can all too easily envision the terrible things death might bring. Our fear paralyzes us and prevents us from exploring that realm on the other side of life. As Whitley Strieber says in *Transformation*, "We think of death as a disaster. Our entire concept of medicine is built around staving off death. When it comes, it is a defeat for doctor and patient and a source of grief for all concerned."[1]

And no wonder. Pervading our culture is the notion that life is a test, and following one's chance at it, we either pass and go to heaven or flunk and

---

1 Whitley Strieber, *Transformation* (New York: Avon, 1988), 177.

suffer eternally in hell. Death is opening the final report card when you have a strong suspicion you flunked Humanity; if you fail, your father will send you to a place worse than military school or the convent, and never speak to you again.

This approach to death could give anyone the jitters. We wonder if heaven is reserved only for the likes of Mother Teresa, Albert Schweitzer, and Gandhi; and whereas the delights of heaven are a little vague, the torments of hell are pretty specific and frightening.

Are magicians any different? Be sure that we have our fears, too! But we have chosen to become agents of transformation. We have chosen to catalyze change, so we must face our fears and move past them again and again. We must face even the fear of death head-on.

What Is Death?

What is death, really? Let's begin with what we know and go on from there. On the physical level, the heart stops beating. Breathing ceases. Electrical activity in the brain ends. The body cools. As the blood stops circulating oxygen to the cells, decomposition sets in. In time, the elements of the body rejoin the great physical cycles of nature: the winds, tides, and slow movements within the earth.

That is the destiny of the physical body. How about the rest of the Self, our thoughts and feelings and memories and desires? What about the part of me that is special, unique in all the universe? The part that surged with pride and loss as my son walked into school for the first time? The part that likes caves and horses and Star Trek and mushroom pizza? I know what's going to happen to the tall, blonde, brown-eyed part of me, but where does the loving, quirky, tenacious, scared, brave, magickal part of me go, if not to heaven or hell?

Let's explore an alternative: as your body ceases to function, your consciousness seems to rise. Soon you can look down upon your body as though you are floating near the ceiling. You can see a cord of silver light reaching from you to your body. Instinctively you know it is time, and you release that cord for the first time since you began inhabiting that body. Below you, your family is grieving. You feel a wave of love for them, and nostalgia for the body and life you are leaving, but mingled with these feelings is a sense of great freedom and relief.

The picture beneath you dwindles. A figure moves toward you—a familiar face and the well-loved voice of someone close to you who died long ago. They move with you toward a sort of tunnel. At the other end of the tunnel is a brilliant light, and you feel drawn toward it.

What I have described so far reflects the near-death experiences related by hundreds of people in hospitals or at the scene of accidents. Technically deceased for a few seconds or minutes, these people were revived and now bring us a glimpse of what lies beyond.

But what is in, or past, the great light? We have very few accounts of this. A few in Western society tell of seeing heaven or hell, angels, or Jesus. Does the religious training of the viewers influence these visions? Mr. Streiber reflects:

> Every religion from Egyptian to Christian has offered a way to the soul after death, a system by which it would go toward its judgment and find its place . . . In a reality made of energy, thoughts may literally be things . . . what if it was intended that we create our own realities after death?[2]

Do faithful Moslems see Paradise, with *houris* moving through fragrant gardens? Did the Vikings have foaming horns of mead thrust into their hands at the portal and greet Father Odin in the great hall at Valhalla? Do Wiccans walk with the Lady and the Hornéd One through the forests and green fields of Summerland? In short, do our expectations shape our experiences in the afterlife?

We shall find out. But whatever the shape of the afterlife, fearing it now will not improve it, so we may as well find our courage and live well in the life we know.

---

2   Ibid., 180.

The Lessons of Past Lives

The Summerland of Wiccan belief is not a final destination but a place to rest, to integrate the experiences of the life just ended, and to chart the broad outlines of the life to come. In common with some other great religions, Craft tradition teaches reincarnation. We have a long succession of lives; in each we make choices and learn from them. Choices resulting in harm to ourselves and others result in imbalance and dislocation: negative karma. Choices that are healing and constructive restore the balance: positive karma. In each life, we learn new lessons or repeat the old ones until we get them right.

So much of who we are is the product of past lives. Reincarnation explains why we have attractions and phobias that nothing in our current childhood caused. It also accounts for déjà vu, or remembering places we have not seen before in this life, and explains why children born to the same parents and raised together can have radically different personalities.

Recalling or re-experiencing past lives can help us understand ourselves. When we know the origin of a habit, attitude, fear, or obsession—when we can see its thread or pattern in a series of lives—then we can more easily guide our own healing and growth.

Several techniques can be used in past-life work. Among them are hypnosis, trancework, guided meditation, ETR (embedded trauma release, or point-holding); and synergetic reverie, where two people who are closely bonded go into light trance and together uncover the memories of a past life they shared.

Obviously we are not approaching this as a party game, to discover who was the most famous in past ages. In most past lives, logically enough, we were not queens or celebrated authors or explorers. We were peasants or hunters and gatherers. A California hypnotist conducted a long series of past-life workshops in which, of over one thousand cases of recall, only one person remembered a life as a historical personage (I believe it was either Benjamin Harrison or Grover Cleveland).

In my very first recall, I found myself in a huge and impressive temple in ancient Sumer, watching several priestesses move about a glittering altar. "Wonderful!" I thought. "I must have been a high priestess!" It was only a fleeting glimpse, so I resolved to return in my next session and discover more details. I did and found out that I was a sort of scullery maid who had crept upstairs to watch the rituals from behind a pillar, when I was supposed to be washing dishes. So much for ego.

Reliving or at least recalling past lives can help conquer the fear of physical death. When you can remember or re-experience your deaths from previous incarnations and realize that your immortal spirit survives and thrives, the fear of extinction begins to melt away.

This sort of work is best done with an experienced guide, at least for the first few times. You may relive ancient traumas and will want some strong support close by. In my own case, I have relived a spear-thrust through the stomach; death by guillotine; death during childbirth; and being raped and left for dead in the desert. Of course I also have access to much more pleasant experiences, but healing requires that we face old traumas. If you are not ready to do so, or do not have the proper guidance and support, your Younger Self may very well refuse access to your most traumatic experiences. This is a sort of built-in safety feature within you. Ordinarily, if you can recall a past life at all, that fact indicates that you are strong enough to deal with it emotionally.

If your religious faith denies the reality of reincarnation and you have no wish to explore it for yourself, then look to the teachings of your religion in order to come to terms with death. Do not stop with doctrines; you must deal with feelings if you would practice magick.

Of course, there are other ways to explore death. You may contact friends or relatives who have passed on, with the help of a medium, if necessary. You can observe nature and her cycles of life, death, and rebirth. You may read books about near-death experiences or about reincarnation. You could volunteer to work at a hospice, and learn from others as they are dying. You may review all the changes in yourself since you were young and accept, even celebrate them, since the death of all those earlier versions of you made the present you possible. Persevere until you understand death as a transition into a new kind of existence and can imagine your own death without fear.

On Dinosaurs, Death, and the Dance

The Wiccan approach to death is celebrated on Samhain, the sabbat or holy night dedicated to the dead. According to tradition, the veil between the worlds is thinnest on the night of October 31, making this the perfect time to communicate with the spirits of departed family and friends, and to work divination of all kinds. Unfortunately, what was originally an occasion for reverence and reunion now has been transformed into Halloween in popular culture, which focuses on monsters and ghosts, the scariness of death, and the quest for candy. Now, there is nothing wrong with a good party, but whereas Samhain encourages people to look squarely at death and change and loss, and to celebrate the life that was and the bonds of love that remain, Halloween simply flirts with death and darkness, titillating our fears and then quickly diverting attention to the goodie bags.

What is it we really need to understand in order to get past the fear and begin to explore the mystery? For answers to such Big Questions, I often turn to wise teachers, the sources of elder wisdom; but for this one, I instead asked the dinosaurs in my ears.

Well, hanging from my ears to be precise. Once when I visited Burnie's Rock Shop, which was a kind of home away from home, there on the counter was a box of little rubber dinosaurs in beautiful bright colors, just begging to become earrings. With the investment of seventy-three cents and five minutes with the jewelry pliers, I soon sported a hot pink tyrannosaurus on one lobe and a lavender one on the other.

Now if you're going to hang rubber reptiles on your ears, you may as well listen to them. So I consulted the Lavender Lizard of Life and the Pink Dinosaur of Death, seeking wisdom. (This may seem a tiny bit eccentric to some, but I learned long ago that any object or entity can catalyze insight; or, to put it another way, you can look through any window and see the sunlight.)

This is what I heard:

"Everything she touches changes. Change is the essence of life, the nature of all reality.

"Dawn breaks, and we change the world, and the world changes us. We dance the dance of daylight.

"Night falls, and our conscious minds rest. But the life of the Deep Mind goes on: reliving, integrating, dreaming, moving, and changing in realms shadowy to our waking selves, but nonetheless real. We dance the dance of darkness.

"In like manner, we are born to dance the dance of life; but when that ends and our living personas rest, the life of the spirit goes on in other realms. We dance the dance of death."

So spoke the dinosaurs, tiny reptile replicas of whole species that danced into the shadows eons before the awakening of humanity, whispering wisdom in my ears from far down the corridors of time. I was reminded that Wiccan high priestesses wear necklaces of alternating amber and jet, symbolizing day and night, life and death and life again—the great cycle through which we move.

Through understanding, it is possible to transcend the fear of death and so live more deeply. I quote once more from a man who moved through his fear and past it, Whitley Strieber:

> Gone was my dread. Now there was . . . a sense of absolute correctness about it. It did not belong to the dark at all. I belonged to the dark. Death was part of the grace of nature . . . I had been so scared and wanted so badly to live. But the peace I touched was so incredibly, transcendentally great that I also now loved death a little, or at least I accepted the truth and presence of it in my own life.[3]

The person you have been must make way for the person you will be. We all learn this lesson at the end of life. If you can learn it sooner, and not only embrace change in yourself but command it, then you are indeed a magician.

---

3   Ibid., 181.

Exercises Toward Mastery

1: Read a Book

Choose one from the list below, and borrow it from the library. Better yet, read several of the books. Afterwards, write down your thoughts and reactions in your journal.

2: Talk It Over

Discuss death with your teacher, or anyone whose wisdom you respect, or a group of your friends. Talk about the various possibilities for the afterlife. Do we go to the Christian heaven or hell? Is that concept more likely than the Muslim Paradise, the Norse Valhalla, or the Greek Elysian Fields? Do we recycle into the great body of the earth, becoming one with the soil and seas and sky? Do we disappear utterly? Do we live on in the deeds we performed, the lives we touched, and the memories of our loved ones? Do we create the afterlife according to our expectations, as a magician creates reality from thought on the astral plane?

3: Describe Your Afterlife

On the chance that the last concept is exactly right, prepare for the afterlife by envisioning it now, in great detail. Write down where you would prefer to go and what you would do there. Describe the environment, your body or vessel, your activities and goals, who would be there, and your relationship with the Deity, deities, or spirit beings in that place.

4: Prepare for the Transition

You may or may not be able to mold the afterlife, but you can certainly take care of business here. Write your will or a living trust, get it witnessed, and put copies in obvious places. Write a living will with instructions on medical intervention, extreme measures to sustain life, and so on. Record, in your will or a separate document, what you want done with your body and special wishes you have for your funeral or memorial service. Record audio or video messages to your family, to be played after you have passed over. These acts mark you as a responsible adult, may slightly comfort you, and will make things easier on your family and friends during and after your passage.

Blesséd be.

To follow this path further, read:

Reincarnation: The Phoenix Fire Mystery; An East-West Dialogue on Death and Rebirth from the Worlds of Religion, Science, Philosophy, and Psychology by Joseph Head and S. L. Cranston, eds. (Theosophical University Press, 1994)

Exploring Reincarnation: The Classic Guide to the Evidence for Past-Life Experiences by Hans Tendam (Rider, 2004)

Transformation: The Breakthrough by Whitley Streiber (Avon Books, 1997)

Life After Life by Raymond A. Moody, Jr. (Bantam, 1986)

Any book by Elisabeth Kübler-Ross.

Conclusion

In these pages, I have written about magick; yet true magick is not in books or tools or incantations, but in the growing heart and spirit.

To the extent that you have ever consciously chosen a new direction for your life and made it happen, you are already a worker of magick. Books and teachers can help you become a more effective magician, but the magick is already in you.

To the extent you have avoided and resisted change in your life, you are not yet the magickal being you can be. Ultimately you can have no idea what any magician is talking about, really, until you begin to work magick and feel it for yourself.

Many people are drawn to the mystery and glamour of magick, but find that they are unable or unwilling to put in the effort that competence demands. They remain dabblers or content themselves with fantasy. This too is all right; such people have another path to follow, and may accomplish much on the earth plane without ever lighting a candle.

But if magick is part of your path, it will lead you to a world that is a deeper, richer, more vivid place than you have known, filled with signs and wonders—*this* world, seen with starlight vision.

Magick can help you find and follow the path that is yours alone, which no other may walk. It can help you to know that you are one with all that is, every tree and hawk and stone . . . and feel the sense of belonging such knowledge brings. It can lead you to the Divine within, and place in your hands such power and responsibility as you have not dreamed of . . . and release the love and wisdom you must have to wield that power "with harm toward none, and for the greatest good of all."

Remember, the magick is within you. Blesséd be.

With harm toward none
and for the greatest good of all
so mote it be!

Glossary of Terms

Note: Terms in ALL CAPS refer to cross-references
within this glossary.

Affirmation: A statement designed as a message to YOUNGER SELF
that, repeated at frequent intervals, aids in self-transformation.

Air: One of the classic four ELEMENTS representing the mind, intellect, or imagination; it often corresponds to the east and the colors
light blue and yellow.

Akashic Records: A record of all that is, was, and will be; usually considered to reside on one of the astral planes and accessible through
TRANCEWORK and MEDITATION.

Alchemy: A philosophical system that flourished during the Middle
Ages and sought to purify and perfect the practitioner while symbol-
ically creating chemical experiments on the material plane; modern
chemistry is an offshoot, though it no longer includes the spiritual
elements.

Altar: A flat surface designed to hold ritual tools and symbols; in many
magickal traditions it is placed in the east.

Amulet: A small item of a natural material such as wood, stone, or
shell, charged for a magickal purpose such as protection and either
carried or worn as a pendant.

Anima: The feminine spirit that exists within males.

Animals: Present in magick as familiars (companions and helpers),
power animals (animal spirits that guide, protect, and empower
individuals), totem animals (those spirits that guide, protect, and

empower clans or tribes), and Huna YOUNGER SELF aspects (the subconscious identified with a particular mammal).

Animus: The masculine spirit that exists within females.

Asana: A position of the entire body having spiritual significance, from yoga. See also MUDRA.

Aspecting: Any advanced magickal activity in which the practitioner manifests a particular aspect of Goddess or God in thought, feelings, behavior, speech, and appearance. Also called "Drawing Down the Moon" or "assuming the godform."

Aspects: Forms, facets, or personas of Deity: for example, Artemis, Persephone, and Kore are aspects of the Maiden, and the Maiden is an aspect of Goddess. Helios, Ra, and Apollo are all solar aspects of God. "All goddesses are one Goddess, all gods are one God; God and Goddess are One."

Asperger *or* Aspergillum: A device used to sprinkle water for purification at the beginning of RITUALS. Some are constructed of brass or silver, but a spray of evergreen, a pine cone, or fingers will do as well.

Asperging: Cleansing the ritual space before casting the circle.

Assuming the Godform: See ASPECTING.

Astral Temple: A mind-created construct on the astral plane, created as a sacred place where members of a lodge or COVEN, or solitary magicians, may go in their spirit-forms to rest, heal, learn, or communicate.

Astrology: The study of the relationships and movements of the planets as they relate to human qualities and events.

Athame: A black-handled, double-edged, knifelike tool used by WITCHES to channel energy, as in CASTING THE CIRCLE, but not used to cut anything material. It may be marked with the owner's name in RUNES and with other symbols, including the PENTAGRAM, and may symbolize either the Fire or the Air ELEMENTS (different traditions vary on this point).

Attunement: An activity that brings the minds, emotions, and psyches of a group into harmony prior to RITUAL; chanting, singing, guided meditation, and breathing exercises are common ways to attune.

Aura: The energy field of the human body, especially that radiant portion visible to the third eye or psychic vision, which can reveal information about an individual's health and emotional state.

Banishing: Causing to depart; used by some traditions as the procedure for releasing the elemental spirits of the QUARTERS at the end of a RITUAL.

Bell: A bell or gong can be used early in the RITUAL to "alert the QUARTERS," that is, to prepare YOUNGER SELF to operate in the modes of Earth, Air, Fire, and Water.

Bindrune: Several RUNES combined into one glyph in order to harness the energy of all of them toward one purpose.

Bolline: A white-handled knife used by WITCHES for cutting, carving, or inscribing things in the course of a RITUAL—CANDLES, TALISMANS, CORDS, etc. It is usually single-edged and sometimes has a sickle-shaped blade. Used in HERBCRAFT to harvest herbs.

Book of Shadows: A magickal journal kept by each WICCAN initiate, in which SPELLS, INVOCATIONS, ritual notes, herbal recipes, dreams, DIVINATION results, and material from the COVEN book can be recorded. Some people write it in Theban script or in other alphabets to keep it from prying eyes. Some keep a disk of shadows.

Broom, *also called a* **Besom:** The magickal STAFFS of WITCHES during the Middle Ages may have been disguised as brooms as a safety measure against the agents of the Inquisition, who would persecute anyone known to own magickal paraphernalia. A besom may be used to sweep the ritual space clear of impurities, as a form of ASPERGING before CASTING THE CIRCLE.

Cakes and Wine: After the magickal work and before the circle is opened, WICCANS and some other groups share food and drink. This custom is a sacrament of thanks for the gifts of Mother Earth, a way of earthing excess psychic energy, and sometimes a time for socializing and merriment.

Calling the Quarters: Invitation for the spirits of Air, Fire, Water, and Earth (from the east, south, west, and north, respectively, in many traditions) to attend a RITUAL and lend their powers to its success. It is also a means of fully engaging the mind, will, emotions, and body in the magickal working.

Candles: These are used frequently in SPELLS. Their colors and the oils they are anointed with, as well as the shapes and inscriptions carved on them, all have a symbolic purpose. See also LAMPS OF ART.

Casting: In DIVINATION, tossing stones, RUNES, or sticks on the ground or on a special board or cloth and gaining insights from their patterns and relationships.

Casting the Circle: The psychic creation of a sphere of energy around the area where RITUAL is to be performed, both to concentrate and focus the power raised and to keep out unwanted influences and distractions. The space enclosed exists outside ordinary space and time.

Cauldron: In RITUAL, a symbol of rebirth from Celtic mythology, and sometimes used to cook food for a SABBAT feast or burn small items as part of a magickal SPELL.

Censer: A container in which INCENSE is burned. See THURIBLE.

Centering: The process of moving one's consciousness to one's spiritual or psychic center, leading to a feeling of great peace, calmness, strength, clarity, and stability.

Ceremonial Magick: A style of magick usually involving complex RITUALS and elaborate tools, apparel, and temple decorations; usually refers to the Western system of magick exemplified by the Order of the Golden Dawn.

Chakras: The nexi or focal points of the human energy field; there are seven major chakras in a line from the top of the head to the base of the spine, as well as many smaller ones. Being able to sense and influence the chakras is an important aspect of HEALING.

Chalice: A goblet or cup, usually holding wine, which is shared around the circle in Wiccan RITUAL. It is both a female and a Water symbol and can be used for SCRYING.

Chanting: The harmonious vocalization of key words, names, or phrases for ritual purposes. Chanting can be used for ATTUNEMENT, CENTERING, RAISING POWER, going into trance, or celebration.

Charcoal: Often INCENSE is burned on a charcoal briquet, placed in a THURIBLE or on a stone. Self-igniting charcoal disks are sold in metaphysical supply stores and are very convenient to use.

Charge: To intentionally imbue with energy, as "to charge a TALISMAN with healing energy." See RAISING POWER. The energy can be transferred from a distance or during physical contact with the object.

Charm: A magick SPELL either chanted or recited; an INCANTATION; also another word for an AMULET or TALISMAN.

Chord: An invisible line of force extending from one being or object to another, through which they influence one another; all things are connected by energy chords, but major chords have a powerful effect and their understanding and use is a key part of magick.

Cingulum: See CHORD.

Circle: See CASTING THE CIRCLE.

Cone of Power: The energy raised during magick is visualized as a cone, which at its peak of power is released toward a specific goal.

Consecration: To solemnly dedicate or devote someone or something to a sacred purpose and/or to the service of a deity; for example, to consecrate a ritual tool to the purpose of protection, or to consecrate a priestess to the service of Artemis.

Cord: Either a heavy string used in binding and releasing magick, or it can refer to the piece of apparel circling the magician's waist (also called a "girdle" or "cingulum"). In many COVENS and magickal lodges, the color of the cord indicates the wearer's degree of attainment.

Correspondence: Something that magickally symbolizes or replaces another thing; for example, the color silver corresponds to the moon or moon goddesses; the god Apollo corresponds to healing, music, and the sun.

Coven: A group of WITCHES who gather regularly to celebrate their faith and work magick. A coven may range in size from three to twenty or more, though most groups limit their size to thirteen or fewer. Covens are self-governing and vary widely in their styles and interests. Some covens are affiliated with a particular tradition (denomination) of the Craft, while others are eclectic.

Craft, the: See WICCA.

Crescent: A lunar symbol popular with many WICCANS and other magicians; the moon goddess rules magick and symbolizes the powers of women. In many traditions of WITCHCRAFT, the high priestess wears a silver crescent on her tiara or headband.

Cunning Man: The male equivalent of the WISE WOMAN; knowledgeable in the ways of nature, HERBCRAFT, and the hunt. One who uses NATURE MAGICK.

Dark of the Moon: The part of the cycle during which the moon is not visible from Earth. This is traditionally the best time in the cycle to do DIVINATION (SCRYING, TAROT, reading the RUNES, etc.).

Deosil: (jesh'-ul) Clockwise or "sunwise." This is the direction the priestess or priest moves when CASTING THE CIRCLE and calling the QUARTERS; it is the direction of attraction, creation, and growth. See WIDDERSHINS for the opposite.

Deva: A spirit, usually the collective nature spirit of a variety of plant life. For example, the chamomile deva is the essence of all chamomile plants, and when planting, tending, harvesting, or using chamomile, many nature-oriented magicians will communicate with its deva.

Diana's Bow: That phase of the moon, approximately three days after the DARK OF THE MOON, when the first slender CRESCENT or bow of the moon is visible low in the western sky just around sunset. A good time to do magicks for beginnings and preparations.

Dismissing the Quarters: Releasing or saying farewell to the spirits of the ELEMENTS. See also BANISHING.

Divination: The art or practice of foreseeing future trends or discovering hidden knowledge by using such tools as the TAROT, the I CHING, RUNES, CASTING stones, or a SHOWSTONE. Useful prior to RITUAL magick.

Drawing Down the Moon: See ASPECTING.

Dreamwork: Any conscious work with dreams, such as recording dreams in a dream journal, dream analysis, and lucid or directed dreaming.

Drumming: Used to raise power for casting a SPELL, for trance induction, or to change consciousness or an emotional state.

Earth: The ELEMENT corresponding to north in many magickal traditions, as well as the body, the material world, health, strength, and prosperity, and the foundation of all things material and solid; and often the colors black, brown, olive green, and yellow.

Earthing: Sending excess energy into the earth; done in RITUAL after RAISING POWER and SENDING it to its goal.

Element: In classical magick, Earth, Air, Fire, or Water, each of which represents a class of energies within the universe, and all of which together (along with Spirit) make up the reality we know. See listings in this section for each element.

Elemental: An entity or spirit expressing the energy of one of the four ELEMENTS. Air elementals are called sylphs, Fire are salamanders, Water are undines, and Earth elementals are gnomes.

Esbat: A gathering of WITCHES to celebrate a certain phase of the moon (the FULL MOON, DARK OF THE MOON, or DIANA'S BOW, usually), work magick, and socialize; from a French word meaning "to frolic."

Evocation: In medieval magick, to summon a "lesser spirit" to do one's bidding; among modern magicians, to draw any particular spiritual or psychic energy from within your own psyche.

Familiar: An animal companion trained to assist in magickal workings.

Fire: The ELEMENT corresponding to south, energy, will, passion, determination, ambition, and the colors red or red-orange and gold.

Full Moon: That phase in the lunar cycle when the moon is at her brightest, and perfectly round; a high point of lunar power when WITCHES traditionally gather to work magick for HEALING and abundance, and to celebrate Goddess. In "The Charge of the Goddess," she says, "Once in the month, and better it be when the moon is full, ye shall gather and adore me . . ."

Girdle: See CORD.

Grimoire: A book of magickal SPELLS and techniques. Although some of the medieval grimoires seem very mysterious and romantic, often they are merely collections of magickal "recipes" that are ineffective in the hands of anyone but a trained magician.

Grounding: Psychically reinforcing one's connections with the earth by reopening an energy channel, often visualized as a golden cord or taproot, between your AURA and the earth.

Healing: The goal of a great deal of magick, especially among healing-oriented spiritual traditions such as WICCA. Healing may be accomplished by the laying-on of hands, mental manipulation of psychic energies, VISUALIZATION, spirit journeys, crystal work, HERBCRAFT, or other means. Ideally, it is performed only with the informed consent of the patient.

Herbcraft: Herbs may be used for HEALING in a very direct and mundane way, using teas, poultices, and tinctures, or in a magickal RITUAL through their CORRESPONDENCES. The WISE WOMEN and CUNNING MEN of old Europe were often skilled herbalists and may have been attacked by the Inquisition because they were seen as competition with the emerging patriarchal medical trades.

Hermetic Magick: A blending of magick and philosophy, in which knowledge and the practice of magick together lead to a knowledge of the divine.

High Magick: See THEURGY.

High Priest: Often the male leader of a COVEN, his duties traditionally include interacting with the outside world on behalf of the coven, and often the initiation of female WITCHES.

High Priestess: Often the female leader of a COVEN, her duties include the spiritual welfare of the members of the coven, and often the initiation of male WITCHES.

Higher Self: That part of the tripartite Self that is in direct contact with Deity, and therefore able to manifest that which MIDDLE SELF desires, when powered by the cooperation of YOUNGER SELF. Often considered to be a male and female pair of souls present in the human psyche. See chapter 5.

I Ching: A Chinese tradition of DIVINATION in which yarrow stalks or coins are CAST and counted to form figures called hexagrams; these are interpreted according to the book of that name.

Incantation: See CHANTING.

Incense: Material burned for its fragrance, which comes in sticks, cones, powders, resinous chunks, and herbal or floral mixtures, and can be purchased or made. The incense used depends on the purpose of the RITUAL and on the energies being invoked, but frankincense and sandalwood are two all-purpose favorites that can be used for almost any ritual.

Initiation: A profound spiritual experience in which one's unity with Deity and the universe is realized; also, the RITUAL by which such an experience is celebrated and/or one is welcomed as a full member of a particular religious tradition or magickal group.

Inner Magick: A style of magick that achieves results through mental concentration and other inner processes without the use of RITUAL tools, costumes, props, movement, or sound. A subset of INTRINSIC MAGICK.

Intoning: See VIBRATING NAMES.

Intrinsic Magick: A style of magick that achieves results through the use of the body and mind alone, without the use of external tools and trappings. The mind, senses, breathing, noises, MUDRAS and ASANAS, VISUALIZATION, and movement may all be employed.

Invocation: Calling on a "higher spirit," Deity, or divine aspect to manifest; also an invocatory prayer or INCANTATION.

Jewelry: Special pendants, rings, bracelets, necklaces, torques, tiaras, garters, or other forms of jewelry are often worn by magicians to symbolize their spiritual path, totem, or chosen aspect of Deity; to hold an energy charge; or to serve as a trigger for altered states of consciousness.

Kitchen Witch Magick: A style of magick focused on home management and other practical matters of daily living (see THAUMATURGY), often using ordinary household items as ritual tools.

Lamps of Art: Two CANDLES on the ALTAR that provide illumination and may represent Goddess and God (Spirit), made preferably of beeswax, although paraffin will do. Choose natural color or white, or use colors based on the season or on the nature of the magick being done.

Law of Contagion: A magickal principle stating that once an object has been part of another object, or even in contact with it, it remains linked by energy CHORDS and can be used magickally to influence it. See OBJECT LINK.

Law of Return: Whatever energy is sent out, positive or negative, is returned to the sender multiplied. Some traditions say it is multiplied by three and therefore call this principle the "Threefold Law."

Libation: Wine or other beverage that is ceremonially poured upon the earth in token of gratitude for the blessings of Deity. Often done after the CHALICE has been passed around the circle in RITUAL.

Lodge: A group of people who gather together to practice magick, usually within a Western ceremonial magickal tradition.

Low Magick: See THAUMATURGY.

Lunar Cycle: The roughly twenty-eight-day cycle during which the moon waxes from dark to full and wanes to dark again; much magickal work is geared to the energies of the different phases of the moon.

Magician: One who uses magick to accomplish their purposes.

Magick: See Chapter 1 for definitions.

Magick Mirror: A dark or black mirror in which a magician may see images with their THIRD EYE or psychic vision; interpretation of these images provides information about distant or likely future events, or insights into the magician's own nature. See SCRYING.

Magickal Journal: A book in which a magician writes notes and observations regarding magickal workings and SPELLS, CHARMS, INCANTATIONS, and other resources. See BOOK OF SHADOWS.

Magister: A formal title for a medieval magician.

Magus: A formal title for a medieval magician.

Meditation: A focused, disciplined form of contemplation or reflection in which the practitioner may alter their emotional state, achieve self-insight, or merge consciousness with another being, object, or process.

Middle Pillar: An exercise in which the major CHAKRAS are serially illuminated or massaged by INTONING names of Deity, and cleansed by running energy through them. Also the middle column of sephiroth in the Qabalistic TREE OF LIFE.

Middle Self: That part of the tripartite Self that works with thought, rationality, logic, and judgment; the part in which most of us operate most of the time; the ego. Also called Talking Head Self or Talking Self. In magick, it is the part that usually decides the desired outcome and plans the RITUAL or SPELL to enlist the aid of YOUNGER SELF, in order to communicate with HIGHER SELF. See chapter 5.

Moon: Symbol of the Triple Goddess (Maiden, Mother, and Crone) in the WICCAN faith, and of feminine powers of intuition and magick, and of female physiological cycles which are attuned to her.

Moon Void-of-Course: An astrological term for the interval when the moon has left her last conjunction in one astrological sign, but not yet made her first conjunction in the next sign; traditionally not a good time in which to do RITUAL work or launch any new project.

Mudra: A gesture or position of the hands and arms that has sacred meaning.

Nature Magick: Magick which focuses on divine powers manifested in nature; uses the energies of the earth, MOON, and SUN; works in cooperation with nature spirits or DEVAS; and uses simple tools such as stones, sticks, or shells.

Necromancy: Communication with discarnate humans, which is to say the spirits of the dead; traditionally practiced at SAMHAIN.

Neopagan: See PAGANISM.

New Moon: See DARK OF THE MOON.

Object Link: An object once associated with someone or something the magician wishes to psychically influence and which is still connected to it with an energy CHORD. Also called a *witness*.

Occult: Knowledge or information that is supposedly hidden from the eyes or the understanding of anyone but adepts, usually referring to magickal principles or techniques. In fact, information formerly considered to be "occult" is freely available to anyone dedicated enough to seek it out in books or from teachers (most of the information in this book, for example).

Offering: A gift to Deity or a particular divine aspect given in gratitude for blessings received or expected. In Neopagan religions today, this might include the burning of INCENSE, a libation of wine, work toward a worthy cause, or providing food for wildlife—but never blood sacrifices.

Opening the Circle: Gathering in the sphere of energy that was CAST at the beginning of the RITUAL, thus returning the space to its mundane state. Sometimes called *banishing the circle*.

Paganism: 1. A collection of mostly pre-Christian, earth- or nature-based religions originating in Europe sometimes called Neopaganism: Asatru, WICCA, Shamanism, etc., based on the old pagan religions but incorporating modern techniques and materials. 2. Any religion apart from Christianity, Judaism, and Islam.

Pen of Art: A special pen that is reserved only for entries into the BOOK OF SHADOWS or for other RITUAL uses. This can be an old-fashioned dip pen or quill pen, but any favored or special writing implement may be assigned this role.

Pentacle: This is a disk of metal, ceramic, or wood with a PENTA-GRAM and other symbols inscribed on it. It is a symbol of the EL-EMENT of Earth, originally designed to be used in RITUALS of protection as a magickal shield. Today Pagan ritualists sometimes place food upon it; see CAKES AND WINE.

Pentagram: A star-like five-pointed figure of very ancient origin, used magickally for blessing, protection, and balance. The five points stand for the four ELEMENTS plus Spirit. WITCHES often wear a silver pentagram encircled, with one point up to symbolize Spirit guiding and balancing the Elements. Also called pentalpha, the "endless knot," and other names.

Planetary Days: Each day of the week is special to one of the planets (or the MOON or Sun) and the energy it represents. See "The Timing of Ritual" in chapter 14.

Planetary Hours: Certain hours of the day correspond to each planet. Traditionally they begin at different times throughout the year and vary in length according to the season, so people new to magick are advised to work their rituals on the appropriate planetary day and not be too concerned with the refinement of planetary hours.

Polarity: The interaction of two differing polarity-energies can raise enormous amounts of magickal power, and this insight is incorporated into most traditions of WICCA, as well as ALCHEMY and other magickal philosophies. The female-male polarity is most commonly discussed, but of course there are others as well: Fire/Water, Yin/Yang, Darkness/Light, etc.

Poppet: A doll used in healing RITUAL to represent a particular patient.

Pranayama: A series of yogic breathing techniques that are extremely useful in magickal work as they can alter consciousness, RAISE POWER, cleanse the AURA, and more.

Quarters: A shorthand term for the four elemental powers and the directions they correspond to; the portions of the magickal circle influenced by the ELEMENTS—each quarter is centered on its direction (e.g., the north quarter [of the circle] is actually from northwest to northeast, centered on north). Some traditions call them "corners," but circles don't actually have corners, so the term quarters is more accurate.

Raising Power: Drawing ambient energy (or specific energies such as solar or lunar) into the circle and the AURA using techniques such as DRUMMING or CHANTING, preparatory to SENDING it to a specific goal.

Ritual: A planned series of events leading to the accomplishment of a goal through magickal means. Can be celebratory, transformative, or both.

Runes: The alphabets used in Old Norse and Teutonic languages. They are an important component in Norse magick and myth, and are still used in DIVINATION today.

Sabbat: One of the eight great holy days of the WICCAN and many other NEOPAGAN religions, celebrating themes (such as birth, fertility, or death) related to the turning of the seasons of the year. Each is known by more than one name, but one set of names is Yule, Imbolc, Ostara, Beltane, Litha, Lughnassad, Mabon, and Samhain.

Sacred Space: Of course all space is sacred, but the term usually refers to the area enclosed after CASTING THE CIRCLE.

Sacred Woods: Wood from trees that were special to the Celtic peoples. Often listed are rowan, hazel, birch, holy, willow, elder, hawthorn, oak, ash, and thorn, among others. Often used to make ritual tools (wands, pentacles, besoms, athame handles) or to build ritual fires.

Salt: Rock salt symbolizes the ELEMENT of Earth, and it is mixed with water and sprinkled over things to purify them. See ASPERGING.

Samhain: The sabbat celebrated on October 31; traditionally the night when the veils between this world and the next are thinnest. See NECROMANCY.

Scrying: The art of divination by gazing into a MAGICK MIRROR, SHOWSTONE, or bowl of water; the images seen with the THIRD EYE or psychic vision can illuminate events or trends in your life.

Seal of Solomon: A protective symbol or design said to have originated with Solomon, usually consisting of two interlaced triangles (now called the "Star of David") surrounded by the TETRAGRAMMATON and other symbols.

Sending: Usually refers to the launching of power raised during a RITUAL toward the intended goal, but can also refer to the transmission of telepathic messages or the sending of an entity to accomplish a specific task.

Shapeshifting: The assumption of an animal form or appearance by a human magician. Everyone has heard scary tales of werewolves, but usually shapeshifting is done purposefully and for entirely benign spiritual purposes by a tribal shaman.

Showstone: A "crystal ball" or other polished stone used for DIVINATION (see SCRYING). Spheres of genuine quartz crystal are comparatively rare and expensive, but balls of obsidian or even leaded glass crystal work very well.

Sigil: A design or symbol representing a specific energy (for example, a planetary sigil) or entity (such as an angelic power).

Sorcery: Often defined as the use of magick for negative purposes, possibly with the aid of, or by controlling "evil spirits." Not recommended; see the LAW OF RETURN.

Speculum: Another term for MAGICK MIRROR.

Spell: A pattern or series of words and/or actions performed with magickal intent, or sometimes simply a spoken INCANTATION. See CHANTING.

Spirit: The nonphysical, immortal component of an entity; the soul. With Earth, Air, Fire, and Water, one of the five basic components of all that is; represented by the top point of the PENTAGRAM. Some spirits are incarnate, that is, they have material bodies; some are discarnate, or are not presently residing in a body; and some have never had a body. There are human spirits of various kinds, nature spirits, spirits of entities on or from other planes, and "higher" or "angelic" spirits. MEDITATION can be used to communicate with spirits, and there are many other ways.

Staff: A tool carried by some magicians that can be used in place of a WAND or even an ATHAME. Traditionally a staff is made of one of the Celtic sacred woods, such as oak or ash, and in medieval times a phallic shape may have been carved on one end, then covered with broomstraw in case the Inquisitors came by (see BROOM). The staff was also used as a hiking stick when traveling on foot to the remote SABBAT sites over rugged ground, and at Beltane the dancers may have ridden staves hobby-horse style.

Stang: A magickal STAFF with a forked end at the top, symbolizing the horns or antlers of the Hornéd Lord. Originally placed in the center of the circle, which represents the Goddess, it is not "for men" or "for women," it is part of the religious furnishings as an altar or pentagram might be.

Starlight Vision: An intuitive, magically and psychically sensitive way of viewing the world, in which processes, things, entities, and possibilities unseen by the logical mind or absent in consensus reality become evident.

Strega: Italian WITCHCRAFT.

Sun: Not simply the star that warms and lights our world, but also a symbol of success, expansiveness, spiritual illumination, HEALING, and a powerful energy source for magick. In some religions the sun is personified as a goddess (Amaterasu Omikami, Arinna, Bast, etc.) and in some as a god (Apollo, Ra, Helios, etc.).

Sword: A sword can be used for CASTING THE CIRCLE and is considered a symbol of either Air or Fire.

Sympathetic Magick: Magick working on the principle that an object or being can be affected by influencing something like it in some way or related to it. For example, one might draw a picture of her horse successfully leaping a high fence, then charge the drawing with energy in order to help her horse become a strong jumper. See also CORRESPONDENCE.

Talisman: A drawn symbol or constructed item that is charged with a very specific energy and carried, worn as jewelry, or put in a special place. If carried on one's person, its energy exerts a continual subtle influence on one; if placed somewhere, the emanation of its energy influences the immediate environment.

Tarot: A DIVINATION tool consisting of a deck of cards (in classic decks, seventy-eight) with powerful scenes or images representing various energies, processes, or spiritual conditions. They are divided into four suits (usually wands or rods, pentacles or disks, cups, and swords) which comprise the minor arcana ("lesser secrets"), and twenty-two other cards that comprise the major arcana ("greater secrets"). Many designs are available, some of which bear little or no resemblance to the original designs of the earliest cards from the fourteenth and fifteenth centuries. Also a card game played using a tarot deck.

Temple: An area reserved, and sometimes decorated and equipped, specifically for religious or magickal activities; also any area consecrated as SACRED SPACE, whether or not it is normally considered so, such as a cast circle in someone's living room.

Tetragrammaton: Another name for the four-letter word for the Name of God in Hebrew: YHVH, later anglicized to "Jehovah." Sometimes used in Jewish- or Christian-oriented magickal traditions.

Thaumaturgy: "Low magick" used to influence things and events in everyday life: to protect your house, get a job, heal your cold, travel safely, etc.

Theurgy: "High magick" employed to connect with Deity and foster spiritual growth.

Third Eye: That CHAKRA most attuned to psychic energy and vibrations, located on the low forehead between the eyebrows.

Threefold Law: See LAW OF RETURN.

Thurible: A metal censer, dish, or burner to hold CHARCOAL and INCENSE. It can either stand on the ALTAR or swing from a chain, and it is often considered to be a symbol of Air, or of Air and Fire.

Trancework: An altered state of consciousness attained by means of breathing (pranayama), CHANTING, MEDITATING, etc., used to retrieve information not readily accessible to logical thought, communicate with discarnate entities, or for other magickal purposes.

Tree of Life: The diagram of the sephiroth and paths of the Qabala or Kabbalah, representing All That Is.

Triangle of Manifestation: A triangular space created outside the protective magick circle, into which medieval magicians would conjure "demons" to do their bidding.

Vibrating Names: Calling the name of a higher power, usually a deity or archangel, in a loud, extended, and resonant voice; either as part of INVOCATION, energy work such as the Middle Pillar exercise, RAISING ENERGY, or clearing blockages from CHAKRAS.

Vibrations: All manifestation is formed by energy vibrating at various wavelengths or frequencies; by working with frequencies unknown or unregarded by most people, a magician can accomplish unusual things—i.e., do magick.

Visualization: Creating an image in the mind, usually thought of as visual but enhanced when auditory and kinesthetic ELEMENTS are added. Imagining something very clearly.

Wand: A stick about eighteen inches long, or "from elbow to fingertips," carved from one of the traditional SACRED WOODS and used to attract, repel, and represent Air or Fire, according to various traditions. It may be carved and decorated, with a phallic shape (acorn or crystal) on one end and a yoni on the other. Also called a *baculum*.

Waning Moon: The period during which the visible part of the moon shrinks from full to dark; an appropriate time for spells of banishing, release, or cleansing.

Ward: A psychic barrier set up for protection from outside influences; may be "anchored" with stones such as hematite, black onyx, or rose quartz.

Water: Mixed with salt, may be used to purify; the bowl (or large shell) containing it is kept on the ALTAR. Also the ELEMENT that corresponds to the west, emotions, love, intuition, and the colors light green, blue, and silver.

Waxing Moon: The period during which the visible part of the moon grows from dark to full; an appropriate time for spells for growth or increase.

Wicca: A nature-oriented religion that includes the practice of magick and celebration of immanent Deity, often in the forms of the Triple Goddess of the MOON and the Hornéd God of nature; also called the Old Religion, the Craft, or WITCHCRAFT. Contrary to fairy-tale stereotypes, it has nothing to do with evil magick or Satanism, but rather focuses on HEALING and spiritual growth.

Wiccan Rede: The ethics of the Craft are summed up in eight words: "An ye harm none, do as ye will," meaning "As long as you do not harm anyone (including yourself), follow your inner guidance, your True Will."

Widdershins: Counterclockwise, the direction a magician moves around the circle when they wish to banish, remove, or release energy; the opposite of DEOSIL.

Wise Woman: The female equivalent of CUNNING MAN, also often a midwife; one who uses NATURE MAGICK.

Witch: A priestess or priest of the Old Religion, WICCA. Real WITCHES bear no resemblance to Halloween's cackling hags on broomsticks; that stereotype was popularized by persecutors in medieval times, for their own reasons. Real Witches look much like any of your other neighbors, and tend to be good neighbors and good citizens.

Witchcraft: See WICCA. May also refer to the magickal arts or skills associated with Wicca, aside from the spiritual ELEMENTS of the religion.

Witness: See OBJECT LINK.

Wizard: A male MAGICIAN.

Words of Power: Names of Deity or other INVOCATIONS or INCANTATIONS that have a powerful effect if properly intoned. Insofar as anything we say has an influence on YOUNGER SELF, all words are words of power. Wise magicians, therefore, use language carefully and accurately.

Younger Self: That part of the tripartite Self that is emotion, the physical body, and memory, and is in touch with HIGHER SELF. Often considered to be a mammalian soul present in the human psyche. In magick, MIDDLE SELF will select the desired outcome and design a ritual or spell to enlist the aid of Younger Self. Younger Self, in turn, sends energy to HIGHER SELF, which is connected to DEITY, which manifests the desired outcome for Middle Self. See chapter 5.

Colors for Magick

The following color correspondences will be familiar to many practitioners of magick, but you should also feel free to choose the colors that seem meaningful and appropriate to you, even if they do not match those given here. Once you have selected your color or colors for a particular working, you can obtain candles, robes, cords, wall hangings, or an altar cloth of the appropriate color.

Abstinence, Sobriety, Temperance, or Moderation: Purple, black

Children: The primary colors—bright yellow, red, blue, and green

Confidence: Royal blue

Courage: Bright red

Fertility: Green, especially a light spring green

Friendship: Royal blue, gold, golden brown, or tan

Healing or Health: Medium green, rose

Home (new): Bright orange, sunlight yellow

Home (blessing): Rose, gold, light blue

Home (purification): White, light blue

Hope: Sky blue

Inner Peace: Light blue, lavender, white

Joy: Rainbow

Love: Rose

Money, Prosperity, or Wealth: Gold, emerald green

Protection (physical): Blue, black

Protection (psychic): Silver

Purification: White

Spiritual Growth: Violet, purple, or lavender

Study or Learning: Orange

Success: Gold, royal blue

Recommended Reading

Magick from a Wiccan/Pagan Perspective

Buckland, Raymond. *Buckland's Complete Book of Witchcraft*. St. Paul: Llewellyn, 1986.

Cabot, Laurie, and Tom Cowan. *Power of the Witch: The Earth, the Moon, and the Magical Path to Enlightenment*. Surrey, UK: Delta, 1990.

Cunningham, Scott. *Wicca: A Guide for the Solitary Practitioner*. St. Paul: Llewellyn, 1990.

———. *Earth Power: Techniques of Practical Magic*. St. Paul: Llewellyn, 1983.

———. *Earth, Air, Fire, and Water: More Techniques of Practical Magic*. St. Paul: Llewellyn, 1983.

Curott, Phyllis. *Witch Crafting: A Spiritual Guide to Making Magic*. New York: Broadway, 2002.

Farrar, Janet, and Stewart Farrar. *A Witches' Bible: The Complete Witches' Handbook*. Custer, WA: Phoenix Publishing, 1996.

Fitch, Ed. *Magical Rites from the Crystal Well*. St. Paul: Llewellyn, 1984.

Galenorn, Yasmine. *Embracing the Moon: A Witch's Guide to Rituals, Spellcrafts, and Shadow Work*. St. Paul: Llewellyn, 1998.

Green, Marian. *A Witch Alone: Thirteen Moons to Master Natural Magic*. Scranton, PA: Thorsons Publishers, 2002.

Grimassi, Raven. *The Witches' Craft: The Roots of Witchcraft and Magical Transformation*. St. Paul: Llewellyn, 2002.

———. *Wiccan Magick: Inner Teachings of the Craft*. St. Paul: Llewellyn, 1998, 1991.

Morrison, Dorothy. *Everyday Magic: Spells & Rituals for Modern Living*. St. Paul: Llewellyn, 1998.

Moura, Ann. *Grimoire for the Green Witch: A Complete Book of Shadows*. St. Paul: Llewellyn, 2003.

Penczak, Christopher. *The Inner Temple of Witchcraft: Magick, Meditation, and Psychic Work*. St. Paul: Llewellyn, 1998.

Polson, Willow. *The Veil's Edge: Exploring the Boundaries of Magic*. New York: Citadel Press, 2003.

Slater, Herman. *A Book of Pagan Rituals*. York Beach, ME: Weiser Books, 1978.

Starhawk. *The Spiral Dance: A Rebirth of the Ancient Religion of the Great Goddess,* 20th anniversary edition. HarperSanFrancisco, 1999.

Telesco, Patricia. *Your Book of Shadows: How to Write Your Own Magical Spells*. New York: Citadel Press, 1999.

Valiente, Doreen. *Natural Magic*. Custer, WA: Phoenix Publishing, 1985.

———. *Witchcraft for Tomorrow*. Custer, WA: Phoenix Publishing, 1988.

Weinstein, Marion. *Earth Magic: A Book of Shadows for Positive Witches*. Franklin Lakes, NJ: New Page, 2003.

———. *Positive Magick: Occult Self-Help*. Custer, WA: Phoenix, 1991.

———. *Positive Magick: Ancient Metaphysical Techniques for Modern Lives*. Franklin Lakes, NJ: New Page, 2002.

. . . and other books by these authors, as well as Gerald Gardner, Margaret Murray, Godfrey Leland, Sybil Leek, and Justine Glass.

Ceremonial Magick in the Western Tradition

Bardon, Franz. *Initiation Into Hermetics*. Salt Lake City, UT: Merker Publishing, 2001.

Bias, Clifford, ed. *Ritual Book of Magic*. North Hollywood, CA: Newcastle Publishing, 1981.

Bonewits, Isaac. *Real Magic: An Introductory Treatise on the Basic Principles of Yellow Magic.* York Beach, ME: Weiser Books, 1989.

Butler, Eliza M. *Ritual Magic.* Kila, MT: Kessinger Publishing, 2003.

Butler, W. E. *Apprenticed to Magic.* Rochester, VT: Thoth Publications, 2003.

———. *Lords of Light: The Path of Initiation in the Western Mysteries.* New York: Destiny Books, 1990.

———. *Magic: Its Ritual, Power, and Purpose.* Wellingborough, Northhamptonshire, UK: HarperCollins, 1952.

———. *Practical Magic in the Western Mystery Tradition.* Dartford, Kent, UK: Aquarian Press, 1986.

———. *The Magician: His Training and Work.* Chatsworth, CA: Wilshire Books, 1940.

Cicero, Chic, and Sandra Tabatha Cicero. *Self-Initiation into the Golden Dawn Tradition: A Complete Curriculum of Study.* St. Paul: Llewellyn, 1995.

———. *The Essential Golden Dawn: An Introduction to High Magic.* St. Paul: Llewellyn, 2003.

Crowley, Aleister. *Magick in Theory and Practice.* New York: Castle Books, 1991.

Denning, Melita, and Osborne Phillips. *Foundations of High Magic: The Magical Philosophy.* New York: Book Sales, 2000.

———. *Mysteria Magica (The Magical Philosophy).* St. Paul: Llewellyn, 1986.

Fortune, Dion. *The Training and Work of an Initiate.* York Beach, ME: Weiser Books, 2000.

Gray, William G. *Magical Ritual Methods.* York Beach, ME: Weiser Books, 1980.

Green, Marian. *The Path Through the Labyrinth: The Quest for Initiation into the Western Mystery Tradition.* Leicestershire, UK: Thoth Publications, 1988.

King, F., and S. Skinner. *The Techniques of High Magic: A Handbook of Divination, Alchemy, and the Evocation of Spirits.* New York: Destiny Books, 2000.

Knight, Gareth. *A Practical Guide to Qabalistic Symbolism.* York Beach, ME: Weiser Books, 2002.

Kraig, Donald Michael. *Modern Magick: Eleven Lessons in the High Magickal Arts.* St. Paul: Llewellyn, 1988.

Matthews, John, and Caitlin Matthews. *Walkers Between the Worlds: The Western Mysteries from Shaman to Magus.* Rochester, VT: Inner Traditions, 2004.

Powell, Arthur E. *The Work of a Lodge of the Theosophical Society.* Kila, MT: Kessinger Publishing, 2004.

———. *The Magic of Freemasonry.* Kila, MT: Kessinger Publishing, 2005.

Regardie, Israel. *Foundations of Practical Magic: An Introduction to Qabalah, Magic, and Meditative Techniques.* London: Aeon Books, 2004.

———. *The One Year Manual* (formerly *Twelve Steps to Spiritual Enlightenment*). York Beach, ME: Weiser Books, 1981.

Waite, Arthur Edward. *The Book of Ceremonial Magic.* Maple Shade, NJ: Lethe Press, 2002.

. . . and other books by these authors.

Shamanism and Magick

Books on shamanism present an interesting challenge. Most tend to fall into three categories: (1) scholarly reports by anthropologists, (2) a few books by outsiders who have lived within a native culture for years or are adopted into it, and then report their experiences, (3) popular how-to books that take some shamanic traditions and practices and simplify them for Western readers. Some of these latter generalize and romanticize so heavily that their version of shamanism bears little resemblance to anything actually practiced by an indigenous culture. Still, the practices may be useful anyway.

Where are the books by indigenous shamans who are fully trained in a living tradition? In some cases, a culture has been largely destroyed by the impact of Western civilization, and no fully trained shamans remain. In other cases, indigenous shamans can't read or write; they work within an oral tradition. Still others are unwilling to train outsiders.

What this means is that you can cobble together your own set of spiritual and magickal practices based on what you have read . . . or enroll in one of the shamanic training programs offered by various modern mystery schools (including Ardantane) . . . or go find an indigenous shaman who is willing to teach you in person.

But if you want to begin your shamanic education by reading, then each of the following books has something to offer.

Campbell, Joseph. *The Way of Animal Powers.* Nashville, TN: Vanderbilt University, 1983.

Cowan, Tom. *Fire in the Head: Shamanism and the Celtic Spirit.* HarperSanFrancisco, 1993.

———. *Shamanism as a Spiritual Practice for Daily Life.* Genealogical Services, 1996.

Drury, Neville. *The Shaman and the Magician: Journeys Between the Worlds.* Arkana, 1987.

Eliade, Mircea. *Shamanism: Archaic Techniques of Ecstasy.* New York: Bollingen, 1972.

Gimbutas, Marija. *The Living Goddesses.* Berkeley, CA: University of California Press, 2001.

Halifax, Joan. *Shaman, The Wounded Healer.* New York: Crossroad Publishing Co., 1982.

———. *Shamanic Voices: A Survey of Visionary Narratives.* New York: Penguin Books, 1994.

Harner, Michael. *The Way of the Shaman: A Guide to Power and Healing,* 10th anniversary edition. HarperSanFrancisco, 1990.

Ingerman, Sandra. *Soul Retrieval: Mending the Fragmented Self Through Shamanic Practice.* HarperSanFrancisco, 1991.

Lee, Patrick. *We Borrow the Earth: An Intimate Portrait of the Gypsy Shamanic Tradition and Culture.* London: Thorsons, 2000.

Madden, Kristin. *The Book of Shamanic Healing.* St. Paul: Llewellyn, 2002.

Moondance, Wolf. *Rainbow Medicine: A Visionary Guide to Native American Shamanism.* New York: Sterling Publishing, 1994.

Prechtel, Martin. *Secrets of the Talking Jaguar: Memoirs from the Living Heart of a Mayan Village.* New York: Jeremy P. Tarcher, 1999.

Rinpoche, Tenzin. *Healing with Form, Energy, and Light: The Five Elements in Tibetan Shamanism, Tantra, and Dzogchen.* Ithaca, NY: Snow Lion, 2002.

Rysdyk, Evelyn. *Modern Shamanic Living: New Explorations of an Ancient Path.* York Beach, ME: Weiser Books, 2002.

Sarangerel. *Riding Windhorses: A Journey into the Heart of Mongolian Shamanism.* Rochester, VT: Destiny Books, 2000.

Somé, Malidoma Patrice. *Of Water and the Spirit: Ritual, Magic, and Initiation in the Life of an African Shaman.* New York: Penguin Books, 1995.

Tedlock, Barbara. *The Woman in the Shaman's Body: Reclaiming the Feminine in Religion and Medicine.* New York: Bantam Books, 2005.

Villoldo, Alberto. *Shaman, Healer, Sage: How to Heal Yourself and Others with the Energy Medicine of the Americas.* New York: Harmony, 2000.

. . . and other books by these authors, as well as Carlos Castenada and Lynn V. Andrews. (Yes, I am aware they can be controversial; but I still recommend them. Sometimes poetic truth is more important than literal accuracy.)

Magickal Traditions from Africa and the Caribbean

Brown, Diana Degroat. *Umbanda.* New York: Columbia University Press, 1994.

Hurbon, Laennec. *Voodoo: Search for the Spirit.* New York: Harry N. Abrams, 1995.

Mason, Michael Atwood. *Living Santeria*. Washington, D.C.: Smithsonian Institution Press, 2002.

Neimark, Philip J. *The Way of Orisa: Empowering Your Life Through the Ancient African Religion of Ifa*. HarperSanFrancisco, 1993.

Voeks, Robert A. *Sacred Leaves of Candomblé*. Austin: University of Texas Press, 1997.

Physics, Magick, and Spirituality

Arntz, William, et al. *What the Bleep Do We Know!? Discovering the Endless Possibilities of Altering Your Everyday Reality*. Deerfield Beach, FL: HCI, 2005.

Burton, Dan, and David Granby. *Magic, Mystery, and Science: The Occult in Western Civilization*. Bloomington, IN: Indiana University Press, 2004.

Capra, Fritjof. *The Tao of Physics*, 2nd edition. New York: Bantam Books, 1984.

Ebert, John David. *Twilight of the Clockwork God: Conversations on Science and Spirituality at the End of an Age*. Tulsa, OK: Council Oak Books, 1999.

Gell-Mann, Murray. *The Quark and the Jaguar: Adventures in the Simple and the Complex*. New York: W. H. Freeman and Co., 1994.

Greene, Brian. *The Elegant Universe: Superstrings, Hidden Dimensions, and the Quest for the Ultimate Theory*. New York: Vintage, 2000.

Gribbin, John. *In Search of Schrödinger's Cat: Quantum Physics Explained*. London: Wildwood House, 1984.

———. *Quantum Physics (Essential Science Series)*. New York: DK Adult, 2002.

Hawking, Stephen William. *The Universe in a Nutshell*. New York: Bantam, 2001.

Herbert, Nick. *Quantum Reality: Beyond the New Physics*. New York: Anchor, 1987.

Hey, Tony, and Patrick Walters. *The New Quantum Universe,* 2nd edition. Cambridge, UK: Cambridge University Press, 2003.

Jargodzki, Christopher P., and Franklin Potter. *Mad About Physics: Braintwisters, Paradoxes, and Curiosities.* New York: John Wiley and Sons, 2001.

What the Bleep Do We Know!? with Marlee Matlin, et al. Fox Home Entertainment, 2005 (DVD).

Zukav, Gary. *The Dancing Wu Li Masters: An Overview of the New Physics.* New York: Bantam, 1984.

Related Areas of Study

You may wish to read books on:

* Huna (Hawaiian indigenous religion; the books by Max Freedom Long discuss Hawaiian magick in some depth.)

* Egyptian religion (E. A. Wallis Budge was an early scholar in this area, and there are several modernized books based on ancient Egyptian magick and religion.)

* Native American traditions (Some are touched upon in the books on shamanism. Be aware that many Native Americans dislike non-Indian dabblers or wannabes who try to adopt Indian spiritual practices without training or permission.)

* Asian spirituality (The various yogas, or Hindu spiritual disciplines, are fascinating; Chinese Taoism also has many associated magickal practices.)

* Alchemy (Charles J. Thompson and Frater Albertus are two established authors; there are more popularized books by modern alchemists.)

* Divinatory techniques (Astrology, tarot, runes, scrying, I Ching, etc.,—all can be used in conjunction with magick.)

Then choose one system or tradition to concentrate on, and set the rest aside for a while.

Seeds for Meditation

Exercise and open your mind by meditating on one of these each day.

We dance around in a ring and suppose, but the Secret sits in the middle and knows.
—*Robert Frost*

Can you be certain that at this very moment you are not a dragonfly dreaming that you are a person?

The adept has the use of everything, but is addicted to nothing.

If you understand, things are just as they are; if you do not understand, things are just as they are.
—*Zen proverb*

Power is so characteristically calm, that calmness in itself has the aspect of power.
—*Bulwer-Lytton*

And what if in your dream you went to heaven and there you plucked a strange and beautiful flower; and what if when you awoke you had the flower in your hand? Oh, what then?
—*Samuel Taylor Coleridge*

In order to draw a limit to thinking, we should have to think both
sides of this limit.
—*Wittgenstein*

The reason angels can fly is that they take themselves so lightly.
—*G. K. Chesterton*

Those in a hurry do not arrive.
—*Zen proverb*

Think with the whole body.
—*Taisen Deshimaru*

A man who as a physical being is always turned toward the outside,
thinking that his happiness lies outside him, finally turns inward
and discovers that the source is within him.
—*Soren Kierkegaard*

Have much and be confused.
—*Tao Te Ching*

To see a world in a grain of sand,
And Heaven in a wild flower,
Hold Infinity in the palm of your hand,
And Eternity in an hour.
—*William Blake*

The way up and the way down are one and the same.
—*Heraclitus*

Act without doing; work without effort.
—*Tao Te Ching*

One never goes so far as when one doesn't know where one is going.
—*Goethe*

Tranquility begins at the water's edge.

The similarity between a spiritual insight and the understanding of a joke must be well known to enlightened men and women, since they almost invariably show a great sense of humor. Zen, especially, is full of funny stories and anecdotes, and in the Tao Te Ching we read, "If it were not laughed at, it would not be sufficient to be Tao."
—*Fritzjof Capra*

Sit quietly, doing nothing, spring comes, and the grass grows by itself.
—*Zen proverb*

We all stand in the midst of eternity. Now.

One moon shows in every pool; in every pool, the one moon.
—*Zen forest saying*

It is the same moon that is reflected in the puddles as in the fountains.

Magic is akin to science in that it always has a definite aim intimately associated with human instincts, needs, and pursuits. The magic art is directed towards the attainment of practical aims. Like other arts and crafts, it is also governed by a theory, by a system of principles which dictate the manner in which the act has to be performed in order to be effective.
—*Bronislaw Malinowski*

Who is the richer, he who has much and wants more or he who has little and wants less?

[E]ffective magic is transcendent nature.
—*George Eliot [Mary Ann (or Marian) Evans]*

Let the flower you hold in your hand be your world for that moment.

Why not walk in the aura of magic that gives to the small things of life their uniqueness and importance? Why not befriend a toad today?
—*Germaine Greer*

You can't think your way into a new way of living—you have to live your way into a new way of thinking.

The four qualities of the adept: to know, to will, to dare, and to keep the silence.
—*Traditional*

Learn to differentiate between the intentional and unintentional contents of the mind.

When you point at the sky, don't mistake your fingernail for the moon.

Do you come to a philosopher as to a cunning man, to learn something by magic or witchcraft, beyond what can be known by common prudence and discretion?
—*David Hume*

Anything that immobilizes you, gets in your way, and keeps you from your goals is part of you and is yours to dispose of as you wish.

You are the sum total of the choices you make.

For us necessity is not as of old an image without us, with whom we can do warfare; it is a magic web woven through and through us, like that magnetic system of which modern science speaks, penetrating us with a network subtler than our subtlest nerves, yet bearing in it the central forces of the world.
—*Walter Pater*

It is impossible to separate yourself from the universe. You are one and the same.

You can't put an ocean in your pocket.

Try being as an infant, knowing nothing except what you hear, see, smell, and feel.

Magic lives in curves, not angles.
—*Attributed to Mason Cooley*

Try too hard to define that central core of tranquility that exists within all of us, and it becomes impossible to reach. Accept it and it will always be there to be tapped into.

You never see animals going through the absurd and often horrible fooleries of magic and religion.... Dogs do not ritually urinate in the hope of persuading heaven to do the same and send down rain. Asses do not bray a liturgy to cloudless skies. Nor do cats attempt, by abstinence from cat's meat, to wheedle the feline spirits into benevolence. Only man behaves with such gratuitous folly. It is the price he has to pay for being intelligent but not, as yet, quite intelligent enough.
—*Aldous Huxley*

Life is like Sanskrit read to a pony.
—*Lou Reed*

We are cups constantly and quietly being filled. The trick is knowing how to tip ourselves over and let the beautiful stuff out.
—*Ray Bradbury*

So an ancient once said, "Accept the anxieties and difficulties of this life." Don't expect your practice to be clear of obstacles. Without hindrances the mind that seeks enlightenment may be burnt out. So an ancient once said, "Attain deliverance in disturbances."
—*Zen Master Kyong Ho*

A master in the art of living draws no sharp distinction between his
work and his play; his labor and his leisure; his mind and his body;
his education and his recreation. He hardly knows which is which.
He simply pursues his vision of excellence through whatever he
is doing, and leaves others to determine whether he is working or
playing. To himself, he always appears to be doing both.
—*Francoise Rene Auguste Chateaubriand*

The obstacle is the path.
—*Zen proverb*

Some of the quotations not otherwise attributed are from *A Thousand
Paths to Tranquility* by David Baird, MQ Publications Limited for Hallmark
Cards, Inc., 2002.

Discussion of Ethical Scenarios

The following are brief discussions of the scenarios presented at the end of chapter 6. They should be discussed with your teacher, and perhaps with friends whose character and judgment you respect. However, if you are isolated for the moment and have no one to talk to about these matters, these comments may help.

a. A teenage friend says her boyfriend has lost interest in her, and would you please do a spell to rekindle his love for her. Do you agree?

Comments: Magicians are often asked to do this kind of "love spell," and the answer is always the same: no. It is not right to manipulate an individual's love (or lack of it) for another; their free will must always be respected. Besides, does she really, deep down inside, want love that has to be forced from another? That is bound to lead to disappointment.

What you CAN do for your friend is healing work to ease the pain of losing that relationship, and sometimes a sympathetic ear is enough. You can also do a spell to "draw the perfect relationship into her life"—one that is perfect for both parties.

b. An uncle whom you love is very ill, and you would like to do some healing magick for him. However, he is part of a religion that discourages magick, and you don't think he would give you permission to work on his behalf. Would you do some remote healing work anyway?

Comments: A wise magician almost never does magick focused on an individual without their express consent. The exceptions are few: if the person cannot give their consent (because they are out of communication range or in a coma, for example), the magician may use their best judgment in doing helpful magick, adding "with harm toward none, and for the greatest good of all." If a parent requests healing or protective magick for their own child, that would also be quite acceptable to most magick-workers.

Getting back to the uncle, you can ask permission to work magick for his healing, and respect his decision. You can help him on the mundane level by cooking healthful meals, offering your company, helping pay his medical bills, or whatever.

There is one other way to help. You can raise healing energy and place it in a "reservoir" on the astral plane, then contact your uncle's Higher Self through meditation and trance. Explain that the healing energy is available for your uncle, and let his Higher Self decide whether to use it.

c. You have been having a lot of problems lately with your job, your health, and your marriage or primary relationship. A friend sends you an e-mail saying, "My group is doing magick to get your life straightened around." You did not ask for magick and don't know what she means by "straightened around." How would you reply to her?

Comments: Personally, I would thank her for her good intentions, but ask that they not do magick on my behalf without checking with me first. Their idea of a better life might not be the same as mine.

If they wanted to do magick for "the best possible outcome" for me, "with harm toward none," I would be fine with that.

d. Someone has been doing a lot of vandalism in your neighborhood—breaking car windows, tagging houses with spray paint, even hacking at trees with a hatchet. A member of your magickal study group suggests that you do a "karmic dumping run" to bring all of the vandal's negativity back on them right now. You don't know exactly how that would manifest in the culprit's life. Would you do this working?

Comments: Interfering with someone's karma and the Law of Return is pretty arrogant. You are doing magick where you have no idea how the result will manifest—maybe a fatal heart attack for the vandal? Do you really want that for some kid because he is angry and misguided?

You can certainly do protective magick for the neighborhood. You can even put healing energy on the astral for the perpetrator's Higher Self to use. And you can work on the mundane level to catch him; for example, by organizing a neighborhood watch group.

e. You would like to buy a neighbor's car, but the price he is asking seems steep. A friend suggests you do a little spell just to nudge him mentally, so he is open to bringing the price down to something more reasonable. Does that seem like an acceptable use of magick?

Comments: Magickally manipulating other people for your own benefit is never all right. Besides, if it ever came out, the reaction would be nasty; even in this "Age of Technology," most people instinctively know that magick is real—and fear it.

By all means, negotiate with the seller. Offer a lower price, or a payment plan over time, or to throw in something extra, like mowing his lawn for the summer. If he refuses, pay the asking price or let it go. There are lots of other cars for sale.

f. You suspect that a neighbor is abusing her children, though you have no direct proof—just occasional yelling and some unexplained bruises. You read about binding spells that can stop a person from acting. Would you perform one on your neighbor?

Comments: We have entered a gray area of magickal ethics. At first glance this seems entirely appropriate . . . but it is still manipulation of another person. And, what if the spell binds them in ways that you didn't intend?

Protecting the children is obviously the highest priority. Is there a way to do it without a binding spell? Can you have a private discussion with your neighbor and ask about the bruises and yelling? She may deny abuse, but knowing that you are aware could discourage further abuse, if that's what's happening. You could also call your local Child and Family Protective Services agency (it may have another name; the police dispatcher will know). You could do protective magick for the children, obviously. You could do all of these.

Bottom line: take action immediately, before the children are harmed. If no other tactic looks possible or effective, maybe the binding spell will be necessary. If you can, talk to your teacher or another experienced magician about setting it.

g. Your country is at war in a foreign land, and a relative is over there in the military. His wife asks you to "do some of that magic stuff to smash the bastards" he is fighting. If you could figure out how, would you do attack magick against the enemy soldiers?

Comments: Is that the best way to protect your cousin? First of all, hurting or killing some of the enemy soldiers won't necessarily save your cousin, or are you such a powerful magician that you can take them all out instantly?

Even if you could, remember the Law of Return: what you send will come back to you, but magnified.

It is always all right to protect those you love, unless they are out there harming innocents. How about starting with a very strong protective spell for your cousin, and then doing some magick to bring an end to the fighting? You can also work on the mundane level, politically, by urging your senators and representatives to work for peace.

You might want to read the "legends" about the Grand Coven of Britain in World War II; all the Witches and magicians gathered to block Hitler's invasion of England, and for whatever reason, the invasion never happened. But even in those desperate days, they did not attack the enemy soldiers magickally.

Have some guidelines emerged here? First, using magick to manipulate other individuals is just nasty. You wouldn't want it done to you; don't do it to others. In fact, you can't do it *only* to others; it always comes back at you, magnified.

Second, wherever there is an unethical way to deal with a problem, there is also a safer and more ethical way—if you look a little further.

Third, magick is not the answer to every problem; sometimes mundane action on the physical plane is quite enough, and sometimes you will want a combination of magick and supportive mundane action.

Blesséd be.

Magicians Through the Ages

These are the stories of some individuals whose names and careers are synonymous with the Art. Some of those mentioned may have been mythical, and others were certainly historical figures. Not all were necessarily great adepts or highly evolved spiritual beings, but all were at least colorful enough to be remembered. They are names worth conjuring with.

Circe

Surely one of the earliest enchantresses of whom we have record, she was a key figure in *The Odyssey* by Homer, written perhaps in 700 BCE. She lived on an island inhabited by many wild animals in the Mediterranean Sea. It was she who changed Odysseus' crew to pigs: even after she restored his men to their original forms, the hero found her so enchanting that he remained on the island for a year. Her magickal skill was hardly surprising: she was the daughter of Hecate, goddess of magick.

Medea

Medea was Circe's niece and a companion to Jason in his quest for the Golden Fleece. They were apparently quite an effective team, until Jason decided to marry royalty. According to legend, Medea killed the bride and disappeared in a chariot drawn by dragons.

Hermes Trismegistus

Hermes Trismegistus, or "Hermes Thrice-Great," was a sage-king of ancient Egypt, or some say a composite god. He is perhaps best known for an event which took place after his death (if he did live and die): according to legend, his tomb was lost for centuries—and when it was at last discovered, an Emerald Tablet was clutched in the hands of the corpse, buried deep in an underground burial chamber. The Tablet is a short and mysterious treatise on magick and the universe: it is a key to great wisdom and power for anyone who can understand its cryptic utterances. It is from this tablet that the famous adage "As above, so below" derives.

Pythagoras

Pythagoras (ca. 560–480 BCE) was a Greek mathematician who formed a secret magickal society about 500 BCE; he was a great numerologist (which seems natural enough in a mathematician), but legend said he could also walk on water and become invisible (skills which my high school geometry teacher never demonstrated).

Mary the Jewess, Maria the Coptic, Maria the Egyptian, Maria Prophetissa, Miriam

(ca. 50 CE—or far earlier). Little is known of the life of Maria, but her skill as an alchemist has been compared with that of Hermes Trismegistus. Many early works on alchemy refer to her as a great master of the art. Some say she was the sister of Moses. She may have lived in Alexandria, and worked with another famous alchemist named Zosimos of Panopolis. She is credited with inventing the process of distillation, and learned the secret of combining sulphur and copper to produce gold. Maria was obviously familiar with the teachings of Aristotle on the quintessence, for she wrote that every chemical, rock, and mineral has both substance and spirit, or body and soul. Her work established the foundation for alchemy for the next thousand years and more.

Apollonius

Apollonius of Tyana (first century CE) lived in Asia Minor, traveled widely all over the ancient world, and was a confidante of kings and emperors. He also raised the dead and performed other miracles. In addition to his skills as a healer and clairvoyant, he could understand and speak to animals. Roman Pagans tremendously admired him during the infancy of the Christian faith—a "legend in his own time." Had the currents of history flowed but a little differently, the Western world might be covered with Apollonian churches today.

Simon Magus

Simon Magus (first century CE) was a great teacher of the Gnostic faith, which was a hybrid of Pagan religion, Jewish teachings, and the fledgling Christian theology. Simon claimed to be an avatar or incarnation of god, come to Earth to rescue the Ennoia or Divine Thought, which had been trapped in a series of mortal women's bodies; this was seen as an act that redeemed all humankind. Gnostics held that with sufficient knowledge, the divine could be experienced and understood by humanity directly, without any need for the mediation of priests and popes. This attitude was not calculated to endear the Gnostics to the emerging Christian hierarchy, and they were wiped out—in God's name, of course. Despite the best efforts of the Roman Church, a great deal of Gnostic lore and teaching has survived.

Morgan Le Fay

Morgan Le Fay was the half-sister of the legendary King Arthur and a sorceress, shapeshifter, and healer. She was one of nine magickal sisters who ruled the Isle of Avalon, and one of the three who bore the dying Arthur away to be healed there and await the time when he would return to Britain in its hour of need. In the earliest stories she is entirely benevolent; later she is depicted as angry at Guinevere for her affair with Lancelot, and still later she has been transformed into Arthur's enemy and the mother of Modred, or Mordred. She may have originally been an aspect of the Celtic mother goddess Modron, or possibly one of the Morganes, water spirits of the Breton coast. In any case, she was both a powerful enchantress and a seductive woman:

For all her looks were full of spells,

And all her words, of sorcery;

And in some way they seemed to say,

"Oh, come with me!"[1]

Christian Rosenkreuz

Christian Rosenkreuz (1378–1484+) was the semi-mythical founder of the Rosicrucian society, a company of adepts who practiced an esoteric system of knowledge and spiritual growth blending Christian mysticism with hermetic philosophy. Legend says that he traveled to the Holy Land, Egypt, Spain, and elsewhere, seeking and sharing esoteric wisdom; finally he established the Brethren of the College of the Holy Spirit, an order of healers and spiritual teachers. However, the first solid evidence we have of the society comes from seventeenth-century Germany, though it popped up later in Paris and other places. Supposedly the member adepts were so skilled that they could move invisibly through the streets of a great metropolis. They operated in total secrecy and anonymity.

The modern heir to this hidden organization is the Ancient Mystical Order Rosae Crucis. Rosicrucians are a worldwide organization, far from secret, who pass on ancient teachings through their website and correpondences. They admit people of all faiths, but are focused on spiritual development (see *theurgy* in appendix I).

Cornelius Agrippa

Cornelius Agrippa (1486–1533+?) was born in Germany but spent much of his career in France and Austria as a physician and astrologer in those royal courts. He did not get on well with the church, and once successfully defended a girl accused of Witchcraft. He was the author of *De Occulta Philosophia* (*The Occult Philosophy*), published in 1531, and could reputedly conjure spirits and turn base metals into gold.

---

1   From "Morgan Le Fay" by Madison Cawein (1865–1914).

John Dee

John Dee (1527–1609?) is known as an alchemist and astrologer, but he was at least as skilled in weaving his way through the political intrigues of sixteenth-century England without getting burned—in either sense of the word. He eventually became a powerful and respected advisor to Queen Elizabeth I.

Dee found an amazing crystal, or showstone, but unfortunately was not particularly adept at divination with it, or scrying. Then he met one whose scrying abilities included seeing and hearing spirits in the crystal. This person happened to be a man of tarnished reputation named Edward Kelly; rumor hinted of his crimes both mystical and mundane, from sorcery to forgery. But Kelly could scry, and from his work came the language and techniques of Enochian magick, as revealed by the spirits of the crystal.

However, eventually Elizabeth withdrew her support of their activities, and Dee and Kelly drifted around Europe looking for new patrons. Years later they split up; Dee went back to England, but died in poverty.

Anna Maria Zieglerin

Anna Maria Zieglerin (ca. 1550–1575) came to the court of Duke Julius of Braunschweig-Wolfenbüttel in the Holy Roman Empire with her alchemist husband in 1571. She set up her own laboratory and quickly attracted attention for her own alchemical studies, partly because she claimed to be the lover and colleague of a mysterious count who was the illegitimate son of the great adept Paracelsus. This relationship, although quite fictional, forced the court to notice her extraordinary knowledge and skill in the alchemical arts. She wrote a single book explaining how to create the legendary Philosopher's Stone and died at age twenty-five, before her brilliance could fully flower.

The Comte De Saint-Germain

The Comte De Saint-Germain (1690?–1784?) cultivated an air of mystery with great success. He arrived in Paris in the year 1748 from parts unknown and was soon a favorite fixture in the salons of high society. Everyone knew (though they had never seen it) that he enjoyed great wealth, and everyone suspected (though they could not prove it) that he had discovered the Elixir of Life, and was far more ancient than he appeared. It was even said that he was the original founder of Freemasonry. He may have died about 1784, but according to another legend he survives to this day.

Count Allendro De Cagliostro

The Count Allendro De Cagliostro (1743–1795) was a Sicilian, born about the time Saint Germain was making his debut in Paris. His tutor was Althotas, a Greek alchemist. Cagliostro traveled throughout Africa, Asia, and Arabia making a living as an alchemist, medium, and fortuneteller. At one point he took the title "The Grand Copt" and created Egyptian Freemasonry—which was progressive for its time in its admittance of women (at least wealthy women, for the fees were more than nominal). He was, for a while, a student of St. Germaine.

After an initial splash in France, the authorities made it clear that his continued presence was not welcome. Cagliostro then made the incredible mistake of trying to start a lodge in Rome, under the very nose of the Vatican. The Inquisition promptly arrested him and sentenced him to death as a sorcerer and heretic, but the Pope commuted his sentence to life in prison and sent his vivacious wife Lorenza to a convent.

Francis Barrett

Francis Barrett (1770?– ?) was a scholar of magick born at an unfortunate time: with the coming of the Enlightenment, interest in magick waned and few pursued the Art. But Barrett delved deeply into "the Rites, Mysteries, Ceremonies, and Principles of the Ancient Philosophers, Magi, Cabalists, Adepts . . . ," and taught magick at his London apartment. He also compiled and edited the works of Agrippa and other early magicians, producing *The Magus: A Complete System of Occult Philosophy* in 1801; this work influenced Levi and others, including, possibly, Joseph Smith—the founder of the Mormon Church. Barrett attempted a second career as a balloonist, but the balloons did not cooperate.

Eliphas Levi

Eliphas Levi (1810–1875) was born in Paris, a city that seems to nurture and attract interest in the occult. He studied for the Catholic priesthood, but attempted to combine his faith with the practice of magick, an endeavor that (as Cagliostro could have explained) was not encouraged by Rome. He was also a political radical and endured two prison sentences for his beliefs. Levi renounced neither magick nor the church and, though he was more a scholar than a practicing theurgist, wrote many popular books on the topic. *The Dogma and Ritual of High Magick* (1855) is one of his major works. His other books on the Qabala, tarot, alchemy, and ritual had a major effect on the Golden Dawn, and are still read by many today. (*The Key to the Great Mysteries*, 1861; *The Science of Spirits*, 1865; *The Great Secret, or Occultism Unveiled*, 1898)

Dr. William Westcott

Dr. William Westcott (1848–1925) was a medical doctor who became a Freemason in his early twenties and promptly accrued a mass of honors and titles in various branches of that organization. He also joined the Rosicrucians (Societas Rosicruciana in Anglia) around 1880, and twelve years later was elected its Supreme Magus. In 1887 he acquired the mysterious Cipher Manuscript, which included some rough rituals and, supposedly, the address of an adept in Germany, who soon gave Westcott authority to found the first Golden Dawn temple in England. Although later it was widely suggested that the "German adept" was a fabrication, Westcott was revered until his death in South Africa, and he is regarded as the founder of the Golden Dawn. (*Sepher Yetzirah*, 1887; *The Magical Ritual of the Sanctum Regnum by Eliphas Levi* (trans.), 1896; and more)

Samuel Liddell MacGregor Mathers

Samuel Liddell MacGregor Mathers (1854–1918) was one of the three founding Chiefs of the Hermetic Order of the Golden Dawn. He lived in London for some time and pursued such diverse interests as boxing, fencing, Celtic studies, feminism, and the campaign against animal vivisection. He became a Mason, then joined the Rosicrucians and rose to the highest level. In 1887 he joined William Westcott in creating the Golden Dawn, and over the next years studied invocation, talismans, divination, alchemy, Egyptology, and Enochian magick extensively; he wrote much of the Golden Dawn curriculum and proved himself to be a gifted ritualist. He was a controversial figure, in that some thought him vain and a shallow scholar, while others found him to be warm-hearted and exceptionally knowledgeable. He and his wife moved to Paris in 1892 to found the Ahathoor Temple #7, and he died of influenza there in 1918. (*The Tarot: Its Occult Significance*, 1888; *The Goetia: The Key of Solomon the King*, trans., 1888, 1972; *The Sacred Magic of Abra-Melin the Mage*, trans., 1898; *The Kabbalah Unveiled*, 1989)

Arthur Edward Waite

Arthur Edward Waite (1857–1942), though born in America, spent most of his life in London. In his thirties he joined the Golden Dawn and then the Societas Rosicruciana in Anglia, and then the Masons. He was more mystic than magician, and was at the center of various schisms and upheavals in the Golden Dawn. Though he wrote many not-very-readable books on magick, Qabala, divination, alchemy, and the Holy Grail, he is best remembered for his involvement with the Rider-Waite tarot deck, in which all seventy-eight cards were fully illustrated with symbolic scenes (*The Rider-Waite Tarot Deck*, art by Pamela Colman Smith, 1910). (*Pictorial Key to the Tarot*, 1960; *Book of Ceremonial Magic*, 1911; and more)

Aleister Crowley

Aleister Crowley (1875–1947) was a very unusual Englishman. Unlike most of his countrymen, Crowley seemed to take great pleasure in shocking people—which was not terribly difficult to do in Victorian England.

He made no secret of his tastes, which included drugs and drink, and he called himself "The Great Beast," a biblical title not calculated to endear him to his more conservative Christian contemporaries. He was a major figure in the Golden Dawn; then left it in a storm of controversy, started another lodge which soon self-destructed, founded Astrum Argentinium (the "Silver Star"), joined the Ordo Templi Orientis in Germany, spent some time in

America, then organized a "Sacred Abbey of Thelema" in Sicily. Apparently the activity schedule at the "Sacred Abbey" would have made a Roman emperor blush, and the government invited him to leave. Like his predecessor John Dee, Crowley wandered for years before returning to England, where he died. (*Book of the Law*, Weiser, 1976; *Collected Works of Aleister Crowley*, 1905)

Pamela Colman Smith

Pamela Colman Smith (1878–1951) is not known as a magician but had a profound effect on modern magick through the tarot. She was born in England, but also lived in New York and Jamaica. Smith was a writer and artist who became involved with the Order of the Golden Dawn about 1903, and was recruited by Arthur Edward Waite to illustrate a new Tarot deck. *The Rider-Waite Tarot*, named for the publisher and Mr. Waite, was the first to include story-like illustrations for all the minor arcana, and became the standard source for most modern decks. There is some controversy as to whether Waite designed the cards and Ms. Smith simply drew them to his specifications, or whether in fact she designed most of them herself. If the latter is true, as seems likely to scholars, then she deserves credit for almost single-handedly reviving the tarot for the present age. Sadly, her career did not prosper, she never married nor had children, and she died alone and in poverty.

Gerald Gardner

A descendent of British Witches, Gerald Gardner (1884–1964) was a studious lad much interested in history and archaeology. As a young man he traveled to Ceylon, Borneo, and Malaysia, where he worked as a British civil servant and wrote about local history and customs. Though he continued to travel a great deal, he retired to the New Forest area of England in 1936, where he became involved with a local group of Co-Masons, and through them met a group of Witches practicing a hereditary Craft passed down through the years. In 1939 he was initiated into the coven by "Old Dorothy" Clutterbuck. Over the years he gathered more occult information and folklore, and blended it with the fragmentary material of the New Forest coven, his own interest in naturism, and perhaps even some Malaysian lore to create his own tradition of Witchcraft, Gardnerian Wicca. When the British Witchcraft laws were repealed in 1951, Gardner became very public as a Witch, and his books sparked a great deal of interest. While Gardner was a controversial figure within the English Craft community, partly because of his love for publicity, he was the single person most responsible for the emergence of Witchcraft as a modern religion. (A novel, *High Magic's Aid*, 1949; *Witchcraft Today*, 1954; *The Meaning of Witchcraft*, 1959)

Dion Fortune

Dion Fortune (1891–1946): this remarkable British mystic and magician was born Violet Firth in Wales and became involved in the Theosophical Society and Stella Matutina, one of the offshoots of the Hermetic Order of the Golden Dawn. Later she created The Society of the Inner Light, part of the Golden Dawn tradition but focused on the mystical aspects of Christianity. The Society is still active today. She was a highly talented psychic, astral traveler, and channeler, as well as a respected psychiatrist and prolific author. She participated in the Magical Battle of Britain, a gathering of magicians who worked to repel a Nazi invasion during World War II, died shortly afterward, and was buried in one of the most sacred spots in Britain, at Glastonbury. (*The Mystical Qabalah*, Weiser, 1984; *The Cosmic Doctrine*, Weiser, 1976; *The Training and Work of an Initiate*, 1940. Novels: *The Sea Priestess*, 1938; *Moon Magic*, Weiser, 1979, and many more)

Israel Regardie

An immigrant and the son of a poor Jewish family, Israel Regardie (1907–1985) joined the Societas Rosicruciana in America before his twentieth birthday. He served as Aleister Crowley's secretary for a few years, though oddly, Crowley refused to teach magick to the young Israel. He later joined a magickal order known as Stella Matutina. In 1937 he published the teachings and rituals in *The Golden Dawn* (1937), to ensure their survival. He practiced as a chiropractor and therapist, and before his death wrote many more classic works on magick, and passed on the Adept Initiation of his order to an

American lineage.[2] (*A Garden of Pomegranates* and *The Tree of Life*, 1932; *The Complete Golden Dawn System of Magic*, 1990; and many more)

Franz Bardon

Franz Bardon (1909?–1958) was the eldest child of a Christian mystic in Germany. Franz had a stage career as an illusionist under the name Frabato, but was secretly studying the true Art; some say that he may have joined a magickal lodge called the Fraternity of Saturn. With the rise of Nazism, all occult organizations were banned; however, it is said that Hitler was deeply involved in black magick. The Nazis learned of Bardon's expertise in the magickal arts, arrested him, and tried to secure his help for the German war effort. Bardon refused and was tortured. He did survive the war and turned to a career as an herbalist and healer in Czechoslovakia, often successfully treating cancer. But in 1958 he was accused of being a spy and arrested by the communist authorities; the exact circumstances of his death are unknown. By all accounts he was a sincere, patient, and kindly person, and as part of his legacy he created a marvelously thorough curriculum for self-instruction in ceremonial magick.[3] (*Initiation Into Hermetics: The Path of the True Adept*, English ed. 1962; *The Practice of Magical Evocation*, English ed. 1967; *The Key to the True Qabalah*, English ed. 1971; and more)

Stewart Farrar

Stewart Farrar (1916–2000) was an English Witch who spent the first decades of his life as an agnostic. He had a long career as a journalist, editor, writer, and army officer. In 1969 he met the self-styled King of the Witches, Alex Sanders, and the next year was initiated into Sanders' coven. There he met Janet Owen, who became his wife and spiritual partner. They created their own covens in England and Ireland, wrote several very popular books on Witchcraft, and as teachers and organizers have had a huge influence on the Craft, not only in their adopted home of Ireland but throughout the Western world. (Several novels, including *The Twelve Maidens*, 1974; with Janet

2 Chic and Sandra Tabatha Cicero, Israel Regardie, www.hermeticgoldendawn.org.
3 Tim Scott, "Who Was Franz Bardon?" www.crow-caw.com, 1991.

Farrar: *What Witches Do*, 1971; *A Witches' Bible Compleat*, 1981, which combines *Eight Sabbats for Witches* and *The Witches' Way*; *The Witches'God*, 1989; *The Witches' Goddess*, 1987)

Sybil Leek

Sybil Leek (1922?–1982) grew up in a well-to-do family (that included some astronomers and astrologers) in the New Forest area of England, and early on hobnobbed with celebrities and aristocrats. But that life was to disappear. During the grim days of World War II, as Britain was bombed incessantly, she joined the Red Cross and then became a nurse. She survived Anzio Beach, served in the remote Hebrides Islands under constant enemy attack, and saw many of her sister nurses die. After the war she became public as a Witch. She made her living as an astrologer and counselor to hundreds of businessmen and to the rich and famous, including President Reagan. With her crow companion, Mr. Hotfoot Jackson, and her boa constrictor, she was a colorful figure, but also a hardheaded businesswoman and probably the premier astrologer of the twentieth century. (*Diary of a Witch*, 1968; *The Complete Art of Witchcraft*, 1975)

Doreen Valiente

Born Doreen Dominy, Doreen Valiente (1922–1999) experimented with magick as a child—to the dismay of her Christian parents, who sent her to convent school (she didn't stay). She moved to Wales, was married at nineteen, and lost her sailor husband just six months later. She married again and moved with her husband to the New Forest area. There, in 1953, she was initiated into Witchcraft by Gerald Gardner, became for a time his high priestess, and collaborated with him in creating much of the liturgy and direction of modern Witchcraft. They took the fragmentary material that Gardner had been given from the New Forest coven and created a complete Book of Shadows. Never interested in publicity, she worked to support and defend the (re)emerging religion of Wicca for decades, emphasizing the Goddess and the importance of feminist and environmental values. (*Natural Magic*, 1975; *An ABC of Witchcraft Past and Present*, 1973; *Witchcraft for Tomorrow*, 1978)

Scott Cunningham

Scott Cunningham (1956–1993) was a Californian who was introduced to Wicca and magick while still in high school. After a couple of years at San Diego State University, he dropped out to research and write full-time. He had more than fifteen magickal works published (in eleven languages), as well as many novels and articles. He will be remembered for his careful research, clear writing, and genuine desire to empower his readers in discovering their own spiritual paths. Cunningham's religion was about people and nature, and he brought magick to a huge audience who would never be drawn to the esoteric studies of Western ceremonialism. Sadly, he passed away at the age of thirty-seven. (*Cunningham's Encyclopedia of Magical Herbs*, 1985; *Earth Power: Techniques of Natural Magic*, 1987; *The Truth About Witchcraft Today*, 1988; *Wicca: A Guide for the Solitary Practitioner*, 1990)

Some common themes run through the stories we have seen here, a pattern that has developed over time. The earliest practitioners on record have miraculous powers ascribed to them, and it is clear they were either completely legendary or else respected figures whose skills were much inflated after death. As we enter the Christian era, the magicians appear more and more like showmen earning a precarious living: one month lionized by fascinated aristocrats as men of learning and amazing skill, the next month denounced as charlatans and hounded by the authorities. This sort of love-hate attitude still exists today. Many are intrigued by the occult but are still not very comfortable with those who study such arts.

Some of the people whose lives were sketched here are not representative of magickal practitioners: these are the ones whose activities were so colorful or outrageous that their names are remembered. Others were serious and admirable people, dedicated to the Art and to the spiritual evolution of humanity. Forgotten are myriad even quieter wonder-workers—the priestesses and healers and ritualists who served their communities without fanfare, and never offered to create gold from lead for a king too wealthy to need it. Especially ignored, in our own patriarchal age, are most of the women who practiced the Art, and who today are the backbone of the magickal resurgence in the West.

So enjoy the tales of magicians of old, but remember that we need not emulate the most flamboyant and egotistic of them. A sense of drama and a strong ego can be useful tools for the magician; but far, far more important are reverence, courage, and love. These are the qualities of the greatest of magicians, and their names were not Cagliostro and Crowley. Their names were Lao-Tzu, and Buddha, and Jesus, and a host of feminine names now forgotten.

Elemental Star Charts

Here are five blank elemental star charts, with space on the pages for notes and reflections. Use them to gauge your progress as you balance your internal elements.

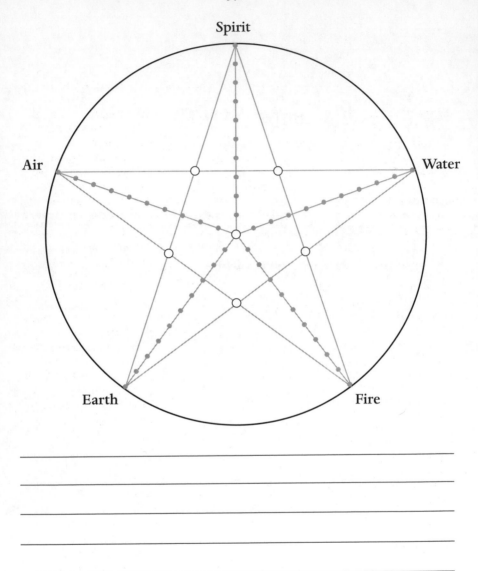

_____

_____

_____

_____

_____

_____

_____

_____

_____

_____

_____

Coven Craft
Witchcraft for Three or More

Amber K

Here is the complete guidebook for anyone who desires to practice Witchcraft in a caring, challenging, well-organized spiritual support group: a coven. Whether you hope to learn more about this ancient spiritual path . . . are a coven member wanting more rewarding experiences in your group . . . are looking for a coven to join, or are thinking of starting one . . . or are a Wiccan elder gathering proven techniques and fresh ideas . . . this book is for you.

Amber K shares what she as learned about beginning and maintaining healthy covens in her twenty years as a Wiccan priestess. Learn what a coven is, how it works, and how you can make your coven experience more effective, enjoyable, and rewarding. Plus, get practical hands-on guidance in the form of sample Articles of Incorporation, internet resources, sample by-laws, and sample budgets. Seventeen ritual scripts are also provided.

1-56718-018-3
480 pp., 7 x 10, illus.   **$19.95**

RitualCraft
Creating Rites for Transformation and Celebration

Amber K and Azrael Arynn K

From sabbat events to magick ceremonies to handfastings, ritual is at the heart of Pagan worship and celebration. Whether you're planning a simple coven initiation or an elaborate outdoor event for hundreds, *RitualCraft* can help you create and conduct meaningful rituals.

Far from a recipe book of rote readings, this modern text explores rituals from many cultures and offers a step-by-step Neopagan framework for creating your own. The authors share their own ritual experiences—the best and the worst—illustrating the elements that contribute to successful ritual. *RitualCraft* covers all kinds of occasions: celebrations for families, a few people, or large groups; rites of passage; esbats and sabbats; and personal transformation. Costumes, ethics, music, physical environment, ritual tools, safety, speech, and timing are all discussed in this all-inclusive guidebook to ritual.

1-56718-009-4

576 pp., 7 x 10, illus. $24.95

To Write to the Author

If you wish to contact the author or would like more information about this book, please write to the author in care of Llewellyn Worldwide and we will forward your request. Both the author and publisher appreciate hearing from you and learning of your enjoyment of this book and how it has helped you. Llewellyn Worldwide cannot guarantee that every letter written to the author can be answered, but all will be forwarded. Please write to:

Amber K
Llewellyn Worldwide
2143 Wooddale Drive
Woodbury, MN 55125-2989

Please enclose a self-addressed stamped envelope for reply,
or $1.00 to cover costs. If outside U.S.A., enclose
international postal reply coupon.

Many of Llewellyn's authors have websites with additional information and resources. For more information, please visit our website:

www.llewellyn.com